THE COOKING COLONEL OF MADRAS

The Cooking Colonel of Madras

DAVID SMITH

The Cooking Colonel of Madras

© David W. Smith, 2018

The right of David W. Smith to be identified as the author of this work has been asserted by him in accordance with the Copyright, Designs and Patents Act 1988.

ISBN: 978-0-244-11322-3

British Library Cataloguing-in-Publication data. A catalogue record for this book is available from the British Library.

All rights reserved. No part of this book may be reproduced, stored in a retrieval system, or transmitted by any other means, electronic, mechanical, photocopying recording or otherwise, without the express prior permission of the author. This book may not be lent, resold, hired out or otherwise disposed of by way of trade in any form of binding or cover other than that in which it is published, without the prior consent of the author.

Cover portrait of Colonel Kenney-Herbert © The British Library Board, Lou.Lon.194.[1894]. Reproduced with permission and under licence.

Cover designed by Emily Lamborn.

Contents

	Preface	1
	Introduction	3
1	Early Years	7
2	Culinary Jottings for Madras	26
3	Furlough Reminiscences	51
4	Madras	69
5	The Great Famine	78
6	Housekeeping and Life on the Move	84
7	On the Hills	97
8	Our Curries	109
9	Later Life in India	123
10	Home to England	133
11	The Servant Problem	151
12	Victorian Celebrity Chef	161
13	Wyvern's Legacy	185

Appendix A: Curry Recipes	193
Appendix B: Chronology	207
Appendix C: Comparison of the First and Fifth Editions of *Culinary Jottings for Madras*	217
Appendix D: Ancestral Relationship between Edward Kenney-Herbert and Lady Jane Hedges-White	221
Notes	223
Glossary	245
Online Pictures	248
Selected Bibliography	249
Index	253

Preface

I first came across Colonel Kenney-Herbert ("Wyvern") many years ago while reading Elizabeth David's book, *Salt, Spices and Aromatics in the English Kitchen*. I was writing an article for my website, The Curry House, on how the British fell in love with curries, and Elizabeth David introduced me to Wyvern, whom she describes as her "Officer of the Kitchen".

The idea of writing a book about Wyvern's life and times grew over a number of years, but I eventually began the research for the book in 2014 and was fortunate enough to be able to make the trip to India, following in Wyvern's footsteps, in February 2015. The book itself was written over the next three years at the cottage of my old friend Richard Cooper in Saint Dogmaels, Pembrokeshire, and at Tim Mercer's lovely Cornish cottage at Crackington Haven.

My trip to India was organised by Hari Daggubaty of TransIndus, who designed the perfect trip for me. He found me the most reliable drivers and the best guides a traveller could ask for. My thanks go to Abirami Shyla who patiently explained Tamil Nadu culture to me, and showed me the magnificent Hindu temples and monuments around Chennai. I learned so much on a cookery course organised by Sandiya Sunderraj of Storytrails, and had such fun buying food in the market and cooking it later under the expert guidance of Chef Smitha. I shall never forget the breathtaking trip up to Ooty on the Nilgiri Mountain Railway, and I would urge anyone who visits southern India to make the journey. Special thanks go to my guide in Ooty, John Bosco, who took me trekking through the tea plantations and forests of the Nilgiri Hills, and introduced me to a Toda family who could not have been more welcoming.

We are extremely fortunate in this country to have resources such as the British Library and The National Archives. The staff at both institutions are highly knowledgeable and unfailingly willing to help a researcher who has got a bit lost while trying to find his way round the system!

The Cooking Colonel of Madras was expertly edited by Lisa Cordaro, who smoothed out my occasionally ragged English with patience and care. I have gratefully accepted her suggestions for changes to the manuscript, which have considerably improved the flow of the narrative. The excellent cover design was created by a talented young artist, Emily Lamborn.

This project could not have been achieved without the support of my wife, Kathy Slack OBE. She encouraged me to take the trip to India, and has always been tolerant of my frequent absences in Wales and Cornwall. Our sons, Alexander and Thomas, never failed to cheer me up when the writing inevitably stalled, and my friends on Facebook kept me sane by sending me encouraging messages while I was away writing.

Without the help and support of the above people, this book might never have been finished. I thank you all.

David Smith
Oxfordshire, August 2018

Introduction

The past is a foreign country; they do things differently there.

L. P. Hartley

The Go-Between (1953)

Writing about the life and times of Colonel Arthur Robert Kenney-Herbert has taken me to two very different countries. First, I travelled to southern India to follow in the colonel's footsteps and then, back in England, I explored an almost unrecognisable place – the past.

Arthur Kenney-Herbert was a cavalry officer with the British Army in India at the time of the Raj. He became famous in colonial India for his cookery book, *Culinary Jottings for Madras*, written under the pen name of "Wyvern". The book was highly popular and ran to seven editions from 1878 to 1904.

Wyvern's times were quite different from our own. Even in his later years in England, only 60% of men and no women at all had the right to vote. In 1918, two years after his death, the campaigning of Millicent Fawcett and her fellow suffragists brought some success, but women still had to be more than thirty years old and own property of a certain value before they were allowed to vote. The same legislation brought the vote to all men over the age of twenty-one. By happy coincidence, Wyvern crossed paths with Millicent Fawcett's sister, Agnes Garrett, in the late 1890s.

At the time of writing, a statue of Millicent Fawcett has been recently erected in Parliament Square, London. It is the first ever statue of a woman in the square, and joins those of eleven illustrious men. One of the men keeping her company is Mahatma Gandhi, famously a leader of the movement for independence for India which brought about the end of British rule.

Wyvern's time in India was some years before Gandhi's, but it coincided with the consolidation of the British colonial rule which Gandhi would later help dissolve. Queen Victoria's government assumed direct rule of India in 1858. The government took over the assets and responsibilities of the British East India

Company, which had first traded with and later dominated much of India. The change came about following the Indian uprising of 1857, and Wyvern was one of the first cohort of British soldiers to be sent to India to enforce colonial rule. Queen Victoria herself was declared Empress of India in 1876, and the British Raj lasted in India until independence was achieved in 1947.

The British in India were vastly outnumbered. There were fewer than 200,000 British (and that includes women and children) ruling over more than 200 million Indians, according to the census of 1891.[1] Militarily, the British used native troops or sepoys to boost their numbers but, in more general terms, the British fostered the mystique of cultural and racial superiority in order to maintain control over the Indian population. However, the British soon learned that setting yourself above and apart from the general population came with its own drawbacks. How, for example, do you prevent your children being drawn into the local culture, especially when they are being brought up by Indian servants? Their solution was to send their children back to England at a very early age (sometimes, like the author Rudyard Kipling, as young as five years old) to reinforce Britishness in their young minds. Unsurprisingly, the children's separation from their parents, caused its own problems. Kipling writes about the psychological damage inflicted on children such as himself in one of his short stories: "Baa Baa, Black Sheep".

Another problem was how to keep up the colonial image of superiority and control without ever relaxing and enjoying oneself. The British response to this dilemma was to retire to the more relaxed social atmosphere of the hill stations for a significant part of the year. The paradox of the British taking their Indian servants with them to cater for their every need, and so not actually being alone with their fellow countrymen, seems to have been glossed over in the collective colonial mind. However, the poor servants were less than pleased. They generally disliked the hill stations because they were cold and damp compared to their homes, and it was they who were now being separated from their families.

Wyvern was a typical member of the colonial regime. He sent his children home to England to be educated, he spent many months of the year at the hill station of Ooty, and he projected the colonial image of superiority in his dealings with his servants. In the chapter from *Culinary Jottings for Madras*, "The Cook and his Management", Wyvern gives us an insight into his dealings with his Indian servants. He tends to use the name "Ramasamy" for a male Indian cook throughout the book. "Ramasamy's" English counterpart, "Mary-Jane", makes an appearance in the book on a number of occasions, and reappears later in Wyvern's books,

INTRODUCTION

Furlough Reminiscences and *Common-Sense Cookery*. An Anglo-Indian dictionary, *Hobson-Jobson*, informs us that "Ramasammy", a common Hindu family name in southern India, was used in the same way that "Tommy Atkins" was frequently used to describe the typical British soldier.[2] It was certainly a term that was in general use by the British in the Madras Presidency. In her book, *Scenes in Southern India*, a missionary named Mrs Murray Mitchell refers to a Hindu boy attending a Madras mission school as a "small Ramasamy".[3] So, when he talks about "Ramasamy", Wyvern is using a kind of shorthand for "your Indian cook". It is difficult not to follow Wyvern's example when reviewing *Culinary Jottings for Madras* so, where relevant to the text, I have also used "Ramasamy" as a generic name for a colonial-era Indian cook. No disrespect is intended to anyone alive today with the name of Ramasamy.

There are many instances in this book where I have used the language of Wyvern's time rather than modern usage. It was necessary to do this in order to satisfactorily explain what Wyvern is talking about, and using modern terminology would have unnecessarily confused matters. For example, the territory referred to as "India" in this book relates to the India of the British Raj, which incorporated the modern-day countries of India, Pakistan and Bangladesh. It is the India that Wyvern and his contemporaries such as Kipling wrote about, and which their readers would have recognised. Since independence, many states, towns and cities in India, Pakistan and Bangladesh have changed their colonial names to more appropriate local names. However, the place names I have used in this book are the ones that Wyvern would have used, which allows for much smoother continuity when referring to books and articles from the time of the British Raj. I have listed these proper names in the Glossary so as to avoid the need to repeatedly qualify their modern equivalents in the text.

Wyvern uses the term "Anglo-Indian" throughout *Culinary Jottings for Madras* and *Furlough Reminiscences*. Anglo-Indians, to Wyvern, are people like himself. They are white British nationals who are living as "exiles" in India. Some Anglo-Indians, like his wife Agnes and their two children, were born in India of British parents. I have adopted Wyvern's usage throughout this book in order to be consistent with his writing, despite it not being current usage in India or elsewhere.

In present-day usage, the term "Anglo-Indian" refers to a person of mixed British and Indian ancestry. The British component of Anglo-Indians' heritage is likely to have come from the days of the East India Company. During that time it was relatively common for British employees of the company, as well as independent businessmen such as tea and indigo planters, to take Indian wives or mistresses. There were very few European women living in India at that time, and those who were resident were probably already married to company officials or military officers. Anglo-Indians, or "Eurasians" as they were called by the British of the Raj, were not fully accepted into British society, and so formed a distinct community of their own.

When Wyvern retired to England in 1892, he reinvented himself as a culinary authority, building on the success of *Culinary Jottings for Madras*. He founded the Common-Sense Cookery Association, wrote many books and articles for prestigious magazines, and became something of a celebrity chef in Victorian London. He even pioneered a Victorian version of home delivery for hot meals.

His life and times, especially in India, may sound foreign to modern ears, but they are fascinating all the same.

1

Early Years

I rub my eyes as I survey the scene to assure myself that I am not the victim of a dreadful nightmare. It is of no avail. There can be no disguising the cruel fact that I am once more enjoying a summer in the plains of Hindustan. A great tear forms itself in my eye, trickles down my parched cheek, and falls upon the paper before me. A tear of unmitigated regret. Only two short months ago I was a "humble cottager in Britain," with my wife and children round me, and with every comfort on a moderate scale that a man could wish for.[1]

So wrote Major Arthur Robert Kenney-Herbert in his book, *Furlough Reminiscences*, on his return to India in 1878 after enjoying a period of leave back in England. By this time, Arthur was well acquainted with the climate and customs of India. He had arrived as an officer-cadet at the age of nineteen in 1859 and had only been back to England once in that time on an earlier furlough (military leave). He would now remain in India until he retired from the army with the rank of colonel in 1892.

He was born Arthur Robert Kenney on 17 August 1840 in the rectory at Bourton-on-Dunsmore, a small village in Warwickshire, England. Old maps of the area give us a clue as to which buildings in Bourton were considered to be the most important at that time. The ones with the largest letters for their names are St Peter's Church and Bourton Hall, with the rectory and Church Farm close behind. Few other buildings are named, but the ones that are tell the story of rural life at that time. There was, of course, a school, post office and blacksmith's forge, but there was also a pheasantry for rearing game birds and a kennels for rearing fox hounds. Arthur would have been brought up in a community which enjoyed country sports, and he continued to enjoy hunting and shooting throughout his military career. Bourton Rectory was demolished many years ago and modern houses now occupy the site, but St Peter's is still a pretty, working church. His mother and father are buried together in its grounds.

Arthur was baptised in St Peter's on 6 September 1840 and the register of baptisms is signed by his father, the Reverend Arthur Robert Kenney, rector of the parish. Reverend Kenney was born in Ireland and had been appointed rector in the year before Arthur was born. (To distinguish in this book between father and son, who share the same Christian names, we will use the name "Wyvern" for the son which is the pen name under which he became famous as a cookery writer. The whole family changed their name from Kenney to Kenney-Herbert in 1875.) Wyvern's mother, Louisa, and Reverend Kenney had seven children who survived early childhood: Catherine (b. 1838), Louisa (b. 1839), Arthur (b. 1840), Harriet (b. 1843), Herbert (b. 1844), Mary (b. 1844) and Edward (b. 1845). Tragically, their mother died of typhus in Brussels on 14 February 1851 after a short illness.

In the census of England for 1851, taken one month after Louisa Kenney's death, Wyvern is recorded as living in Leamington, Warwickshire with his aunt, Mary Kenney, described on the form as a "Fund Holder". The rest of the family were not living at Bourton Rectory when the census was taken. It is possible that Reverend Kenney took most of his children back to Ireland to recover from his grief, but was forced to leave Wyvern behind because he was attending school. Wyvern was only ten years old at the time, and we can but guess at how his mother's death and separation from his family might have traumatised the young boy. Tragedy was soon to visit the Kenney family once again: Wyvern's brother, Herbert, died on 19 January 1856 aged eleven, and was buried a few days later.

Not much is known about Wyvern's early years. We do get a glimpse into his home life from a chapter in *Furlough Reminiscences*, "The Sabbath Day at Home", and it does not sound especially happy. His father comes across as a strict disciplinarian who dispenses severe corporal punishment, even for minor misdemeanours. In one sad little passage, Wyvern recalls:

> One of the severest whippings I ever received during these tender years was, I remember, for taking a hedge-sparrow's nest on a Sunday afternoon, the sin being aggravated by its having been committed in my Sunday clothes.[2]

Later, his nurse goes up to his bedroom to comfort him and tend his wounds. She also feeds him because he has been sent to bed without eating supper. He wistfully remarks: "O! How I loved her, and how I hated Sunday!"[3]

In *Furlough Reminiscences*, Wyvern tells how he visited his relatives while he was home on leave in England. He disguises his father as "the old parson" – which is just as well, because he is not very complimentary about him – describing him as:

> A high churchman of the old school, an uncompromising Tory, and, once upon a time, an ardent sportsman, he looks upon any one who holds opinions contrary to his own as a traitor to his Queen and country, and unworthy of the name of an Englishman.[4]

We do not know which schools Wyvern attended prior to 1855, but we do know that he attended Rugby, the prestigious public school,[*] from February 1855, aged fourteen, until summer 1859. The records at Rugby School confirm that he was a student of Town House, which means he was a day pupil, not a boarder. In those days there was a railway station in the nearby village of Birdingbury,[†] so Wyvern may well have caught the train to and from Rugby every day.

In *Furlough Reminiscences*, Wyvern disguises the name of the school, calling it "Avonby", but they are one and the same. Chapter XI in *Furlough Reminiscences* sees Wyvern revisiting his old school, and it becomes clear that he was not exactly a brilliant and hard-working scholar. There are numerous references to his being one of the "big idle boys", with detailed accounts of the punishments he received. Wyvern meets the old school marshal or "proctor" who tells him that current times are quieter than in Wyvern's day. The proctor recalls Wyvern and his friends' various misdemeanours, such as "beer and tobacco parties at Barby", "hunting on the sly from Dunchurch" and "game[s] of billiards at The George".[5] Discipline at Rugby was strict, and corporal punishment was the norm.[‡] Although Wyvern claims to have revered the headmaster of his day, he also quotes a contemporary who used to say that "it was a downright honour to be birched, he conducted the ceremony with so much dignity, and good feeling".[6] Wyvern felt his greatest accomplishment at Rugby was to be appointed Captain of the Eleven – the school's top cricket team. He writes:

> Not only had I spent five happy years at Avonby, but I had carried away from it

---

[*] In England, the term "public school" refers to a private, fee-paying secondary school, not a school supported by public funds (OED).
[†] The remains of the old platforms can still be seen today, although what used to be the railway line is now a long-distance cycle path.
[‡] Rugby School was the setting for the book *Tom Brown's School Days* (Thomas Hughes, 1857).

a guerdon* for which I must ever remain thankful. Besides, had I not been Captain of the Eleven, and in that position had I not possessed an amount of sublime authority the like of which can never be mine again?[7]

His obituary in the 1917 edition of Wisden's *Cricketers' Almanack* includes the following passage:

> He was in the Rugby Eleven from 1856 until 1859, in the last-mentioned year (when he was captain) playing a hard-hit innings of 90 at Lord's against M.C.C†.[8]

Wyvern paints a telling self-portrait of his time at Rugby:

> The once idle boy [...] whose only first class was won in the cricket field, who frittered away his golden opportunities, and was in the end fain to take the Queen's shilling, and sail for India.[9]

A local newspaper, the *Northampton Mercury*, reported that:

> After a lengthened examination, the Rev. D. Temple, Head Master of Rugby School, has recommended Mr Arthur Robert Kenney, oldest son of the Rev. Arthur Robert Kenney, Rector of Bourton, Warwickshire, for the Madras Light Cavalry Cadetship, placed at his disposal by Lord Stanley. He is this year Captain of the Eleven.[10]

Wyvern's cadet nomination papers have survived and today are safely housed in the Asian and African Studies reading room of the British Library.[11] It was a privilege to examine these original documents, some of which are written in Wyvern's own hand, and imagine him completing the forms at his desk at Rugby School in May 1859.

The nomination papers confirm that Wyvern was recommended as a cadet by the headmaster of Rugby School, Reverend Dr Temple. The Rt Hon. Lord Stanley[12] endorsed Wyvern's nomination on 6 June 1859. Wyvern had to complete the

---

* reward
† Marylebone Cricket Club, which owns Lord's Cricket Ground in St John's Wood, London.

examination form in the presence of an officer appointed by the Secretary of State for India. He confirms that he is being educated at Rugby School and is a confirmed member of the Church of England. There are handwritten reference letters attached to the nomination from Reverend Dr Temple and Wyvern's tutor, Reverend Charles Evans, as to his good character.

Temple's reference reads:

> Arthur Robert Kenney has been a scholar of Rugby School since 8 February 1855 and has always conducted himself to my satisfaction and with perfect propriety. I believe him to be a conscientious and well principled young man.
>
> *Frederick Temple (28 May 1859)*[13]

Evans' reference reads:

> Mr. Arthur Robert Kenney has been a member of Rugby School and my private pupil during the last four years. His conduct has always been most exemplary, and by his industry and ability he has attained to a most creditable position in the school. I have the greatest confidence in his integrity and high principles.
>
> *Charles Evans, late Fellow of Trinity College, Cambridge and Assistant Master in Rugby School (28 May 1859)*[14]

On 16 August 1859, Wyvern took examinations at the East India Military College, where they found him "to be qualified for admission into the Indian Army".[15] He took and passed examinations in mathematics and classics, fortifications, Hindustani and French. He also had to undergo a medical examination, certifying him as fit to join the Madras Cavalry.

Our young cadet arrived in India on 31 October 1859 and started off his military life as a cornet, the lowest rank of commissioned officer in the Madras Cavalry. Wyvern had been officially appointed cornet on 20 September 1859 and, less than two years later on 14 March 1861, was promoted to the rank of lieutenant. Unfortunately, from October to December of that year he was away from duties on sick leave, but once he was well again he did not waste any time. Four months later, on 23 April 1862, he married Agnes Emily Cleveland.

Agnes Cleveland was born in Bangalore in the Madras Presidency:* her father was Lieutenant-General John Wheeler Cleveland of the Madras Infantry, so she would have been accustomed to life in India. It is likely that she would have spent her early years there with her parents, then sent to boarding school in England before the age of ten. Once she had finished school at around the age of eighteen, she would have returned to India to rejoin her family. Her companions on the voyage back would almost certainly have included young women who were affectionately known as the "fishing fleet", because they were "fishing" for a husband. In her fascinating book, *The Fishing Fleet: Husband-Hunting in the Raj*, Anne de Courcy explains that men outnumbered women in the British community in India by as much as four to one at that time. The eligible young women travelling out to India were very much in demand and, according to de Courcy, would have been "besieged by suitors" as soon as they arrived at their destinations.[16]

Agnes probably returned to India at much the same time as Wyvern made his own journey out for the first time. The journey took many weeks, although by this time not the months it had previously taken to sail around the Cape of Good Hope. By the 1850s, steamships had superseded sailing boats and the journey was made in several stages. Passengers would embark from England, head south across the Bay of Biscay, steam into the Mediterranean Sea and head for Egypt. After disembarking in Alexandria, they would travel to Cairo on a Nile steamer. From there, the journey proceeded overland to Suez (after the Suez Canal opened in November 1869, passengers were able to remain on their original boat for the whole journey to India). Travellers would then pick up a new ship at Suez and go on to their chosen port in India. Those heading to the Madras Presidency would have disembarked at Bombay (modern-day Mumbai) although some went on to Ceylon (Sri Lanka) and, from there, across the Palk Strait to southern India.

Because Agnes had been born in India and was the daughter of a lieutenant-general in the army, she would have been familiar with the social life of the Madras Presidency and probably had many suitors for her hand in marriage – but it was Lieutenant Arthur Kenney whose proposal she accepted. Wyvern was exactly the sort of man that the fishing fleet were angling for: young, sociable and with a bright future in the military. His grandson, H. R. C. Carr, describes Wyvern as follows:

---

* Each presidency in India had its own government, which was presided over by a governor.

He was, like many soldiers, a man of varied talents. A good artist, an amateur actor in great request at parties, a fine cricketer, a good shot, in short he had much that ensures social success.[17]

De Courcy tells us that after members of the Indian Civil Service, army officers were considered to be the next prime catch for the fishing fleet. Young officers in the "good" regiments, such as the Madras Light Cavalry to which Wyvern belonged, were particularly sought after on account of their excellent career prospects and relatively good salaries.[18]

Agnes was born on 5 June 1840,[19] two months before Wyvern, so they were both aged twenty-one when they married in April 1862. Because Agnes was not a true member of the fishing fleet and not in a hurry to find a husband, she could afford to take her time. Those poor members of the fishing fleet who did fail to find a husband within a reasonable period often had to go back to England as one of the so-called "returned empties" – a cruel allusion to empty beer bottles being returned to the brewery.

As a dutiful husband, Wyvern was already making provision for his wife should anything happen to him, and he started subscribing to the Madras Military Fund. According to the India Office records at the British Library:

The Madras Military Fund was established in 1808 and closed to new subscribers in 1862. It applied to regular officers and chaplains of the Madras Army and provided pensions for their dependants. It was optional for Madras medical officers up to 1847. On the officer's death, pensions were provided for his widow and legitimate children. Sons benefited until their twenty-first birthday, and daughters until they married. Daughters who were widowed or divorced were often re-admitted to the Fund.[20]

Wyvern was one of the last subscribers to be allowed to join the Fund before it closed. The List of Members of the Fund is a massive volume showing, along with hundreds of others, the complete record of Wyvern's military career in addition to personal details such as the date of his marriage, change of surname and death.[21] There is also a companion volume listing potential beneficiaries of the Fund showing the dates of birth, marriage and death for Agnes and their children.[22]

The next major event in the life of Lieutenant and Mrs Kenney was the birth of a son, Arthur Herbert Cleveland, on 24 September 1863. Their baby was baptised at St Mark's Cathedral, Bangalore on 3 November the same year. Arthur Herbert Cleveland Kenney was a healthy baby and survived the rigours of the Indian climate to grow into a military man like his father. At the time, many babies died in their early years; Agnes had a total of three children but only two survived. (The couple's third child, Ida Louisa, was born in 1871, but died at the age of seven-and-a-half months.)

It is worth noting that Agnes' mother, Louisa Elizabeth, had suffered even more tragedy in relation to her children. The India Office records tell us that Louisa married John Cleveland on her sixteenth birthday and went on to give birth to fourteen children. Tragically, Agnes was one of only five who survived beyond childhood. Giving birth to all those children and the heartache at the loss of so many must have taken a huge toll on Louisa, but she must have been a tough woman as she lived until the age of seventy-five. After Louisa died, Agnes' father went on to remarry at the age of eighty-four and died at the age of ninety-two. Unsurprisingly, he did not father any children in his second marriage.

Wyvern's military record[23] shows that he attended a course in Madras from 1 September 1864 until the end of the year. In September the following year he was appointed Adjutant to the Governor of Madras' Body Guard. On Christmas Eve 1865 he was promoted to captain. Wyvern was now aged twenty-five, and had been a serving officer in the Madras Light Cavalry for just six years.

Wyvern was then appointed as Officiating Interpreter to the 16th Lancers on 19 April 1866, so he was making good use of the Hindustani studies that he had undertaken while training at the East India Military College. The next entry in his service record is not so welcome: on 8 September 1866 he was invalided back to England on a medical certificate. A local newspaper, *The Rugby Advertiser*, records Wyvern's return to England on sick leave:

> On Monday last [22 October 1866,] Captain Kenney, (an Old Rugbeian) eldest son of the Rev. A. R. Kenney, arrived home from India, from which country he had been obliged to return in consequence of a sun-stroke. On the Captain leaving the train at Birdingbury Station, and taking his seat in a carriage, the horses were taken out and he was drawn to his home by the inhabitants of Bourton, amid the shouts and welcome of the inhabitants.[24]

That must have been quite a homecoming, and we can imagine Wyvern thoroughly enjoying the short journey from the train station to Bourton Rectory.

Wyvern writes in *Furlough Reminiscences* that he was able to watch the Oxford and Cambridge boat race* in April 1867 and 1868. Sir Mountstuart Grant Duff,[25] Governor of the Madras Presidency from 1881 to 1886 and to whom Wyvern was military secretary in his later career, writes in his diary that: "A day or two ago, at breakfast, Colonel K. Herbert mentioned that he had, in 1867, been [in England]."[26] *Furlough Reminiscences* cannot always be relied upon to be quite as accurate on account of Wyvern's tendency to discreetly disguise people, dates and places, but Wyvern's military record and Grant Duff's diary entry confirm that *Furlough Reminiscences* is, on this occasion, correct (see Chapter 3).

Wyvern returned to India on 5 June 1868. He resumed his duties as Officiating Interpreter on the following day, so he was away from his post for a year and nine months.

Arthur and Agnes' second child, Enid Agnes, was born on 2 May 1869. So they now have a son and a daughter. Enid was baptised two months later at Trinity Church in Bangalore. In the baptism record, the family are stated to be living in Bangalore at the time, so Wyvern must have been stationed at one of the many barracks in the city which are still in existence today, and are now used by the Indian armed forces.

In August 1869, Wyvern was appointed Officiating Quartermaster to the 16th Lancers in addition to Officiating Interpreter.† Between 6 April 1873 and 14 June 1873, a total of 70 days, Wyvern took private leave in India. There is no record of where he and Agnes were living during that period, but the hill station of Ootacamund (known as Ooty) on the Nilgiri Hills would have been a cool and pleasant place at that time of year. It is easy to imagine Wyvern tending his garden and taking part in amateur theatricals there while he took a break from his duties.

Back from leave, Wyvern was appointed Deputy Assistant Quartermaster-General of the 1st Division Bangalore Camp on 5 December 1873, and moved to the Centre District two months later. Wyvern's army career was progressing nicely. In July 1874 he was released from his duties by his commanding officer, Colonel Bolton, in order to attend a garrison course of instruction. We know from one of Wyvern's articles in the Madras newspaper, *The Athenaeum and Daily News*, that he had attended a garrison course in surveying, so this may well be the course to

---

* An annual rowing race held on the River Thames from Putney to Mortlake, contested by crews from the Universities of Oxford and Cambridge.

† A quartermaster is a staff officer in charge of army supplies.

which the record is referring. The course lasted until late October, and he then recommenced his duties as Deputy Assistant Quartermaster-General at the Centre District until the end of February 1876.

The next development in Wyvern's life is very interesting indeed, but we can only guess at the reasons behind what happened. His whole family changed their name from Kenney to Kenney-Herbert – except for Wyvern's married sisters, who had taken their husbands' names. First to make the change were Wyvern's father, his brother Edward and his sister Mary. Legal notices dated 1 July 1875 of intention to change name by deed poll appeared in the London newspapers.[27] His father describes himself as "the Reverend Arthur Robert Kenney-Herbert, clerk in Holy Orders, and Rector of Bourton-upon-Dunsmore, in the county of Warwick". Mary is described as "a spinster of Bourton Rectory", and Edward is "of Merton College, Oxford, Master of Arts and one of Her Majesty's inspector of schools". Wyvern's notice was dated 6 September 1875 and issued in Bangalore, although it also appears later in the London newspapers. It is very similar in wording to his family's notice from July:

CHANGE OF SURNAME – KENNEY-HERBERT formerly KENNEY

I, ARTHUR ROBERT KENNEY-HERBERT, a captain in her Majesty's Madras Cavalry, the eldest son of the Reverend Arthur Robert Kenney-Herbert, clerk in Holy Orders, and Rector of Bourton-upon-Dunsmore, in the county of Warwick, who is the only son of the Very Reverend Arthur Henry Kenney, Doctor in Divinity, formerly Fellow of Trinity College, Dublin, afterwards Dean of Achonry, and Mary Lucinda, his wife, who was a daughter of Robert Herbert of Currens and Catherine, his wife (daughter of Edward Herbert Esq., of Muckruss, and the Honourable Frances Browne, his wife, and the only grandson of the said Robert Herbert and Catherine, his wife); and I, AGNES EMILY KENNEY-HERBERT, his wife, by a Deed Poll, under our several hands and seals, bearing date the 6th day of September, 1875, and duly enrolled in Her Majesty's High Court of Chancery, have severally ASSUMED the SURNAME of HERBERT in addition to our former surname of Kenney, for ourselves and for our children already born or to be hereafter born, and for all our future issue and descendants, and in the execution of all deeds and documents, and for all purposes, we intend in future to use the surname of Kenney-Herbert instead of Kenney for ourselves and for our children already born, or to be hereafter born, and for all our future issue and dependants, and we and they shall accordingly be designated by the surname of Kenney-Herbert instead of Kenney.

– Dated the 6th day of September, 1875.

ARTH. R. KENNEY-HERBERT

A. KENNEY-HERBERT

Signed and executed in my presence by Arthur Robert Kenney-Herbert and Agnes Emily Kenney-Herbert, this 6th day of September, 1875

E. PEREIRA, Magistrate, Q.C.

Bangalore Cantonment, Q.C. Magistrates Court,

6 September, 1875[28]

So why did they change their name, and why include all that detail if it was not actually necessary for the legal notice?

The clue lies in the extensive family lineage, going back three generations in the family tree from Wyvern's father. The timing here is relevant. In the following year, Wyvern's brother, Edward, married Lady Jane Hedges-White, daughter of the 3rd Earl of Bantry – the two families were distantly related. The Catherine (*née* Herbert) mentioned twice in the legal notice and married to Robert Herbert of Currens was Wyvern and Edward's great-grandmother. She was also Thomas Herbert's sister. Thomas Herbert, in turn, was Lady Jane Hedges-White's great-great-grandfather. So the families of both Edward and Lady Jane were descended from Catherine and Thomas' parents – Edward Herbert of Muckruss and the Hon. Frances Browne (see Appendix D for a family history). It is possible that Wyvern's father was trying to establish his own family's noble credentials in advance of his son marrying into the aristocracy. Or perhaps there was pressure from Lady Jane's mother for her ancestral name of Herbert to be continued after her daughter was married. We do not know, but from now on Kenney-Herbert it is.

The newly-named Captain Arthur Robert Kenney-Herbert was appointed to the staff of the Government of Madras as Deputy Assistant Quartermaster-General on 4 April 1876, a post which he held for five years until his tour of service expired in April 1881.

The Prince of Wales (the future Edward VII) visited India from November 1875 to March 1876. He arrived in Madras from Ceylon (now Sri Lanka) on 13 December 1875. In his contemporary book *India in 1875–76: The Visit of the Prince of Wales*, George Wheeler describes the scene:

> Society at Madras were obliged to get up at five A.M. on Wednesday [18 December] to attend the races.
> The turf exhaled a sweet, fresh, earthy perfume, and fitful breezes chased away from young faces the pallor of the morning light. The racecourse, viewed from the stand, was – as the Prince himself described it – "altogether European" – save for the tropical sky, and the presence of a crowd dressed in bright, instead of sombre raiment. There was a grand stand, filled tier above tier with ladies, military men, and yellow-gloved dandies, who are understood to form the Jockey Club of India. The riders are nearly all English, wearing caps and silk just as jockeys do at Epsom, and the course itself is marked out in the orthodox way.
> The races were named in compliment to the Prince: The Rothesay, the Denmark, the Prince of Wales, and Alexandra Plates, and the Sandringham Steeplechase. The last-named was most exciting, Mr. Taaffe, of the 16th Lancers, an excellent rider, winning easily with his horse Artaxerxes. Some of the nine animals entered came back to the paddock in a white lather.[29]

A correspondent for *The Morning Post* attended the races and set the scene:

> The grand stand and enclosure were not as crowded as usual but the prince and his suite, in sporting costume, the batch of richly-clad rajahs, and the groups of gentlemen and gaily dressed and beautiful ladies, gave great animation to the scene. Never before, say the local papers, have so many persons been seen at a Madras race, which is a sufficient evidence that many came to see the prince as much as the races.[30]

One of the horses entered in the Sandringham Steeplechase was named "Warwick". It was owned by a certain Captain Kenney-Herbert and was ridden by Mr Elmhurst. We can imagine Wyvern's disappointment that his horse did not win, but also his pride at seeing "Warwick" being cheered on by the Prince of Wales as it gallantly chased the winner over one-and-a-half miles. Mr Taaffe, the owner of the winning horse and also its jockey, collected prize money of 1,000 rupees.

On 22 December 1876 Wyvern was promoted to brevet major after serving as captain for eleven years. A brevet rank is not the same as a full or substantive rank, the brevet promotion being one where the officer performs the duties of a higher rank but without the associated pay and benefits. Wyvern had to wait for another three-and-a-half years before he would receive full promotion to major in the Madras Cavalry.

We are told in the prologue to *Furlough Reminiscences* (see Chapter 3) that Wyvern returned home on leave to England for eighteen months. In fact, his military records show that he was on furlough for fifteen-and-a-half months so, once again, the book is not entirely accurate in its detail. Wyvern's furlough started on 1 September 1876 and he returned to his duties in India on 17 December 1877.

While on furlough, Wyvern wrote a regular column, "Etcætera from Town", for a Madras newspaper, *The Athenaeum and Daily News*. Credited as "Wyvern", this was the first time he had used the pseudonym in print. His first article is dated London, 28 June 1877 and appeared in the newspaper some three weeks later. The delay between writing and publication was due to the fact that the article would have been posted in London and sent by mail boat to Madras.

Wyvern describes what he has been doing since he returned to England:

> As an Anglo-Indian, dwelling in London for a short holiday, I have tried to see as much of what is going on round me as possible, without making a penance of my pleasure; and what with the Opera, the theatres, picture galleries, Epsom and Ascot, Hurlingham, the Orleans, Lords, and little dinners my time has been well employed.[31]

In other words, Wyvern has been enjoying "The Season", which saw the social elite gathered in London from their country estates – Wyvern certainly seems to have enjoyed all the key events in the calendar. Epsom and Ascot are famous horse racing events, Hurlingham was the home of polo and an exclusive social club, and Orleans House was a riverside villa at Twickenham which hosted society garden parties. He reviews operas and theatre plays, remarks in great detail on the latest ladies' fashions, reports on cricket matches he has attended, and relays society gossip. He is credited as being *The Athenaeum and Daily News'* correspondent and, as such, the proud owner of an accredited press pass. He uses it to enter the press enclosure at events such as the Windsor Review, a military display on which he reports in one of his articles.

Some of the anecdotes in Wyvern's "Etcætera from Town" column reappear in *Furlough Reminiscences*, even though he states in its preface that it is based on articles that appeared in the *Madras Mail*. The reunion with old friends from India at Epsom and Ascot is familiar but, on this occasion, Wyvern names the people "upon whose faces there still lingers traces of Madras sunshine". Curiously, he includes the name of Major Kenney-Herbert as if he were an old friend rather than actually talking about himself. The story of making mayonnaise with an attractive young woman in the kitchen of a large country house is also reprised in *Furlough Reminiscences* (see Chapter 3).

As we might expect, Wyvern is keen to update his readers in Madras on the latest developments in dining in London. He lists a number of menus for meals he has enjoyed and remarks on the latest fashion, already popular in Europe, of serving vegetable courses at a meal in their own right as opposed to being a secondary accompaniment to roast meats. Here is a menu for a meal that Wyvern particularly enjoyed, which was served at the Orleans Club:[32]

Potage Brunoise (Brown soup)

***

Saumon Froid, sauce Ravigotte (Cold salmon)

Anguilles grillees à l'Anglaise (Grilled eels)

***

Boudins à la Richelieu (Savoury puddings)

Filet de boeuf pique aux champignons (Fillet of beef with mushrooms)

Selle de mouton (Saddle of lamb)

Asperges en branches (Asparagus)

Petits pois verts à la Française (Young peas)

Mirlitons à la Roennaise (Chayote gourd)

***

Gelee, au vior de Madère (Jelly with Madeira wine)

Glace aux fraises (Strawberry ice cream)

***

Dessert

It is fascinating that Wyvern describes the above meal as a "little dinner" rather than the formal banquet that it sounds like to modern ears. He remarks that culinary reform has been at work in London just as much as in India, and that "light and artistic dinners" have become more commonly served at smaller gatherings. He gives an example of the courses for a typical modern dinner for eight people:

>Soup
>Fish
>Two *entrées* (separately served)
>One joint of meat
>Dish of dressed vegetables (or game when in season)
>Sweet
>Iced pudding
>Cheese
>Dessert

Wyvern attends and reports on many cricket matches at Lord's and, according to *Furlough Reminiscences*, he is living nearby at this time. On his first visit, he is embarrassed to find that he is not known as an old member of the MCC. On being challenged at the members' gate, the secretary of the club, who is new to the job, can only find Wyvern's brother's name on the register of members. The secretary is eventually persuaded to allow Wyvern entry on his word as a gentleman, and his name is rightfully restored to the list of members.

The Season in London comes to an end towards the end of July, when high society heads out of London for their country estates, the seaside or across the Channel to Europe. The Royal Opera has closed for the summer, as have many of the art exhibitions which Wyvern has been reviewing in his articles. In August, Wyvern pays a visit to his home county of Warwickshire and stays for a few weeks in a cottage visiting friends and, presumably, relatives. We know from the 1881 census that Wyvern's father and sister Mary were still living at Bourton Rectory at that time, so Wyvern would have been sure to visit them while he was at home on furlough. He paid another visit to Warwickshire in September 1877 for some game shooting with friends, and he is despondent that the journey took most of the day:

> I was downright thankful for a heavy box cloth great coat at Rugby Station, where I enjoyed a happy hour waiting for the branch line train, by which I was eventually deposited, with my traps, on the dripping wooden platform of a tiny station about the size of an ordinary turnpike lodge. The single official of the little place was, however, civility itself, and the brougham* which had been sent for me was punctual. Half an hour's drive brought me to the end of my journey.[33]

This sounds very much like the same journey that Wyvern made on his previous furlough eleven years earlier where he had alighted at Birdingbury Station, but on this occasion there was no welcoming committee to cheer him home.

Wyvern liked to include recipes and menus in his articles that his readers in Madras would have been able to make with the resources available there. For example, in his article written on 31 August he notes that the snipe-shooting season had just begun in Madras, so he offers a recipe for roasting the bird and making gravy to accompany it, as well as some suggestions for sauces which can be served with cold, roast snipe.[34] In his next article he gives recipes for making soup from snipe.[35]

Wyvern's last article in his "Etcætera from Town" series is dated 2 November 1877. The column itself continues, but was taken over by a new writer with the pseudonym of "Griffin". In his maiden article, dated 9 November 1877 but published on 4 December, Griffin concludes by wishing Wyvern a fond farewell from England:

> Many will be glad to welcome back to India Major and Mrs. Kenney Herbert. His loss to us is your gain; they leave for Madras by this Mail.[36]

The use of pen names was popular in *The Athenaeum and Daily News*. Not only do we have Wyvern succeeded by Griffin, but a regular correspondent from Ooty calls himself "Juvenis" and another from Calcutta, "Hotspur". Since Griffin actually mentions Arthur and Agnes Kenney-Herbert by name, Wyvern's identity cannot

---

* horse-drawn carriage

have been a very great secret.

An interesting question is: why did Arthur Kenney-Herbert choose the pen name of "Wyvern"? A Wyvern is a mythical beast which, according to the *Oxford English Dictionary*, is a heraldic symbol of a "winged two-legged dragon with a barbed tail". It is the symbol for the ancient English kingdom of Wessex, but Wessex did not stretch to Warwickshire, Kenney-Herbert's home county, so that connection does not sound likely. A more likely source for the name is William Herbert, 3rd Earl of Pembroke. According to Cracroft's Peerage, the Earl of Pembroke's crest was: "A Wyvern with wings elevated Vert holding in the mouth a Sinister Hand couped at the wrist Gules."[37]

William Herbert was one of the "incomparable pair of brethren" to whom the First Folio of Shakespeare's plays was dedicated. So here we have two connections: first, the Herbert family name and crest; second, the Shakespearean connection – since William Shakespeare was, like Kenney-Herbert, a native of Warwickshire.

Writing in *Country Life* magazine in 1968, Wyvern's grandson, H. R. C. Carr, suggests another, simpler possibility. He concludes that the pen name was: "A sly Irish pleasantry, perhaps, aimed at the dragons of Anglo-Indian society he proposed to advise."[38] In the end, only Arthur himself knows why he chose Wyvern as his pen name – and he isn't telling.

It is possible that Wyvern's duties as Deputy Assistant Quartermaster-General left him with some time on his hands, because it is during this period of his career that he began to write a new column for *The Athenaeum and the Daily News*. The first article was published on 5 January 1878, under the series title "Culinary Jottings for Madras". Initially the column was published weekly throughout January, February and March 1878, but from early April it was subsequently published fortnightly until the end of September.

In the first of his newspaper articles Wyvern mentions how his recipes and menu suggestions from his earlier "Etcætera from Town" series were well received by his readers; he goes on to say how much this had encouraged him to write more articles solely about cookery. He concludes his first article, or "letter" as he calls it, with the words:

> I beg to say that I shall at all times receive with gratitude any corrections, hints, advice, or assistance that my readers may feel disposed to offer me. Letters should be sent to the *Athenaeum Office* addressed to "Wyvern".[39]

Later that year, Wyvern would use the articles published in *The Athenaeum and Daily News* (presumably amended using the feedback he had received) as the basis for his first and most well-known book for which he used the same title: *Culinary Jottings for Madras*. The titles of the book chapters are identical to the titles of each of the newspaper articles, and follow almost exactly the same sequence. Only the book's chapters on "Fritters", "Salads", "Hors d'oeuvres", "Eggs, Macaroni, and Cheese" and "Camp Cookery" are missing from the articles, because Wyvern ran out of time. It is interesting to note that Wyvern must have planned out the chapters of his book right from the beginning – the sequence of articles in *The Athenaeum and Daily News* were not just topics that he had dreamed up week-by-week. In an article from as early as 23 February he mentions he will be writing in future about camp cookery, even though that topic never did make it into his newspaper articles.

The main difference between the book and the newspaper articles is that the latter each include one of Wyvern's menus for a little dinner that was seasonal to the current time of year. In the book, the menus have their own section in Part II. Wyvern mentions in his second letter that he was going to follow the book's format in the articles, but he was taken to task by "a friend whom I deeply respect" for not including a menu in his first article. The friend remarked: "I have read Wyvern's letter, and am sorry to find nothing in it whatever", which is a bit harsh – but Wyvern takes his point and changes the format.[40]

Wyvern's last complete article, "Our Luncheons", was published on 30 September. He concludes:

With these hints for luncheons I regret to say that I must conclude the "Culinary Jottings" in the columns of this paper. I promise however with the kind permission of the proprietors of the *Athenaeum* past and present, to publish what I have already written as soon as possible together with a few additional chapters which time forbids my bringing out in the form of my previous communications. I shall continue, I am happy to say, to suggest a *menu* for Madras dinner tables once a week with brief explanations. So his kind readers have not yet got rid of...

Wyvern.[41]

The menus that he promised appeared weekly in *The Athenaeum and Daily News* from the beginning of October until 9 December 1878, and form the basis of Part II of Wyvern's soon-to-be-published book. In his final menu, Wyvern includes

Potatoes *à l'Américaine*, noting that the recipe can be found on p. 102 "in the Culinary Jottings". Page 102 of the first edition of *Culinary Jottings for Madras* does indeed include the recipe for Potatoes *à l'Américaine*, so the book must have been published already at that time.

The response to Wyvern's *Athenaeum* articles was a good omen for the future. *The Athenaeum*'s editor had to put a notice in the newspaper following Wyvern's last article, asking his readers not to request any more back numbers of earlier articles because they had completely sold out the previous month.

In his preface to the first edition of *Culinary Jottings for Madras*, dated 1 November 1878, Wyvern tells us:

> When I first began to write about Cookery I flattered myself that I had undertaken a very easy, and pleasant task. I thought my jottings would be composed *currente calamo*,[*] and that I should be able to carry out my project with satisfaction and success. But at the hour of launching my frail shallop[†] from the shore, I am compassed about with grave doubts concerning its seaworthiness.[42]

So, on the eve of his book's publication, Wyvern is anxious of failure and worried about his own shortcomings, but he needn't have worried. It was a huge success.

We take a look at the book in detail in the next chapter.

---

[*] without deliberation, off-the-cuff
[†] a light sailing boat (OED)

2

Culinary Jottings for Madras

CULINARY JOTTINGS FOR MADRAS
A TREATISE IN THIRTY CHAPTERS
ON
REFORMED COOKERY
FOR ANGLO-INDIAN EXILES,
BASED UPON
MODERN ENGLISH, AND CONTINENTAL PRINCIPLES,
WITH
THIRTY MENUS
FOR LITTLE DINNERS WORKED OUT IN DETAIL,
AND
AN ESSAY ON OUR KITCHENS IN INDIA.

Culinary Jottings for Madras is the book which made Arthur Robert Kenney-Herbert famous in British India. Except, of course, that the book was not published under his own name, but under the pseudonym "Wyvern". The book ran to six editions published in Madras between 1878 and 1891. The fifth and sixth editions dropped the words "for Madras" from the main title, so it became simply *Culinary Jottings*. The publishers issued a seventh edition under the new title of *Wyvern's Indian Cookery Book*, released in Madras by Higginbotham & Co. and in London by Simpkin, Marshall & Co. in 1904. The publisher notes that the seventh edition "is entirely reconstructed and rewritten, and, while it retains the leading features of *Culinary Jottings*, is essentially a new work".

The first edition of *Culinary Jottings for Madras* was published in November

1878. A second edition with corrections to the text came out the following year. The book was later revised and expanded for the fourth edition, which was published in February 1883. Wyvern corrected errors and expanded the book for each successive edition. In his preface to the fourth edition, written in February 1883, Wyvern notes that he has added one hundred pages of new material. Three articles on curries and *mulligatunny* (mulligatawny soup) which had been published in *The Pioneer* newspaper were incorporated into the book, the chapter on vegetables was expanded, and several new recipes for rice and vegetarian dishes were introduced. Wyvern added a few extra chapters to the fourth edition, including "Our Kitchens in India", as well as amending the full title of the book (shown above) accordingly. (See Appendix C for a full list of chapters and a comparison between the contents of the first and fifth editions.)

Culinary Jottings tells us much about the British colonial experience in India, as well as Wyvern's not-untypical attitude to the Indian servants under his command. Many of the chapters paint a colourful picture of life at the time and how the British adapted (or not) to the conditions in which they found themselves. A constant theme runs through the book concerning native chefs' poor cooking skills. To put this into perspective, Wyvern is not talking about Indian cooks' ability to make their own traditional dishes, far from it: the whole purpose of the book is to explain to the British ladies of Madras how to organise the cooking of European-style food under Indian conditions. To that end, native cooks would need to be taught cooking methods which were beyond their experience, and *Culinary Jottings for Madras* sets out to clarify exactly how to do that.

In his introduction, Wyvern sets out what he hopes to achieve. He stresses the importance of being economical in the kitchen and keeping costs within the means of the average household, stating that he intends to write his book based on those principles. He explains that there are no contemporary cookery books available to the Madras housewife to teach her how to cook modern English and European dishes using the resources available at the time.

Wyvern refers to a well-known Anglo-Indian cookery book which he calls "Indian Domestic Cookery", but which is almost certainly *Indian Domestic Economy and Receipt Book* by Dr R. Riddell. It was first published in 1849 but still in print in 1877, even though the author had died some years previously. Wyvern thought that the book was an excellent work in its day, but he believed that the housewives of Madras needed a more contemporary book to help them in the kitchen. He relates a story from a couple of years previously when he was trying to find a suitable book to use himself. He ends up purchasing a copy of a cookery book which had been recently published at Madras. Wyvern thinks that the book had been written for returned colonials living in England rather than the English living in India, and considers it to include "much dangerous counsel proffered which should be most carefully avoided". The first draft of his introduction, which appeared in one of his articles for *The Athenaeum and Daily News*, actually names the book as "*The Original Madras Cookery Book* by An Old Lady Resident" and goes on to give a lengthy and highly critical review of it, concluding sarcastically that:

> the intention of the "old lady resident" had been to bring before the retired Anglo-Indian sundry painful visions of the past: of days of jolting travel and the dishes that were presented to him at the "public bungalow"; or of quondam[*] visits at the Presidency and a happy day at a Madras hotel![1]

Perhaps the author took offence at Wyvern's review of her book, or maybe his publisher thought it wiser to omit such caustic comments. Whatever the reason, the original critique had been edited out by the time *Culinary Jottings for Madras* was first published.

Wyvern goes on to explain, in two glorious paragraphs, how things have changed since the early days of the British presence in India, and how formal dining has been reformed:

> Our dinners of to-day would indeed astonish our Anglo-Indian forefathers. With a taste for light wines, and a far more moderate indulgence in stimulating drinks, has been germinated a desire for delicate and artistic cookery. Quality has superseded quantity, and the molten curries and florid oriental compositions of the olden time – so fearfully and wonderfully made – have been gradually banished from our dinner tables.
>
> For although a well-considered curry, or mulligatunny – capital things in their way – are still very frequently given at breakfast or at luncheon, they no longer occupy a position in the dinner menu of establishments conducted according to the new *régime*.[2]

It is important here to understand that the British ladies of Madras were unlikely

---

[*] former

to be doing the cooking themselves. *Culinary Jottings for Madras* is aimed primarily at explaining how they should instruct their servants in making the recipes in the book. It would have been the lady's job to plan the menu and possibly oversee the cooking, but she certainly would not have bought the ingredients in the bazaar, nor cooked the meals herself.

I have not included any of Wyvern's recipes here (with one exception – see "Savoury Omelettes" below).[3] I have selected the most informative chapters in *Culinary Jottings for Madras* to look at in greater depth: they are set out below. Wyvern's writing on curries and his curry recipes deserves a chapter of their own (see Chapter 8), because it is his curry making for which he is best remembered.

"The Menu"

Wyvern sets the scene:

> All who have studied the reformed system of dinner-giving will, I think, agree with me when I say that the *menu* of a dinner anywhere, but in India especially, should be reduced to the smallest compass possible.[4]

He suggests that the menu for a "cosy dinner" should include:

Soup
Fish
Two well contrasted *entrées* served separately
One joint of meat (*relevé*)
Game and a dressed vegetable
One *entremet sucré*
An iced pudding
Cheese with hors d'oeuvres
Dessert

– which he describes as "ample", but which to the modern ear sounds more like a banquet.

It may be useful to explain some of the culinary terms that Wyvern uses here, because they are referred to frequently in the present book. The *entrée* is part of the first service, but supplementary to and smaller than the *relevé*. The joint or *relevé* (also anglicised as "remove") is a large cut of roasted or braised meat carved at the table by the host.

The main attraction in the second service is the *rôt* – roast game (partridge, quail, hare, etc.) accompanied by a dressed vegetable (i.e. served with a sauce). An *entremet* is a light dish served alongside more substantial courses, while *sucré* implies sweet rather than savoury. An iced pudding is self-explanatory, but the mere fact that the holder of this formal dinner would have had the resources to serve an iced pudding in the days before refrigeration is worth noting.

Cheese with hors d'oeuvres sounds wrong to modern ears. Today we are used to hors d'oeuvres being served as a savoury appetiser before a meal. Wyvern is serving his hors d'oeuvres near the end of the meal and to accompany his cheese course. He notes that the European custom of offering hors d'oeuvres as a prelude to the meal is becoming more common (he also notes that it was becoming fashionable to serve oysters before the soup course).

At first glance, "dessert" would appear to be self-explanatory, but Wyvern does not use the term in the modern sense – otherwise, why would there be yet another substantial sweet dish following on from an *entremet sucré* and an iced pudding? We need to turn to Wyvern's companion book to *Culinary Jottings for Madras*, appropriately titled *Sweet Dishes*, to find out:

> [Dessert] must be laid out as tastefully as possible before dinner is served, and, as it is continually before the eyes of the assembled guests, it must be composed of nice dishes.[5]

So the dessert is composed of attractive little sweet dishes which are on display throughout the meal. Wyvern notes that prepared fresh fruit is the exception to this custom, in order to avoid the aroma of ripe fruit disturbing the diners during their savoury courses. Dessert consisted of two parts. The first was primarily ornamental and consisted of crystallised fruit, nuts, fancy biscuits and so forth displayed on elaborate table settings to impress the guests. The second was sweet creations to be eaten and enjoyed: fresh fruit, fruit salads, macaroons, chocolate creams and suchlike.

Wyvern explains that the menus in his book are "adapted to a great extent, of course, from that of France".[6] This style of dining, known as *service à la Française*, has two main "services" where a group of dishes are placed on the table at the same time. Wyvern gives an example of such a dinner:

Premier Service:

Potage	Soup
Poisson	Fish
Entrées	Side-dishes
Relevés	Joint, or remove

Second Service:

Rôts	The roast (game or poultry)
Entremets	Savoury and sweet dishes
Fromage	Cheese
Dessert	Dessert[7]

The courses in each service would be eaten in the order shown on the menu, although there was some considerable contemporary debate about whether the *entrée* should precede the *relevé* or vice versa. Some authorities such as Wyvern's culinary hero, the epicure Jean Anthelme Brillat-Savarin,[8] were convinced that the order should be "from the more substantial dishes to the lighter",[9] and so the *entrée* should follow the *relevé* and separate the *relevé* from the other substantial course on the menu, the *rôt*, which began the second service. However, Wyvern has chosen the more traditional order of courses – probably to indulge the preferences of his more conservative readers.

"The Cook and His Management"

Wyvern introduces us to his Indian cook and recommends ways in which to manage the running of the kitchen. Throughout the book, Wyvern uses the name "Ramasamy" as shorthand for "your Indian cook" and "Mary-Jane" for his English counterpart (see Introduction).

Wyvern suggests that the mistress of the house befriends her cook if at all possible:

> After some years of observation I have come to the conclusion that if you want to put nice little dinners upon your table, you must not only be prepared to take an infinite amount of trouble, but you must make a *friend* of your *chef*. Unless

amicable relations exist between the cook and his mistress or master, the work will never be carried out satisfactorily. There will be a thousand and one annoying failures, your mind will never know what repose means, and, in the end – utterly wearied with the daily struggle against petty larceny, carelessness, ignorance, stupidity, and an apparently wayward desire to thwart your desires to the utmost – you will resign the *bâton* to your butler,[*] and submit in sheer desperation to that style of dinner unto which it may please him to call you.[10]

So according to Wyvern, unless he is befriended – or at least kept under strict control – "Ramasamy" is a petty thief, careless, ignorant, stupid and out to sabotage the dinner plans of the lady of the house with his incompetence. In one paragraph, we have an insight into Wyvern's colonial mentality. It is the same mindset which enables Wyvern to think of him, a grown man, as a "child of this world". Wyvern explains that although "Ramasamy" has the potential to be a good cook, his employers should

> take heed lest he grow up at random, clinging affectionately to the ancient barbarisms of his forefathers. We should watch for his besetting sins, and root them out whenever they manifest themselves.[11]

In Wyvern's view, "Ramasamy" is an adult but he needs to "grow up" and forego his traditional ways in order to become part of a colonial household. He even addresses "Ramasamy" as he would a child. Wyvern and his contemporaries were dismissive of the Indians' ability to fully understand English and he talks disparagingly about his *munshi* (secretary) who "never admitted himself to be puzzled by the most intricate passage in English that you could place before him".[12] The result was that Wyvern would talk to his cook in the native patois which, he asserts, "is easily acquired. [...] You will even talk of 'putting that troople,' 'mashing bones all,' 'minching,' 'chimmering,' &c., &c., without a blush".[13]

On occasion, when being patronised for his lack of English skills, "Ramasamy" worked the situation to his own advantage. Wyvern laments that the trimmings of meat from the preparation of mutton cutlets often end up in the cook's own curry, rather than as the basis for the sauce to accompany the cutlets. On being taken to task for his appropriations, the cook replies (in Wyvern's approximation of his

---

[*] Head servant of the household

accent): "missus din't give arder for using bits all".[14] *Touché!*

Despite Wyvern's frustration with his servants' difficulties in speaking English, Mrs Murray Mitchell remarks on how much easier she found it to communicate in English in Madras compared with Bombay or Calcutta (modern-day Mumbai and Kolkata). Mitchell had learned Hindustani, as had Wyvern during his cadet training, and enjoyed being able to speak to the local people in their own language; but she was disappointed to find that in Madras, the natives only spoke Tamil. However, her language difficulties were lessened because she found that her servants all spoke "tolerably good English", and even the labourers in the streets "know a smattering".[15]

"Certain Kitchen Requisites"

The chapter starts with a note of optimism for "Ramasamy's" skills:

> Allowing then, that our native cooks are, by nature, adapted to their calling, and that by judicious treatment we can develop the talent which they possess, one of the next things for consideration is our kitchen equipment, and the kind of utensils which will be found best suited for Ramasamy's use, bearing in mind the sort of dishes we shall hereafter call upon him to prepare.

But the mood soon changes:

> In introducing novelties of European construction to the Indian cook-room it is, a *sine quâ non* to proceed with caution. Ramasamy is intensely conservative, and a sworn foe to innovations.[16]

Wyvern warns his readers that if they have brought some favourite kitchen utensil out with them from England, they might be bitterly disappointed to see the gadget misused or discarded by their Indian servants. He tells the story of being a guest at a house on the Nilgiri Hills. He is astonished to see one of the servants bring out his bathwater in a Warren's Patent Cooking Pot. When Wyvern questions why such a useful kitchen device is being used for bath water, his host sadly explains that his servants will not employ it for its intended purpose, and that he has given up trying to make them use it properly. Wyvern is of the view that:

> Left entirely alone, with articles of his own selection around him, the native

cook is, however, a singularly ingenious creature. [...] Given a hold in the ground, and a couple of stones for her range, with a bundle of jungle sticks, a chatty or two, *perhaps* a *degchee*,* and a fan, wherewithal to prepare a dinner, can you picture to yourself the face of Martha,† the "thorough good cook" of an English household?[17]

Wyvern tells the story of young colonel who is ordered to march his regiment to a new camp. The colonel is delighted because he likes to go by the book on all military procedures, and now has the opportunity to start from scratch with a new camp. He gives orders for the kitchens to be set up in advance of the regiment's arrival, but when they do arrive the kitchen area is empty – not a soul in sight. The colonel dispatches his orderlies to find out what has happened to the native cooks – they find them busy preparing the regiment's breakfast in a dry riverbed beside the camp. The colonel is furious and demands to know why the camp kitchen has not been used. The reply from the boldest of the cooks is: "What sar! that bad sense kitchin, sar, I beg your pardon: too much firewood taking: see sar this prâper kitchin only".[18]

Recognising he cannot win, the colonel reluctantly allows the cooks to remain where they are.

The chapter finishes with Wyvern's advice on cleanliness. He urges that the kitchen utensils should always be clean, and therefore inspected at least once a week. The inspection should take place on the verandah of the house, with all the pots and pans laid out on a mat, so that the lady of the house can check them; if not spotless, they should be thoroughly cleansed with washing soda.

"In the Store-Room"

Wyvern wonders how a lady learns what she needs for her storeroom, when she first starts housekeeping in India. He has been invited to some grand houses in Madras, and seen that the *châtelaine* (the mistress of an important household) often has a huge collection of tinned goods, bottled sauces and the like in her pantry. Wyvern imagines the mistress has dictated a list of items to her butler and sent him off to buy the goods, but he believes that the butler may be too enthusiastic about what he would call "Europe articles", and encourages his mistress to buy far more

---

* chatty – earthenware pot; *degchee* – cooking pan, saucepan
† An alternative name for "Mary-Jane".

than she possibly needs.

In Wyvern's opinion, the storage of tinned goods should be kept to a minimum. He remarks:

> In Madras we have all the materials for soup-making at hand, we have excellent fish, very fair flesh and fowl, good wild fowl and game when in season, and vegetables from Bangalore and the Neilgherries[*] in addition to the standard produce of the country. If, therefore, we concentrate our attention sufficiently upon what we can get from market, our demand on tinned food should be very small indeed.[19]

He tells the story of a colonel in the artillery who had served all over the British Empire, but was recently posted to India for the first time. The colonel is passionate about food and enthuses about the dinners he has enjoyed in the officers' mess in India. However, when he is invited to a ceremonial dinner, he is severely disappointed. No expense had been spared for the formal dinner, but the money had been spent on tinned goods which were ruined by the cooking. The colonel would have far preferred to have been served fresh ingredients sourced from the local market.

All too often, Wyvern tell us, when a lady is allocating stores for a dinner party, she freely issues tinned goods but will skimp on fresh ingredients such as cream, butter, eggs and meat for the gravy. Wyvern believes that the poor quality of cooking in India has a great deal to do with economising on what he considers to be essential foodstuffs. He has some sympathy for "Ramasamy":

> If an English cook, surrounded with the best market supplies in the world, be helpless without her stock, her kitchen butter, and her cream and eggs, how much more should Ramasamy be pitied if he be refused those necessaries, for his materials stand in far greater need of assistance.[20]

Firewood and charcoal for cooking are another bone of contention between the lady of the house and the cook. The British tended to believe that Indian cooks would ask for more fuel than was actually needed, and that the extra charcoal was destined to be spirited away for the cooks' own use. Occasionally, having such a

---

[*] The Nilgiri Hills

suspicious attitude could give rise to unintended consequences. Wyvern tells the story of a dinner party that was going smoothly until the game and dressed vegetables were due to be served. When they arrived, they were stone cold. The cook was interrogated about the affair the next day and explains: "charcoal all done finish, and Missis only got godown* key in the pocket".[21] At least here the lady of the house had taken Wyvern's advice about locking the storeroom at night (see below), but this time, unfortunately, her caution had backfired on her.

The final anecdote in this chapter relates to an article published in *Vanity Fair* magazine, "Curry and Rice". Wyvern is outraged at its inaccuracies and generalisations: he contends that they do not apply to any part of the Madras Presidency. The article claims that Anglo-Indians eat tinned beef with yams, and make stock from the bones of meat left over from the lunch table. Wyvern is horrified, considering the author to be an "ignoramus". The author tells his readers in England that no dinner in India is complete without a "burning curry", and that no meal is made without tinned food. Wyvern is clearly incandescent at this misrepresentation of life in Madras, and declares sniffily: "we can do pretty well without either".[22]

"Our Kitchens in India"

Wyvern added an essay on "Our Kitchens in India" to the fourth edition of *Culinary Jottings for Madras*. The essay gives us a graphic vision of how in many cases, the kitchens in which food was prepared were filthy and grossly unhygienic. The chapter was first published in the *Madras Mail* and added to the book later with the *Mail*'s permission.

It is no wonder that many of the British developed gastroenteritis while stationed in India. It was so widespread that colloquialisms such as "Delhi belly" and "Simla trots" came into common usage. The prime cause was bacterial infections such as E. coli, acquired through poor kitchen hygiene or drinking contaminated water.

Wyvern describes the horror of the kitchen:

> Now follow me into the room. It is as black as Erebus. The pungent smoke from yonder wood fire, upon which some water for a bath is being boiled, penetrates

---

* An outbuilding, often located near the property's stables.

every crevice. There is no chimney, you see, so the wall, up which the smoke is creeping towards an opening in the roof, is lined by an ancient coating of soot. Observe the mass of patriarchal looking cobwebs depending from the rafters, and the floor of mother-earth, greasy, black, and cruelly uneven in its surface.

Pull yourself together now, for we are about to examine the kitchen table. It is, to begin with, a piece of furniture which it would be gross flattery to call a dresser. It is small, and very rickety. In colour it is a remarkably warm burnt umber. The legs which support it are begrimed with dust which has become coagulated from time to time by grease, and smoked a rich sable. If you wished to do so, you could scrape off this filthy tegument[*] with your pen-knife to the depth of the sixteenth of an inch. The top of the table is notched and scored all over with wounds inflicted by the chopper, the edges are all worn down, and there are tell-tale marks which prove that it is the custom of the *chef* and his assistants to mince parsley, herbs, onions, aye the meat itself of which those "chicken cutlets" that he delights to give you are made, upon the oily, nut-brown board.[23]

So far, so disgusting – but there is more. Just about everything that a modern environmental health inspector would fail in a restaurant kitchen takes place in the Anglo-Indian kitchen. We have seen above that raw meat and vegetables are being prepared on the same surface – a sure-fire way to spread the animal-borne bacteria which causes acute food poisoning. However, it is the location of the kitchen itself that causes even more alarm.

Anglo-Indian kitchens were not usually part of the main house: they would be located in one of the godowns. There was no running water and no drainage in the kitchen, so the area immediately outside received all the waste food and unwanted liquids: imagine the stench of that festering in the heat of Madras. There was no place to clean kitchen utensils and, in fact, there were precious few utensils to clean. Wyvern points out that there are no spoons in the kitchen, and poses the question of how the cook might serve the puréed dishes made there. He leaves the answer to the reader's imagination, but the implication is via the cook's hands (which might not have been washed). What utensils there were, like the stone slab and rolling pin for making pickles or puréed vegetables, were probably never cleaned either. Wyvern paints a picture of traces of the previous night's spinach on the rolling pin he sees being used to make today's dishes.

---

[*] Tough outer layer

Because the kitchen was located away from the house, regular supervision of food preparation was almost impossible. Not only that, but the friends and families of the kitchen staff also tended to congregate there too. Wyvern thinks that the servants' children in particular were "a fruitful source of dirtiness".[24] The kitchen was always open, and Wyvern is particularly distressed to think that the servants and their families actually might be sleeping there too. He notes "the idea of the kitchen being used by a number of native *employés* as a sleeping chamber is obviously too horrible to need more than a passing remark".[25]

There is now a twist in the tale of the kitchen. Wyvern unexpectedly takes the Indian cook's side in the matter, but only to the extent that he knows no better and there is "positively no reason to expect him to be clean".[26] Instead, he points the finger of blame at the cook's employers. Wisely (since he does not want to offend his more conscientious readers), Wyvern makes it clear that there are many exceptions to the deplorable kitchen conditions outlined previously.

Wyvern has strong views on changing the existing arrangements for the kitchen. He asks:

> Why on earth should we continue to accept as places fit for the cooking of our food the dismal hovels that are attached to our godowns, and called cook-rooms? These places may have sufficed for the culinary necessities of our forefathers, who chiefly preyed upon curry and rice, and lived to all intents and purposes *à la mode Indienne*. But *nous avons changé tout cela*.* The delicate cookery which day by day gains popularity in India now demands a clean airy room, properly furnished, with plenty of *light*, and many accessories borrowed from civilized Europe.[27]

What Wyvern wants is more like an English kitchen: a kitchen from "civilised Europe" (as opposed to uncivilised India?). His solution is to move the kitchen nearer to the main house: specifically, to construct a new building next to its rear verandah. He suggests that the building should consist of three rooms: a workroom, cook-room and scullery. The food and pastry should be prepared in the workroom. The cook-room should be furnished with a modern range cooker (Wyvern recommends buying English or American), and used to transfer cooked dishes to serving plates. The scullery should be used for washing up and the

---

* "We have changed all that."

"plucking of poultry". Most importantly, the doors of all three rooms should be locked at the end of the day, and the keys handed back to the lady of the house.

Wyvern anticipates the disapproval of the British residents of Madras for such a venture. He admits that in practical terms his ideal kitchen is virtually impossible to achieve, either through lack of space or because of the cost of building and equipping it – so he offers a compromise. He observes that many houses still have a small building close to the back verandah that was formerly used as a "coolers' godown", but which had been made redundant when ice became more readily available. At the very least, Wyvern recommends walling off part of the rear verandah of the house, so that a small room is created to act as the workroom. This is where all the food would be prepared and the pastry made, as far away as possible from the heat, dust and smoke of the kitchen.

In the final part of his essay on "Our Kitchens in India", Wyvern offers "Ramasamy" some redemption:

> It is downright nonsense to say that native cooks cannot work upon English principles. They manage very well on board ship, where their services are highly prized, yet their appliances are wholly European. The kitchen at the Madras Club, and those of several private houses, both here, and on the Hills, are fitted up entirely upon the Home system, yet the cooks do not complain. No: it seems pretty clear that if no other alternative present itself, Ramasamy can fall into the way of using a range readily enough.[28]

Wyvern tells the tale of a native chef who begged his mistress to let him use a spare room in the house away from the heat and smoke of the kitchen, in order that he might make his jellies and pastries successfully there. Wyvern can see no reason why other cooks might not follow the keen young chef's example.

So there we have it: Wyvern wants to anglicise the kitchens of British India. He yearns after the "cheerful aspect of the English kitchen, its trimness, its comfort, and its cleanliness" against the backdrop of the all-too-common Indian kitchen – a room which, he believes, is the "foulest in our premises".[29]

"Our Vegetables"

As with the chapter on "Our Curries", this one is all about *our* – British – vegetables. Wyvern dives straight in by acknowledging the poor reputation that the English have for cooking vegetables. He hopes to educate the Madras housewife in serving vegetables the European way, rather than providing a few over-boiled vegetables with some roasted meat. He points out that in the climate of India, it is often more desirable to eat vegetables only and forego meat completely. In that case, the vegetables need to have been cooked carefully, and perhaps dressed with a well-flavoured sauce.

Wyvern starts by cataloguing the vegetables commonly found in the Madras markets:

Let us consider what we have got under three heads :–

(a) English vegetables grown in India.
(b) Country vegetables.
(c) Vegetables preserved in tins.

At different periods during the year we can get in Madras: potatoes, green peas, cauliflowers, cabbages, spinach, artichokes (Jerusalem), and globe artichokes from the [Nilgiri] Hills, French beans, carrots, parsnips, turnips, knolkhol,* celery, marrows, leeks, cucumbers, tomatoes, lettuces, beetroot, endive, and onions: all under head number one.

Under head number two we have brinjals,† bandecai,‡ various beans, country cucumber, and greens (which cook well as spinach), moringa pods,§ small tomato or love apple, maize, (*mucka cholum*),** sorrel, pumpkin, yams, onions large and small, garlic, and sweet potato.

For head number three, which we will take separately, we must consult the list of preserved French and American vegetables published by any well-known Firm.[30]

Many of Wyvern's English vegetables would have been grown on the Nilgiri Hills (see Chapter 7), which are mentioned many times in the book as a place where the choicest vegetables are cultivated. Wyvern is also a keen gardener, and has grown vegetables in his gardens in Ootacamund, Bangalore and Secunderabad. He is

---

* kohlrabi
† aubergine (eggplant)
‡ okra (ladies' fingers)
§ Known as drumsticks, on account of their shape.
** maize

particularly proud of his peas: he complains that the ones sold in the Madras markets have been allowed to grow too large, and are too old to be sweet and tender like the ones he has grown himself.

Culinary Jottings for Madras contains many recipes for English vegetables, but Wyvern also writes about the native Indian vegetables mentioned in his second heading above. He declares, "I have the highest respect for all country vegetables",[31] so his menus are not so narrow that vegetables have to be of the English kind – Wyvern gives recipes for them all.

"The Savoury Omelette"

The Savoury Omelette is one of my favourite chapters in *Culinary Jottings for Madras*. These days, I make my omelettes only according to Wyvern's method. I think that the simplicity of the recipes in this chapter is what holds them apart from many of the dinner party dishes which make up so much the book. In Wyvern's own words:

> [W]ith moderate forethought we ought never to be unable to make a good savoury *omelette*, whether in camp, at a traveller's bungalow, at a picnic, or in the privacy of our back verandah in cantonment*.[32]

However, at this point Wyvern launches into another of his complaints about poor "Ramasamy's" abilities:

> Before I proceed to the discussion of *omelette*-making, however, let me point out that Ramasamy has been led astray altogether with regard to this branch of his art. He sends you up a very nice pudding, symmetrical in design, of a goodly consistency, and of a rich brown colour. You almost require a dessert-knife to help it. It is, of course, lighter somewhat, than a 'roly-poly' pudding made of paste,† but it greatly resembles that homely composition. It is a first cousin of the pancake, and Ramasamy evidently uses the stuff of which it is made to coat his plantains when bidden to make fritters.[33]

Wyvern does not exactly think that "Ramasamy" is one of the world's natural omelette-makers, but all is not lost in pursuit of the perfect omelette. Wyvern

---

* A military garrison or camp, especially in India
† pastry

maintains that "native cooks are nevertheless very easily taught how to make one properly, and rarely fail after a patient exemplification of the correct method". (Thank goodness for that.)

Here is Wyvern's basic recipe:

1. Use a proper utensil, with narrow, well sloping sides; see that it is clean, and quite dry.

2. Do not overdo the amount of butter, or salad oil, that you use for the frying.

3. Mix, do not beat the eggs, and never use more than six as in the Pennaconda omelette. It is better to make two of six, than one of twelve eggs.

4. Three eggs, mixed whole, make a nice sized omelette.

5. Be sure that your pan is ready to receive your mixture. If not hot enough, the omelette will be leathery, or you will have to mix it in the pan like "scrambled eggs" (oeufs brouillés).

6. The moment the butter ceases to fizz, and assumes a pale brown tint, the pan is ready.

7. Instantly lift up the part of the omelette that sets at the moment of contact, and let the unformed mixture run under it; repeat this if the pan be very full, keep the left hand at work with a gentle see-saw motion to encourage rapidity in setting, give a finishing shake, and turn it into the hot dish before the whole of the mixture has quite set.

8. The omelette will roll over of its own accord, if the sides of the pan be sloped as I have described, it will not require folding.

9. Three quarters of a minute is ample time for the whole operation, if the pan be properly hot when the mixture is poured into it.

10. Have the hot dish close by the fire, so that you can turn the omelette into it instanter. A little melted butter, with some chopped parsley, may, with advantage, be put into the dish.

It is above all things necessary to have a very brisk fire under the pan while the omelette is being cooked.[34]

The "Pennaconda omelette" mentioned in the method was a breakfast omelette cooked for Wyvern by a member of the Madras Civil Service at Pennaconda (located between Bangalore and Secunderabad), when Wyvern stopped there on a march with his regiment. The omelette is made by adding chopped shallots, chopped parsley, salt and cream to the egg mixture. Wyvern was so impressed with it that he adopted the civil servant's method as his own from then onwards. He finishes the chapter by describing the many and various ingredients you can add to a plain omelette, but the above recipe is the basis for all the flavoured omelettes, including the Pennaconda.

"Réchauffés"

According to Wyvern's philosophy of economical cooking, making *réchauffés* is an absolute necessity. A *réchauffé* is, literally speaking, food that has been reheated. But it is more than that: it is a way of using up leftover food by making it into something new which might turn out quite differently from the original. Wyvern is enthusiastic:

> If the art of dishing up nicely the remains of cold meat, fish, and vegetables were more closely studied than it is, the fair *châtelaine* would not look upon cold mutton, cold beef, &c., with the feelings of despair that I fear too often possess her, there would be much less wastefulness, and our breakfast and luncheon tables would be far more easily supplied than they are.[35]

Wyvern urges his readers to avoid making the same *réchauffés* over and over again, and to experiment with some of his recipes instead. He also warns against the native cook's propensity to smother everything in bottled sauces and condiments. If the mistress take his advice, he asserts, she will no longer find that her leftover meat is always served in fat slices swimming in sea of watered-down Worcestershire sauce. (I'm sure the mistress would be pleased about that!)

Wyvern suggests that previously cooked meat should have any burnt pieces removed. The trimmings, together with any bones, should be used to make a stock. Another of his suggestions is to mince the leftover pieces of meat and enrich them with a thick sauce made from a reduced stock flavoured with vegetables, herbs, a little Marsala wine and some egg yolks. The resulting mixture can then be used in a number of ways.

Some of Wyvern's serving suggestions:

> Make an omelette, spread the mince over the top and roll it out onto a plate.

> "Make a case of mashed potato, with high sides like a *vol-au-vent* case, and pour your mince into it."[36]

> Hollow out some bread rolls, butter them and fry until golden, pour the mince mixture into the hollow and, finally, bake the filled rolls in the oven.

> Make some puff-pastry cases and bake them, then fill the cooked cases with the mince mixture.

> Serve the mince, as it is, in a hot serving dish garnished with pieces of fried bread, crispy bacon, slices of lime and, on the top, a few poached eggs.

Leftover fish has many uses in Wyvern's book, especially for making "little breakfast dishes". His suggestions include making croquettes (flaked fish mixed with mashed potato) and *croustades* (pastry cases filled with fish mixed with a sauce), but the most familiar to the Anglo-Indian community would have been kedgeree. His method for making kedgeree is as follows:

> Kegeree (*kitchri*) of the English type is composed of boiled rice, chopped hard-boiled egg, cold minced fish, and a lump of fresh butter: these are all tossed together in the frying-pan, flavoured with pepper, salt, and any minced garden herb such as cress, parsley, or marjoram, and served smoking hot.[37]

The original Indian dish of *khitchiri* was made with butter, rice, dhal[*] and spices, but the British omitted the dhal and added cooked fish and eggs instead. Nineteenth-century Anglo-Indian recipes such as Wyvern's and Steel and Gardiner's[38] make their kedgeree without any spices, except maybe for black or cayenne pepper. It seems that spices in the form of curry powder were reintroduced

---

[*] Pulses – lentils, beans, peas, etc.

to the dish by former colonials after they had returned to Britain.

"Pastry-making, etcetera"

Not unexpectedly, "Ramasamy" is not the hero of this chapter. Pastry making is very much a European tradition, and Indian cooks seem to have had trouble acquiring the skill (at least according to Wyvern). His opinion is that "Ramasamy stands in great need of instruction here, for his ideas of pastry are, as a rule, crude in the extreme".[39] Wyvern himself admits that the biggest problem for anyone attempting to make pastry in Madras is the hot climate. His solution is to use a marble slab rather than wood, and to pour iced water over the slab to keep it cool. He contrasts the city heat with the cooler climate of the hill stations, and enthuses about the pastry which could be made "on the Hills" (see Chapter 7).

According to Wyvern, "Ramasamy" has only two types of pastry in his repertoire: "butter crust", used for sweet dishes, and "suet crust" for savoury ones. He thinks "Ramasamy's" butter crust is "a humble apology for puff paste", and should be avoided if possible. However, his suet crust has more potential, and "with a little careful teaching Ramasamy is capable of achieving very fair results with it".[40]

Wyvern's solution is to teach his cook to make three basic types of pastry: puff, pie crust and raised pie crust. Puff pastry is to be used for such things as *vol-au-vents*, fruit tarts and patties. Pie crust is suitable for all those savoury pies that the British like so much – beef-steak pie would be a good example. Raised pie crust is used for savoury pies such as pork pies, where the pastry is firm enough to hold the filling without the need for a pie dish.

The colonial Englishman's dreaded thought of an Indian cook touching his food with unwashed hands resurfaces here. Wyvern is insistent that the cook must wash his hands before starting to make the pastry. Even so, he suggests that the cook should be encouraged to use two spoons, rather than his hands, to mix the dough and turn it over after being rolled out. Wyvern insists on the same method being used for bread making. In his chapter on "Camp Cookery", he writes:

> I have taught my servant to use two wooden spoons to work his dough with, the result is satisfactory as regards the lightness of the bread, and to those who dislike eating food mauled by native fingers, the system is especially attractive.[41]

The poor quality of the ingredients to be found in the Madras is another source of problems for pastry making. Wyvern suggests that the flour should be imported and, on account of the high humidity in Madras, dried thoroughly in the oven before being used. Another significant problem is the quality of the butter found in the markets. The local butter had a high water content and had to be pressed to remove as much moisture as possible before being used. Wyvern thinks that the Indian chefs' preference for using beef suet rather than butter is a good practical adaptation in the circumstances, and recommends using it if imported tinned butter is not available, or too expensive.

"Roasting and Braising"
This summary of Wyvern's manifesto for good cookery cannot pass without mentioning his chapter on "Roasting and Braising". It starts with a declaration:

> "Give me," says the Englishman, "a good cut of a well-cooked joint, with a nicely boiled potato, and a fresh vegetable, and I will ask for nothing more." Now, it must be admitted that honest slices of meat constitute the favorite dinner of a Briton. […] And verily the well roasted haunch or saddle of mutton, the sirloin or round of beef, the fillet of veal, and the loin or leg of pork, are dishes peculiar to England, of which we may well boast.[42]

"John Bull", the archetypal Englishman, does not change just because he is no longer living in his home country:

> Our *penchant* for solid food follows us withersoever we wander away from home, and we find John Bull in India as fond of his beef and mutton, as he was when "a humble cottager in Britain." He sighs for a Southdown saddle or a Scotch sirloin.[43]

How does "John Bull" cope with roasting joints of meat in India? Badly, it seems. The animals are not well fed, and good meat is relatively scarce. The scarcity was made worse by the Great Famine of 1877 (see Chapter 5), although by the time of writing the fourth edition of *Culinary Jottings for Madras* in 1883, the situation had improved – at least for the British – and a steady supply of meat could be found once again in the markets. There was even some excellent meat to be found, but at a very high price and equivalent to what they would have had to pay in England.

As mentioned previously, Wyvern is concerned with economy and so chooses to restrict his recipes to cooking the meat that could be found in the bazaars of the

Madras Presidency. He believes that the difficulty in obtaining good meat is partly the fault of the British themselves: they insist on paying the lowest possible price, and the quality of meat reflects that (some things never change).

Wyvern gives some advice and a warning:

> Now, although a vast quantity of wretched meat is sold in the Indian market, I think that people who are willing to pay a good price, and whose servants are not unusually dishonest, can generally get fair beef and mutton at the large stations of this Presidency. A really bad servant will, of course, cheat you with greater cruelty in buying your meat than in anything.[44]

Working on the premise that the lady of the house employs an honest servant who has been able to buy a nice joint of beef or mutton in the bazaar, Wyvern explains that inevitably it will be on the small side, and so needs cooking with care. He strongly recommends braising the joint rather than roasting it. If a larger joint can be acquired for, say, a dinner party, then traditional roasting is perfectly acceptable; but for a small family dinner, braising is the best method. He explains:

> This admirable method of cookery is far too rarely adopted: so for the benefit of those who do not understand the process, I had better mention that braising consists in placing meat in a closed pan, with some made-gravy or stock round it, vegetables cut up, and a judicious allowance of salt and pepper. In this the meat is very slowly simmered, whilst it is browned externally by live coals placed on the braising-pan lid. There is thus heat from above and below the pan, and the joint is cooked in its own gravy, while it derives additional flavour from the vegetables, &c., associated with it.[45]

If the joint of meat *has* to be roasted, then Wyvern issues some rules for its cooking. It must be remembered that in Wyvern's India, roasting would not have taken place inside a closed oven as it would today, but on a rotating spit over hot charcoal. The reason why Wyvern prefers braising is that the roasting process can easily dry out a small joint. He also cautions against running the spit through the meat, so as not to lose any of the juices; rather, he suggests tying the joint onto the spit and cooking it that way. The joint must be frequently basted and a little flour dredged over the meat towards the end of the cooking to create a "crisp, brown, frothy surface".[46]

"Part II: Thirty Menus Worked Out in Detail"
The second part of the fifth edition of *Culinary Jotting for Madras* contains Wyvern's suggestions for thirty full menus. Wyvern revised the menus and corrected errors in each subsequent edition of the book (see Appendix C for a comparison of the first and fifth editions). The names of each of the dishes in a menu are given in French, but English equivalents are provided in the body of the recipes. The hostess could copy the French names to her menu cards to be placed on the table in front of each guest, while perhaps understanding the dishes a little better from their English descriptions.

Wyvern does not provide recipes for the sweet dishes contained in the menus, although many of them can be found in his companion volume, *Sweet Dishes*. In the fifth edition of *Culinary Jottings for Madras* there are ten menus for dinner parties for eight people, a further ten for six people, and a final ten for what Wyvern calls "little home dinners".

The first menu for eight people is set out as follows:[47]

Consommé aux quenelles	Clear soup with quenelles
Seer aux concombres	Seer* with cucumbers
Crème de volaille truffée	Mould of chicken cream
Grenadins de boeuf a la Béarnaise	Fillets of beef Béarnaise fashion
Selle de mouton aux haricots verts	Saddle of mutton with French beans
Galantines de cailles, sauce tartare	Quails boned and rolled, with tartare sauce
Epinards à la crème	Spinach with cream
Pain de fraises	Mould of strawberries
"*Pudding*" *glacé aux abricots*	Iced apricot cream pudding
Fromage, hors d'oeuvres	Cheese, hors d'oeuvres

---

* a local fish

| *Dessert* | Dessert |

Wyvern attaches a note to the end of each menu for eight people, with instructions on how to convert it to the modern style. Here is his note for the above menu:

> To adapt this *menu* according to the new *régime*, serve the saddle after the fish, and instead of galantines of quails, let the birds be roasted with a slice of fat bacon over their breasts, and sent round with bread sauce, fried crumbs, and filbert chips* of potato. A plain *salade* or water-cress should accompany the *rôt*.[48]

Here's the first of the menus for six people:[49]

Potage à la crème d'orge	Pearl barley soup
Orlys de seer, à la Hollandaise	Seer fritters with Hollandaise sauce
Poulet à la St Lambert	Chicken St Lambert fashion
Carré de mouton farci	Shoulder of mutton stuffed
Bécassines rôties	Roast snipes
Petits pois au lard	Green peas with fried bacon
Tartelettes de limon	Lemon cheesecakes
Fromage, hors d'oeuvres	Cheese, hors d'oeuvres
Dessert	Dessert

And finally, a sample menu for a little home dinner:[50]

Potage à la Crécy	Carrot soup
Pomfret sauce ravigote	Pomfret† and ravigote sauce
Poitrine de mouton à la	Breast of mutton à la Wyvern

---

* oval-shaped, deep-fried potatoes
† A local fish.

Wyvern

Purée de pommes de terre	Mashed potatoes
Aubergines au gratin	Brinjals au gratin
Blanc-manger à la vanille	Blancmange with vanilla
Fromage, hors d'oeuvres	Cheese, hors d'oeuvres
Dessert	Dessert
Café noir	Black coffee

In the time between the publications of the second and the fourth editions of *Culinary Jottings for Madras*, Wyvern kept himself busy by writing two new books. *Furlough Reminiscences* was published in 1880, and *Sweet Dishes* a year later in June 1881.

We have seen previously in Chapter 1 that Wyvern was back home in England on furlough for fifteen months between September 1876 and December 1877, and kept a diary of what he describes as a "happy holiday in England". After he had returned to India, he turned the diary into a series of newspaper articles, then later into a book – *Furlough Reminiscences*. The next chapter gives an account of Wyvern's time in England based on the reflections, observations and incidents he relates in the book.

3

Furlough Reminiscences

FURLOUGH REMINISCENCES.

A

POTPOURRI

OF

REFLECTIONS, OBSERVATIONS AND INCIDENTS,

COMPILED

FROM THE DIARY OF A HAPPY HOLIDAY IN ENGLAND.

Wyvern's second book was published in Madras by Higginbotham and Co. in 1880, and written at a time when *Culinary Jottings for Madras* was already proving to be a success in India. In his undated preface, Wyvern informs us that:

> The *"Furlough Reminiscences"* appeared originally in the form of letters from "Exsul" in the *Madras Mail*, and are now republished by the kind permission of the proprietors of that journal.[1]

Wyvern is using the same process for writing that he used very successfully with *Culinary Jottings for Madras*. The book declares its author to be "Wyvern", not "Exsul", which is presumably because he has now become something of a celebrity in Madras, and using his familiar pseudonym would help to sell more copies of the new book.

Furlough Reminiscences was only published in one edition, and is almost impossible to find in antiquarian booksellers' lists. It is probably safe to conclude that the book did not sell anywhere near as many copies as Wyvern's cookery books, especially *Culinary Jottings for Madras*, which ran to seven editions over twenty-six years. However, there are some original copies in the British Library, which has published a facsimile edition in paperback format as part of its historical collection.[2]

Furlough Reminiscences is a frustrating book for the purpose of conducting research into Wyvern's life. He uses pseudonyms throughout the book, presumably to avoid embarrassing his friends and relatives; also to conceal his own identity, because he was a serving officer in the Madras Cavalry at the time. It is possible that Wyvern included some incidents and adventures in the book which happened to fellow officers, but which he claims to have happened to himself. Moreover, it may be the case that some incidents which happened during Wyvern's previous furlough have been woven into *Furlough Reminiscences* as if they had happened in his current one. Even so, we can try to piece together the significant events of Wyvern's fifteen months back in England from September 1876 to December 1877.

Wyvern set sail for England on 1 September. He boarded an Italian mail steamer which he calls "the *Tasmania*" in Bombay, and sailed to Italy: the journey took twenty days. Wyvern discusses at length the merits of travelling on the Italian Rubattino Line rather than the more popular but British P&O Line. The Italian vessel was cheaper, and did not charge for excess luggage or on-board refreshments. The cost of travelling with Rubattino was £50 (including wine, ales and soda water) but the journey with P&O cost £60 with drinks as chargeable extras. P&O also charged a supplement if the passenger's luggage was over a certain weight. The Italian line had yet another advantage: the traveller could break their journey at any of the ports of call, and make their way overland by train if they wanted. The company would forward on a passenger's heavy luggage from the ship's final port of call of Genoa, and Wyvern's was scheduled to be delivered to shipping agents in London.

The Rubattino Line did exist in Wyvern's day, and it did operate a route between Genoa and Bombay via the Suez Canal. However, I can find no evidence of the Rubattino Line owning a ship called the *Tasmania*, so it is likely that this is the first of many instances in the book of Wyvern disguising proper names. Advertisements in contemporary newspapers tell us that Rubattino – or Royal Italian Mail Steamers, to give the company its official title – owned a ship, the *Australia*, that worked the Genoa–Bombay route, and that the first-class fare was indeed £50, including wine and beer at table. A notice in *The Homeward Mail* newspaper confirms that the *Australia* left Bombay for Genoa on 1 September 1876, so it looks like this was in fact Wyvern's *Tasmania* with its name changed. (It is fortunate that Wyvern had already returned to India because in April 1879, the

Australia struck a rock off the coast of Vada in Italy on its way from Genoa to Bombay, and sank – fortunately, everyone on board was saved.)

The *Tasmania/Australia* steamed from Bombay through the Suez Canal and into the Mediterranean Sea. The vessel's final ports of call were Messina in Sicily, Naples and Genoa. Unlike the P&O Line, which employed Asian "Lascars",* Wyvern notes that the crew of the Italian ship were all native Italians and that "the discipline of the vessel was admirable". Wyvern is enthusiastic about the food on board the *Tasmania*, noting that it was not "tainted with oil and garlic" as many British people would have expected on an Italian ship. He remarks:

> I feel sure that many travellers, especially ladies, would prefer the little Italian *menu* to the ponderous bill-of-fare of a P & O Steamer.[3]

The menu included *antipasto*, *pot-au-feu* (the meat from which was served with tomatoes and macaroni), an *entrée*, dressed vegetables, a roast joint of meat, a sweet, cheese and dessert.[4]

Wyvern disembarks at Naples and remarks that it is almost ten years since he last stood on European soil. His previous furlough in England was taken between September 1866 and June 1868, so it was actually little more than eight years since he was last in Europe. After sightseeing in Naples, Wyvern makes his way to Foggia where he catches the train that will "set my face straight for England".[5] He sketches out a little tableau of his fellow passengers and conversations on the train, and proves to be a keen observer of people and manners.

On one occasion he makes an embarrassing assumption that an attractive French companion in his railway compartment is a lady. (By that, I do not mean that he mistakes a male for a female, but a servant for an upper-class woman who, in Wyvern's time, would be called "a lady".) Wyvern confesses: "[I] lost my heart for fully two hours to *Lady D----'s 'own maid'!*"[6] This is first example in the book of Wyvern's acute class-consciousness, and he is downcast when it turns out that the object of his admiration is not of a higher social rank. He has been charming to the young woman and tells her he is "a soldier from India, homeward bound".[7] She is dressed like a lady, while he feels the need to apologise for his own shabby Indian suit and the cuffs of his "*dhoby*-destroyed shirt".† It is the French "lady's"

---

* A sailor from India or SE Asia (OED)
† A *dhoby* is a laundry servant

companion who gives the game away. He turns out to be Lord D----'s valet, but because he is English, Wyvern can tell from the moment the man starts to speak all that he needs to know about his class from his accent. Wyvern is shocked that he thought the couple were a lady and gentleman. He writes about the valet: "his roughly-toned, badly-pronounced English completely staggered me".[8]

Wyvern's railway journey finally ends at the Channel port and he catches the mail boat to England. His luggage was booked through to Charing Cross in London, but he needed to intercept it because he wanted to spend the day with his wife who, he claims, had come down to meet him. Wyvern says that he and his wife stayed the night at the Lord Warden Hotel in Dover. He tells how he was acutely embarrassed to see everyone smiling and smirking at him, and vows not to stay in a hotel "much frequented by honeymooning couples, and by ladies about to greet their long lost husbands" ever again.[9]

If the above anecdote is true then Wyvern's wife, Agnes, must have travelled to England ahead of him. The most likely explanation is that she took their daughter Enid back to England in advance of Wyvern's furlough, so that she could start school. Dane Kennedy tells us in his book *The Magic Mountains: Hill Stations and the British Raj* that it was common for boys to be sent back to England at the age of six or seven, but for girls it was usually a few years later.[10] Although Enid would have been only six years old when Agnes took her back to England, her parents would have been with her until they returned to India in December 1877, by which time she had reached the age of eight and a half. In that scenario, Wyvern would indeed have travelled alone. What we do know is that Wyvern and Agnes were bid a fond farewell on their return to India fifteen months later (see Chapter 1), so she certainly accompanied him back to Madras at the end of his furlough.

Wyvern's new life as a "humble cottager in Britain" is about to begin. The next few chapters in *Furlough Reminiscences* give an account of the Kenney-Herberts' trials and tribulations in finding somewhere suitable to live in London. But first, Wyvern needed new clothes to replace the "rusty garb" he had worn on his journey back from India. Wyvern changes people's names or refers to them by a single letter, as he does with "Lady D----" on the train; this time, his tailor is "Mr Snippage". Wyvern and his tailor talk about one of Wyvern's friends, a certain "Major Blank of the * Hussars" (no names, no pack drill). Finally, "the captain", as all the tradespeople address Wyvern, is kitted out in the contemporary London fashion suitable for a gentleman: suits, shirts, hat, boots and a smart new haircut.

Again, Wyvern is rather taken with an attractive young woman: this time it is the cashier at his hairdressers. He thinks she is one of the "nicest girls in London" and, when he meets her in Kensington Gardens on another occasion, he cannot resist taking off his hat to her because "she was so well turned out, and looked so lady-like".[11] A gentleman such as Wyvern would normally only take his hat off for a lady, not a shop girl.

House hunting does not go well for Wyvern. At first he and his wife stay in lodgings but they prove too expensive, so they decide to move out even though the landlady is "irresistible" and they were "capitally fed". Instead, they decide to rent a house of their own. Most of the areas of London suitable for a gentleman to live were too expensive for Wyvern, so he is persuaded by a slick-talking estate agent to rent a house at an address given in the book as 13 Blenheim Terrace. The address exists today and is now an estate agent, with two floors of accommodation above. The census records for 13 Blenheim Terrace for 1871 and 1881 show that the same family, the Rodwells, lived in the whole building for at least that ten-year period. They were bakers, so it is very likely that during Wyvern's time in London the shop was a bakery (it may even have been the place from which Wyvern bought his daily loaf). If 13 Blenheim Terrace is a smokescreen, then the address of the estate agent's office is more of the same. The office is supposedly located at 713 Westbourne Grove, Bayswater. The problem is that the numbers for buildings in Westbourne Grove, then or now, do not go much higher than 300.

Even though Wyvern was not actually living at 13 Blenheim Terrace, it is probably safe to assume that his real address was somewhere nearby, as many of his stories revolve around the general location.[12] However, in Wyvern's time, the area was out in the suburbs. The Metropolitan Railway had reached the area as early as 1868 with a single branch line.[13] The railway's outward expansion was already extending the boundaries of London, creating what would later became known as "Metroland". The estate agent assures Wyvern that he can easily get to the smarter parts of London because there is a station within three minutes' walk of his house. (The nearest station, St John's Wood Road, was about 15 minutes' walk from Blenheim Terrace. so it seems estate agents were a little economical with the truth, even in those days. The station was later renamed "Lord's", but closed in 1939.)

After some unpleasant legal wrangling, the Kenney-Herberts finally moved into their new home. It seems that their daughter is with them, but not their son. Arthur was born in 1863, so he would have just turned 13 at this time and was probably away at boarding school.

Wyvern, who calls himself "Philip" throughout the book, entertains his uncle for dinner one evening. The uncle enjoys his dinner but complains to Wyvern: "Well, Philip, [...] you're close to Kensal Green, – the cemetery Sir! – miles away from everybody, a part of London I've never heard of anyone living in before!"[14] By that, of course, the uncle means he has never heard of anyone of their *class* living in the area. Wyvern himself is outraged when a clerk at the gas supply company tells him he lives in a neighbourhood where the houses were "run up cheap". Wyvern splutters: "Why here was an impertinent snob of a third-rate clerk telling me to my face that I lived in a lath-and-plaster neighbourhood"!"[15]

Wyvern is more generous in his attitude towards some of the local tradespeople. He takes a liking to Mr Welby, his butterman, whom Wyvern thinks is "one of those chatty, smiling, intelligent fellows who generally know everything". One day, Wyvern walks into Welby's shop and asks if he has any Devonshire cream. Welby replies: "Excuse my saying so, Sir, but we've no haristocracy of your sort living here; so there's no good getting in of delicacies."[16] (Wyvern likes to write exactly how people speak, including his approximation of their accent – as we can see in the above quote, he often modifies his spelling to produce the desired effect.) Welby is an expert on cheeses and impresses Wyvern with his knowledge; he even gets hold of some mature cheddar cheese, which he maintains is as good as any Stilton cheese, from his brother who has a shop in the City of London. Wyvern is very grateful.

If Wyvern was pleased with the local tradespeople, then finding good servants was an entirely different matter. The chapter on "Concerning Servants" is especially interesting because when Wyvern eventually retired from the army in India and returned to England, he would set up exactly the sort of employment agency for servants that he describes using for himself in this chapter. He tells us that his wife entrusted him with the selection of a cook and a parlour-maid which – if true and not one of Wyvern's smokescreens – makes the Kenney-Herberts a very modern-sounding couple. This is unusual for the time because when Wyvern arrived at the servants' registry, he was the only man in the place. The registry employees, the people looking for servants and the servants themselves were all women, and everyone turned to look at the hapless Wyvern. He confesses:

> I am habitually shy when alone with *one* lady; I leave you, therefore, to imagine what I felt on discovering myself entirely surrounded by the fair sex – my retreat cut off, a bevy of expectant cooks in front of me [...]. I felt hot up to the roots

of my hair.[17]

To cap it all, after he had chosen a cook and a parlour-maid, one "saucy looking girl" asked if he also needed a nurse, which the other young women apparently found hilarious. Wyvern beat a hasty retreat.

It is not surprising that, given Wyvern's hasty choice of a cook and a parlour-maid, things did not turn out too well. Everything was fine for a few months: the cook was "well up to her work", and the parlour-maid was "a clean industrious girl". Wyvern blames himself for not being strict enough with the staff. First, the cook was too ill to work after drinking too much gin the previous night. Then she gets the parlour-maid and the lady's-maid drunk on a Sunday afternoon. When Wyvern asks a French chef from a nearby restaurant to bring over some *vol-au-vents* for his wife's lunch, the cook, worse the wear for drink, physically attacks the little chef and screams that she does not want any of his "beastly messes" in *her* kitchen.[18] There was a reconciliation of sorts after Wyvern's wife had spoken to the cook, but it was short-lived.

A little while after the incident with the French chef, Agnes Kenney-Herbert's *ayah** arrives from India to be with her mistress. We then observe the first of a number of instances of casual racism described in the book. On the *ayah*'s arrival, Wyvern's cook promptly resigns, saying that she never could "abide a black",[19] and the parlour-maid follows her out the door. Wyvern resolves the problem by paying higher wages to secure the services of a more experienced (and less bigoted) cook and parlour-maid, who ended up staying with the Kenney-Herberts until they broke up their household and returned to India.

As we have already seen, Wyvern comes across as a man with an eye for the ladies. He describes a visit to a library as follows:

> I admit that I dawdled with this delightful librarian. I became very doubtful with regard to my selections, and artfully courted as much conversation and assistance as possible, observing with aesthetic pleasure the pose of her lissom figure, as she stood upon the ladder in order to get me books from the upper shelves.[20]

This does not sound very much like the man who is shy in the company of women

---

* lady's maid

that he claimed to be during his visit to the servants' registry! "Lissom" – slim, supple and graceful – appears more than once as a description of the young women that Wyvern meets. He recalls seeing "a bevy of lissom hand-maidens"[21] in one particular shop, for example. On a visit to a country house he enthuses about cooking alongside his fellow (female) guests and sighs that:

> Kitchen floors demand that skirts be pinned up; dainty ankles are therefore cunningly revealed, and you find that mixing a *Mayonnaise* sauce with an accompaniment of mirthful chatter, silvery laughter, and the pattering of pretty little shoon,* is far from disagreeable work.[22]

Once he has settled in to his new life in England, Wyvern decides that he ought to visit his relations who live in the country. He is not looking forward to the visit. Wyvern is a well-travelled man with experience of the wider world; the thought of the parochial nature of life in the country fills him with dread:

> The mind of the domesticated Briton is narrow enough, no matter where he may live; but for downright Pharisaical exclusiveness, can any folk on earth be compared with those of our kith and kin who have been born bred, and educated within the sacred pale of "county society"?[23]

Wyvern tells the story of a fellow officer who has found a wife in India. Even though the officer's wife was as English as his sisters and sisters-in-law (and in many ways "superior" to them), they look down on her and do not think she is a suitable wife for a man in their social circle. As we know, Wyvern met and married Agnes in India, so it is more than likely that he is talking about himself without directly saying so.

Wyvern met up with his brother-in-law and went shooting, after which he "pushed on to my birth place". He does not, of course, mention the place by name, but we know that he was born and brought up at Bourton-on-Dunsmore. He meets "A flippant younger brother who had come up specially to greet me from Oxford".[24] As Wyvern has only one brother, this must be Edward Maxwell Kenney-Herbert, who was indeed associated with Merton College, Oxford.

Wyvern recalls a church service he attended with Edward which was presided

---

* shoes

over by the "old parson". As previously mentioned in Chapter 1, the parson sounds like someone unconnected with Wyvern; yet we know from the census of 1881, some four years later, that his father was still living at Bourton Rectory – so presumably it is his father, dutifully disguised. This is probably just as well, as Wyvern goes on to say that he and his brother made fun of the sermon because it was exactly the same one, told in exactly the same way, as they had heard many times before in their youth. (Interestingly, it was on "The Prodigal Son" – Wyvern perhaps?)

Another instance of casual racism occurs when Wyvern meets an old family servant who, incidentally, still calls Wyvern "*Master* Philip". The servant is a gardener and he takes Wyvern aside to ask him how many men he has killed. Wyvern replies that he has never been to the wars. The gardener responds: "'ow many of them blacks now 'ave you fairly killed?" Wyvern quickly realises that "the dear old creature was under the impression that officers in India were in the habit of slaying any native that displeased them".[25] The gardener takes offence and believes Wyvern is trying to deceive him when he tries to explain that a native would be tried for a crime in India, just like an Englishman, and not summarily shot.

Wyvern's next port of call is his old school. As we already know, Wyvern went to the prestigious Rugby School in Warwickshire, but he cannot bring himself to name the school, so he calls it "Avonby" (the town of Rugby is on the River Avon). He meets old employees of the school and chats about old times, but we must assume that the names mentioned are heavily disguised. In one conversation an old school servant says to Wyvern: "O! It'll take years to make the school what it was in your time, Sir – in Dr G's days, I mean."[26]

Back in London after his visit to Warwickshire, Wyvern settles into life in the bustling metropolis. He takes great care with his appearance and feels very satisfied with himself when he is walking down the street with his neck-cloth neatly tied, his boots shining like mirrors and his cherished umbrella nicely balanced in his hand. He is also perfectly comfortable shopping with his wife. He declares that most men think of shopping as a "feminine treat, and a masculine penance".[27] Not Wyvern – he freely admits that he likes clothes shopping with his wife, although that may have something to do with his fondness for talking with the "charming young ladies" he meets on their retail expeditions. Wyvern reveals that he has a "sort of rough knowledge of millinery mysteries" but is quick to distance himself from the "lady-like man" who is obsessed with shopping and who, Wyvern believes, should really have been born female.[28] He even provides the shop assistant with some watercolour sketches of dresses he thinks his wife might like, although quite what Agnes thought of this, we do not know.

Like many of the civil servants, lawyers, merchants and soldiers coming home from India, Wyvern is keen to attend the major sporting and social events while he is back in England. Horse racing at Ascot and Epsom are particular favourites for the returnees, even if they attend no other events while back in their home country. While at the Epsom Derby, Wyvern meets fellow officers from the Madras Cavalry "comprising many a well-known name in Southern India", who are gathered around their carriage, eating picnics and drinking champagne. He tells us that "cheery greetings resounded as each unexpected sunburnt wanderer turned up".[29] Wyvern, true to form, does not name names, but the cheering and shouting came to a crescendo when:

> A very popular ex-member of the Quarter Master General's Department, whose connection with the secretariat of the Bangalore races will not soon be forgotten, came up to the place. On recognising this new arrival, a subaltern of the Regiment, seated on the roof of the coach [...] sprang to his feet with a wild "view halloo"* exclaiming "*Shabásh!*† here we are again at Bangalore!"[30]

The civilians in the neighbouring carriages were evidently startled by this outburst and thought that the subaltern must be completely mad, but the old soldiers of Madras didn't care; they were having a merry reunion and thoroughly enjoying themselves.

If the Epsom Derby was a good excuse to meet up with fellow officers from India, then the Oxford and Cambridge boat race gives Wyvern an opportunity to meet a whole new social circle. The chapter describing his adventures is titled "At the Boat Race with a Bohemian Party". The evening before the boat race, Wyvern gets a telegram from an old army colleague inviting him – no refusal accepted – to join him at the race. Their carriage arrives early in the morning, and off they set. Wyvern is a little puzzled as to why the most comfortable seat in the carriage is vacant, but he soon learns the answer. The carriage diverts to a house in the suburbs and out comes "a young lady dressed in black velvet, with a lovely pale blue bonnet".

---

* A call used to incite dogs to the chase during a hunt (OED).
† Bravo!

Wyvern recognises the young lady as a famous actress from a fashionable theatre. Wyvern helps the actress into her seat and off they go. But once again, they head away from the course of the boat race, and stop at another house. Out comes "a second fair passenger". Wyvern has to help her into the carriage by letting her use his boot as a step. She is also an actress, but not yet as successful as their first passenger, and she and Wyvern strike up an immediate friendship. It is a cold morning and Wyvern whispers that the actress, whom he calls "Lotty", "nestled up close to me very cosily".[31]

Eventually, they reach Barnes, which is on the River Thames and close to the finishing line of the race. They are invited into a house where the main room is lined with dining tables and waiters are bustling about, setting places for about forty people. Most of the other guests are in the garden which looks directly out onto the river. Wyvern describes them as "a few richly attired, and a few eccentric looking ladies, and a motley gathering of men". He recognises a comedian, a professional singer, a barrister who is also a writer, an artist and a few soldiers. Everyone gets very excited when the competing boats approach, with each person shouting for their favourite team. When the race is over, the guests return to the dining room. Wyvern describes the scene:

> The tables groaned with good food; the champagne flowed like water; breakfast was dovetailed into luncheon, luncheon into afternoon tea. Merriment, songs, and clever stories followed each other, and we did not break up till it was growing dusk.[32]

Wyvern appears to have enjoyed Lotty's company all day long and, when they part, she gives him her bouquet, which he absent-mindedly puts in his buttonhole. Wyvern is in trouble with his wife when he eventually arrives home at half-past eight in the evening. Not only is he more than an hour late for dinner, but Agnes was expecting him back for breakfast! She demands to know where he has been since the race finished, and is less than impressed that he has an actress's bouquet in his buttonhole. Wyvern consoles himself with the realisation that "Bohemian feasts [do] not occur every day".

It is curious that in a book where Wyvern takes a great deal of trouble to disguise the true identity of the people he is writing about, he specifically tells an uncomplimentary story about his own wife in the chapter "A Fashionable Craze – Spiritualism". (Perhaps Agnes gave him a hard time over his exploits at the boat race, and this was his way of getting his own back!) It seems that Agnes took to going to seances to keep a friend company, after the friend's son had been murdered. Agnes then adopted spiritualism herself: Wyvern complains that it is like having a newborn baby in the house, and his own needs are very much being given a back seat. He is not even allowed to speak to his wife if she is being "visited" by spirits.

At the time, there had been a recent and well-reported court case where a self-professed medium, Henry Slade, had been caught fraudulently producing evidence of paranormal activity during a seance. Slade's trick was to claim that spirits had written a message in chalk on a slate, but investigators proved that Slade had written on it prior to the proceedings, and swapped a blank slate for the pre-written one to fool his audience.[33] Despite the court case, Agnes remains a fan of "poor, dear, Dr Slade", and Wyvern is driven to distraction by her obsession.

Desperate to find a way out of his wife's new-found devotion to the supernatural, Wyvern consults a friend who advises him to humour Agnes and to go along with her to her meetings, pretending that he has become interested himself. Wyvern is unsure at first because he believes that the followers of spiritualism are:

> composed almost wholly of fashionable people, with time and money (for it is an expensive creed) to throw away. The fair sex, as may be expected, predominates among them, for though there are a few male devotees in their ranks [...] the true believer is woman [sic].[34]

Even so, Wyvern decides to take his friend's advice and accompanies Agnes to a seance. Fortunately for him, there are other husbands present who have also paid their "fifteen and six per head"* to attend the meeting with their wives, and they are just as sceptical as him. Between them they make life very difficult for the medium: at one point the medium is tied to a chair and the spirits are supposed to untie him (in reality, he is a escapologist). Unfortunately for the medium, the man who insists on tying him up is a yachtsman, and the medium is forced to claim that the spirits are asking for a knife in order to free himself. When the medium invites the attendees to put forward questions to ask the spirits, the men start asking frivolous ones and fall about laughing. The medium abruptly ends the proceedings,

---

* Fifteen shillings and sixpence – a considerable sum of money in Wyvern's day.

complaining that he is being ridiculed; but it does not stop him suggesting to the ladies that they have a private seance the following week – for which they will be charged once again, but at a specially discounted price.

At this point, Agnes is beginning to have some doubts about the medium's good intentions. Wyvern concludes his plan by taking Agnes to see "an amusing performance at Maskelyne and Cooke's". John Maskelyne was a famous stage magician of his day and, along with George Cooke, put on shows of magic and illusion at the Egyptian Hall in London's Piccadilly.[35] After seeing the tricks in the show, Agnes changes her mind and returns to being "as rational as she had been before her supernatural conversion".

There are numerous observations on the British class system throughout the book. In one scene, where Wyvern is waiting at a photographer's studio, he is looking around at the other people in the room and remarks of a grand woman and her daughters that they are "evidently wealthy people, but *not* belonging to *haut ton* exactly".[36] The *haut ton* is the Upper Ten Thousand – a collective name for the British ruling classes – of which *he* is a part, and *she* is not.

An article in *The Spectator* of 1 April 1871 reads:

> The Upper Ten Thousand of London had a field-day on Wednesday. The Queen opened the "Royal Albert Hall," that huge and ugly copy in brick of the Colosseum, down there in Kensington, and eight thousand persons in their finest clothes went to see Her Majesty and each other.[37]

In case anyone was in any doubt about who qualified for inclusion in the Upper Ten, they could consult *The Upper Ten Thousand* by Adam Bissett Thom, published in 1875, which provides:

> An alphabetical list of all members of Noble Families, Bishops, Privy Councillors, Judges, Baronets, Members of the House of Commons, Lords-Lieutenant, Governors of Colonies, Knights and Companions of Orders, Deans and Archdeacons, and the Superior Officers of the Army and the Navy, with their official descriptions and addresses.[38]

There is no one by the name of Kenney or Kenney-Herbert included in the book so maybe Wyvern, being a mere captain at the time, did not qualify. As we have noted already, it was also in 1875 that the Kenney family changed their name *en masse* to Kenney-Herbert, and there are numerous entries for the name Herbert, some of whom were distantly related to Wyvern's family. So the Kenney-Herberts were on the fringes of the Upper Ten, if not important enough to be listed in the book. By the time Wyvern retired from his post as Secretary to the Government of Madras at the rank of colonel, he would surely have qualified for an entry in his own right. However, there is no doubt that when Wyvern was writing *Furlough Reminiscences*, he firmly believed he belonged within the ranks of the Upper Ten.

It is not so much that Wyvern despises the lower or middle classes, it is more that he is part of a rigid class system and has sensitive antennae as to who belongs in which class. The classes do get together on occasion in some mutually enjoyable pastime. For example, Wyvern describes the Oxford and Cambridge boat race as:

> a grand national holiday for the male upper ten, the middle and lower classes, and the tag-rag and bobtail of London alike. The social pack is shuffled with a vengeance.[39]

At the Epsom Derby too, Wyvern is certain that he will be "buffeted by a throng of uncouth folk, or swayed about amidst a well-dressed mob of fashionable people. It mattered not".[40]

During his time on holiday in England, Wyvern makes a point of observing the habits and customs of classes other than his own. He comes to the very interesting conclusion that there is:

> one grand, co-existing trait of character amongst all classes, which asserted itself wherever I saw my countrymen assembled *en masse*: it consisted in their common devotion to eating and drinking.[41]

Wyvern maintains that the picnic itself is the essential part of the great British open-air festivals. He is not snobbish about the food his social inferiors are eating:

> It is of little consequence to compare the materials which compose these dearly loved *al fresco* festivals. The giant sandwich of cold boiled pork, and the lukewarm Bass in a stone bottle passed round from mouth to mouth, of the one circle, are no doubt as delightful as the iced champagne cup, and *galantines truffée* of the other.[42]

Wyvern quizzes his greengrocer's wife about the contents of their picnic basket, which they are planning to take to the Windsor Review. This is her reply (in Wyvern's approximation of her accent):

> We mostly allas takes a nice leg of cold boiled pork, a few pounds of sliced 'am, a cold kidney pie, and some sausages. A bit of pickled 'erring or mackerel and a few 'eads of lettuce, with a cucumber if they're reasonable, is what few can say no to; and then to be sure, there's bread, and butter, cheese, spring honions, and radishes; jam turn-overs, fruit puffs, and such like, a sweet raisin cake, and hany fruit that's plentiful. Has for liquor we in general sticks to a porter in a stone jar for it is so coolin, is a porter, of a 'ot day.[43]

Wyvern is impressed with the variety and quality of the food in the greengrocer's picnic basket, even if it is not the kind of fare he would take to the Windsor Review himself. There is not much doubt that his own basket would contain refreshment more in the vein of the *galantines truffée* and the iced champagne cup.

Focusing on his own class, Wyvern reprises some observations that he first made in his column, "Etcætera from Town", in *The Athenaeum and Daily News* (see Chapter 1) about places a little way outside London where high society goes to relax away from the dust and noise of the metropolis. He is particularly fond of Hurlingham, located in Fulham, and the Orleans Club in Twickenham. Both locations were semi-rural in Wyvern's day and border the River Thames. Wyvern waxes lyrical about his experiences:

> To find yourself wandering in luxury over velvet turf, and among lovely flower beds, is, of course, a great attraction. But even that pleasure would fade, and appear scarcely worth the candle, were it not for the delicate little luncheon, the afternoon tea on the lawn under the cedars, and the perfect dinner which you know you can rely upon. There is, I confess, a charm in this combination of nice things, that baffles description.[44]

At the Orleans Club, Wyvern walks through the gardens down to the river, watching the pretty young women in their summer dresses and, later in the day, eats in the well-appointed dining room. He points out that the atmosphere at the club is nothing like that of a stuffy London club, not least because women are not only welcome but are encouraged to enjoy themselves. Because the guests are from the same class and from similar backgrounds, it seems as if they all know each other and no one is made to feel uncomfortable. Wyvern is particularly keen on visiting the club on a Sunday so he can enjoy an expertly cooked dinner whereas, at home, it would be the cook's day off and she would be spending her time having a "happy day with her young man".

There is a chapter devoted to "English Dinners" in which Wyvern welcomes the modern trend for dinners to be served *à la Russe* (see Chapter 10), rather than the long-held custom of *service à la Française* (see Chapter 2). With *service à la Russe* the courses are served one after the other, with the food already plated. Wyvern despondently describes the scene at the dinner tables of old where four different joints of roasted meat, each competing with the others with their steamy aromas, are placed on the table together surrounded by vegetables which have been "ruined by ignorant cookery". Wyvern does not regret the passing of a system of dining where "quantity was held in honour before quality, and size was at a premium".[45] Instead, he rejoices in the new regime where:

> You now sit down to dinner with your aesthetic senses gratified, an air of refinement pervades everything, the decorations of the table, the well-toned light, and the general attractiveness of the scene pleases you. The little *menu* card, quaintly illuminated, tells you that you are only to have a few things; but each dish, you notice, has been considered well with reference to its predecessor, and you feel that you may therefore take a little of each *plat* without fear. The wine, you find, is sound, deliciously cold, and beautifully dry.[46]

Wyvern relates a tale of being invited to a meal which he was especially looking forward to because the quality of his hosts' dinners was legendary. The evening did not go well, but not because of the food. The menu cards at each place setting were held between the outstretched wings of a china butterfly. The cards themselves would be completely unacceptable today because they were illustrated with ten black characters who were dressed "in the orthodox evening dress of the Christy Minstrels".[47] When the modern reader encounters this passage, we expect some of the guests to be upset by the racism depicted on the cards, but it is not the case for Wyvern's contemporaries. The ensuing commotion is created by his dinner companion who, bizarrely, objects to the cruelty of stretching a butterfly's wings, even though they are made of china. The worst thought that anyone, including Wyvern, has about the representation on the cards themselves is that they are "in bad taste" because the tenth character is drunk and falls over (and then there were nine).

Life was not all fun and games for Wyvern while he was back home in England. He seems to have done some freelance work as well. He writes: "I worked as picture gallery gossip-monger – I cannot claim the loftier title of art critic – for a fashionable weekly journal."[48] He gains experience in writing reviews and critiques which, no doubt, he would find extremely helpful when he eventually retired to England and started writing newspaper articles on the art of dining. He also takes on the job of completing a review of art galleries from a critic who has fallen ill. Wyvern has to travel to the "semi-rural suburb beyond Fulham"[49] to meet the critic. (Anyone who knows modern London will be amused at the Fulham area being described as "semi-rural", because it is now just as built-up and traffic-clogged as any other part of the city.)

There is another fascinating insight into Wyvern's future career when he is talking about the cost of living in London, compared with running a household in the Madras Presidency. Wyvern has found two establishments run by foreign chefs where he could buy ready prepared meals at very reasonable prices, and which only needed their final cooking in the customer's own kitchen. After his retirement from the army, Wyvern established the Common-Sense Cookery Association in London, whose advertisements announce: "Dishes cooked in the school on sale daily. Complete dinners or single dishes supplied."[50]

With his furlough nearly over, Wyvern has to steel himself to complete one last task before returning to India. It was customary for returning officers to have their photograph taken, but he is uncomfortable about the whole experience, grumbling that he is "condemned to be photographed". He is outraged that he has pay in advance for the service, which he feels is "plainly implying doubt as to one's honesty".[51] Wyvern is an English gentleman, and as such he does not understand why he has to pay for any article before he has even seen it.

It seems that his whole family had their photos taken because, on one visit to the photographer's studio, Wyvern has to approve some proofs of his daughter's photographs. He relates the unpleasant experiences of having his picture taken at a number of famous photographers' studios (one of which he humorously describes as being the studio of "Messrs Slurrit and Blurr"), although he does find one lesser-known studio where being photographed is just about tolerable. It is possible that he is referring here to the studio of C. Naudin on High Street, Kensington, because we know that he uses its services for a portrait taken after he had retired to England (see Chapter 13).

So, the time has come for Wyvern to leave England and return to military life in India: he arrived back on 16 December 1877. His days of being a "humble cottager" in England are over. "Today" he laments, "I am at work again, an exile and alone".[52] As we know, he was not exactly alone because Agnes returned to Madras with him, but he makes the point dramatically enough. However, it is quite possible that his duties included being posted away from his cantonment in Madras to some remote and fiercely hot area in the *mofussil* (outlying country districts), and that is why the quotation cited at the beginning of this book sounds so plausible and heart-rending.

4

Madras

Wyvern spent most of his years in India in the region known as the Madras Presidency, which covered the modern Indian states of Tamil Nadu and Andhra Pradesh as well as parts of Odisha, Kerala, Karnataka and Telangana – in other words, nearly all of southern India. The presidencies were similar to modern states: they had their own governments which had devolved powers, but which ultimately answered to the national government in Calcutta, headed by the viceroy.

The strange thing about the development of the City of Madras is that there was no fully functioning harbour until 1900, by which time Wyvern had retired to England. The Madras expert, S. Muthiah, tells us in his book *Madras Discovered* that for the first 250 years in the history of Madras, the East India Company's boats would anchor offshore, their goods offloaded and passengers disembarking on small, local boats called *masula*.[1] The illustrated newspapers of the time employed artists to illustrate their stories, just as modern newspapers use photographs. (I have a small collection of such prints from late nineteenth-century Madras, including one of a *masula* carrying passengers and their belongings from their ship to the shore. There is an unmistakable look of fear on a British woman's face, as she and her worldly goods are transported through the surf.) Cavalry officers such as Wyvern would even have had their horses landed by rowing boats, which must have been quite an achievement. Another picture shows how the boat was rested on its side, and the horse gently encouraged to step inside, at which time the boat was righted and launched into the sea.

In 1868 the Madras Chamber of Commerce began to lobby the Madras government to construct a purpose-built harbour. It was concerned that the *masula* boatmen were charging exorbitant fees for their services and, on occasion, deliberately dropping their cargo into the sea, declaring it lost, then employing strong swimmers to retrieve it later from the waves. Mrs Murray Mitchell, a missionary visiting Madras in February 1882, remarks on the lack of a working harbour:

It was an odd idea to plant a great city down on a long sea-shore without reference to bays or harbors, or even a reasonably safe approach by the natural way to it, the sea. On this coast the surf-wave is very dangerous; even in fine weather it rises several feet; and every one knows what it means to land at Madras when the weather is at all tempestuous. I have found it quite exciting to watch the catamarans cut through the boiling surf on a stormy evening. They disappear entirely for a few moments, and you think it is all over with the poor fishermen crew. But no; they hold on somehow to their frail-looking barks and emerge presently none the worse, shaking themselves free from the white foam like so many water-dogs. The dark skins, happily, do not seem to attract the numerous sharks so readily as white ones would do in similar circumstances.[2]

Work on the harbour began in 1876. Wyvern, then a captain, would have seen the construction taking shape. Muthiah describes how two parallel masonry breakwaters, each 3,000 feet (900 m) long, were built, which turned in towards each other on their seaward end to form a 515-foot (157-m) entrance. The harbour could accommodate nine large ships and was completed in 1881. Unfortunately, disaster struck just months later: in November 1881 a severe cyclone hit Madras, and the new harbour was all but destroyed, along with two ships that were sheltering inside. It must have been a terrifying spectacle to see the harbour reduced to rubble and two of the huge Titan cranes, which had carried out the building work, pitched into the sea.[3]

When the newly-appointed governor, Sir Mountstuart Grant Duff, arrived in Madras in 1881, he quickly set to work realising a plan he had conceived on an earlier trip there in the 1870s to build The Marina. The Marina is not a harbour for small boats, which is what we would think of today if we heard the name, but a promenade running along the landward side of the beach. The promenade was opened by Grant Duff in 1884 and extends for 6 km along the beach, although the natural beach itself stretches for some further 7 km. Today, it is a popular place to stroll, buy an ice cream or snack and admire the fine statue of Mahatma Gandhi erected in 1959. However, the sea is as dangerous as ever, and swimming off the beach is banned because of the strong undertow. When looking out to sea from the promenade it is easy to imagine that somewhere on the seabed, deep under the surf, there is probably still some "lost" cargo which the *masula* boatmen never managed to retrieve.

Fort St George had long been established as a military base by the time Wyvern arrived in India, and it is still so today for the Indian armed forces. St Mary's Church, consecrated in 1680 and proudly claiming to be "the oldest Church East of the Suez", was built within the ramparts of the fort and itself is fortified against sieges and cyclones. Muthiah tell us that the original church was built "with outer walls four feet thick and a bomb-proof curved roof two feet thick".[4] Wyvern would almost certainly have worshipped in St Mary's while he was garrisoned at Fort St George. Today, the church is only under siege from the many tourists who visit, and yet remains a haven of peace and tranquility among the busy comings and goings of the fort.

Mitchell gives us her impression of the European houses in Madras:

> Madras differs in a good many points from the other cities of India we have seen. The European part is of immense extent and has far more beauty to show than I remembered. The houses are large, two-storied, and exceedingly handsome. They are surrounded by extensive gardens and grounds, wonderfully green, and ornamented by clumps of fine trees and shrubs and evergreens in all the luxuriance of beautiful tropical foliage. These residences, standing in their park-like inclosures, extend for miles chiefly along the shore, and there is a sense of delightful expansiveness everywhere as if space counted for nothing, which is extremely pleasant in so very hot a climate.[5]

As we have already seen, *Culinary Jottings for Madras* was published in Madras by Higginbotham and Co., which was founded in 1844 as both a publisher and a bookseller. The present Higginbotham's bookshop – the oldest and largest in India – was not built until 1904, but Wyvern would certainly have visited Higginbotham's former premises, also on Mount Road, in advance of his first edition in 1878. (All seven editions of *Culinary Jottings for Madras* as well as Wyvern's *Furlough Reminiscences* and *Sweet Dishes* were published by Higginbotham and Co.)

A short way from The Marina is a curious building known today as Vivekanandar Illam. It is circular in design and its original name, the Ice House, gives away its past history. The Ice House was built in 1842 by an American, Frederic Tudor – the self-styled "Ice King", whose company transported huge blocks of ice to Madras by clipper from the Great Lakes of North America. The ice was unloaded and stored in the ice house, which has double walls for insulation against the fierce heat of Madras.

Many of Wyvern's recipes call for the use of ice, and it is quite possible that his butler would have been sent out to buy it from the Ice King. Sometimes the ice supply could be erratic, so its cost was determined by availability. Prices rose steeply in 1868 when an ice ship failed to arrive from North America: the Madras Club had to pacify some of its members because the price of its iced drinks rose considerably. In February 1877, the agent for the Tudor Company wrote to the Madras newspapers, requesting its customers to limit their consumption to the absolute minimum necessary until the next ice ship arrived in 78 days' time. The previous ship had had difficulties in unloading all of its cargo, and the full amount ordered by customers in Madras had not been delivered.

However, soon the Ice King would have some competition. An editorial in *The Athenaeum and Daily News* from March 1877 remarks on a letter to the newspaper from The General Ice Factory Company in London, announcing that it intended to set up an ice factory in Madras.[6] The editor is all in favour of the proposal, making the point that the previous irregularities in the ice supply would cease to occur because it would be made locally in a purpose-built factory, rather than needing to be transported by sea from America. The editorial concludes that competition to supply ice should also bring down prices – which would be very welcome to the citizens of Madras.

Perhaps the most famous institution in Madras was the Madras Club. We know from *The Asylum Press Almanac and Compendium of Intelligence for 1882* that Wyvern was a member of the club's General Committee at that time.[7] It was founded in 1832 and, according to the *Short Historical Notice of the Madras Club* by Henry Davison Love, those allowed membership were:

> Civil Servants on quitting the College; Officers of His Majesty's and the Honourable Company's Military Service of two years' standing, or the rank of Captain; Officers of the Medical Department; members of the Bench and Bar; the Clergy, and all who form part of society at Madras.[8]

In other words, the upper echelons of society and, in line with the racial segregation of the times, certainly no Indians – even if they were maharajahs. The Madras Club soon relaxed its rules a little to allow men (it was, of course, a male-only club) who were on the "Government House List" to become members. The Club bought its first permanent premises on Mount Road towards the end of 1832.

Even in its early days, the Madras Club had a reciprocal arrangement with Bengal Club in Calcutta and the Byculla Club in Bombay, whereby each club's members were allowed to use the others' facilities. Right from the outset, the club appears to have has a gambling problem. It looks like the members would bet on almost anything, not just card games – racket games, billiards and even quoits are mentioned in the history. The committee took a dim view of this and tried to limit the stakes to a moderate level, but the move does not appear to have been very successful. Various rumours concerning the high stakes being gambled appeared in the gossip columns of the local newspapers in the 1850s, but none were ever proven.[9]

When the "Ice King" formed The Tudor Ice Company in Madras in 1840, the Madras Club bought shares in the project. The minutes of the club's committee meeting note that ice was "a new article of consumption in this Presidency".[10] The club started to serve iced drinks in its new "Ice Bar" at first at considerable loss, but later at a reasonable profit despite occasional shortages.

A ball was held at the club on 25 March 1870 in honour of the Duke of Edinburgh, who was making a royal visit to India. Wyvern was a captain then, so it is likely that he would have attended the ball if he was stationed in Madras at the time. We know for sure that Wyvern was stationed in Madras for the Prince of Wales' visit in 1875, because his horse took part in the Madras races, watched by the prince himself (see Chapter 1). The Madras Club held a grand ball in the prince's honour: members dined in a marquee on the lawn while the ball committee and the prince used the main building. Tents were pitched in the grounds of the club for the "up-country" members because there was not enough accommodation available in the club itself. The *Short Historical Notice of the Madras Club* makes a point of noting that these two balls were the only known occasions when women were "freely admitted" to the clubhouse.[11] The cost of the ball was split between 288 members, who later received a photograph of the official engraving depicting the Prince and Princess of Wales.

George Wheeler tells us in his book, *India in 1875–76: The Visit of the Prince of Wales*, that the prince returned to the club the following day and took lunch there:

> It was a day for "curries," for the making of which the institution has gained a reputation. The Prince remained two hours and a quarter within the building, during which time nine different curries and fifteen chutnees were set before the guests. His Royal Highness's chef de cuisine, Monsieur Bonnemain, went

into the club kitchen to see how the native Consamas* made their famous dishes.[12]

The prince is reported in the minutes of the Madras Club to have been so pleased with the curries he was served during his stay that he took one of the club's cooks back to England with him. He was especially keen to introduce chutneys made from fresh herbs into English cuisine. The Madras Club kept a complaints book, and it makes for interesting reading. Despite the prince's praise for the club's curries (or possibly because he had sequestered its best chef), one entry reveals a club member complaining that "the Club curries are notoriously bad".[13] Maybe the committee should have asked Wyvern to give instructions to the curry-cook!

Wyvern mentions the Madras Club on a number of occasions in his "Culinary Jottings for Madras" column for *The Athenaeum and Daily News*, and not always in good way. On one occasion, in 1876, he claims a formal dinner was spoiled by poor service. The cause, in Wyvern's opinion, was not so much the waiting staff but the menu itself. There were too many items and the waiting staff were falling over themselves to serve all the courses at the appropriate time. On another occasion, Wyvern is more positive, remarking that the mutton served at the club is always excellent and that the saddle of mutton is particularly good.[14]

There were many places of entertainment in Madras apart from the club which, as we have seen, was a white male preserve and did not allow membership to women or Indians. The Museum Theatre was popular and is still in operation today. The Theatre Royal at Fort St George regularly presented amateur productions, and the Regimental Theatre Company had a residency there throughout 1878. The performances seem to have been to a high standard, and the theatre critic of *The Athenaeum and Daily News* is full of praise for their production of a farce called "Poor Pillicoddy". The farce was followed by an orchestral interlude and a burlesque, "Blue-Beard", which had the performers singing and dancing to great applause from the audience. The reporter notes that there were so many calls for encores that the audience's carriages were not called to take them home until well after the appointed time.[15]

Circuses were popular, and Wilson's Great World Circus was a regular visitor to Madras. It set up its big top on the open space of the Esplanade, just to the north

---

* house-steward, chef.

of Fort St George.* The circus toured southern India in 1878 and its performances in Madras were so popular that they regularly sold out. Despite the midday heat, Wilson's Circus put on an afternoon performance so that families with children and people who lived some distance from Madras could attend. There was a second performance in the relative cool of the evening. An advertisement in the Madras newspapers for their opening show of 3 July 1878 trumpeted:

> The Public of Madras is respectfully informed that this Mammoth Combination will remain in the City for a short season only, so embrace the opportunity of witnessing this first class entertainment, all the great performers, all the highly educated and trained horses, and that comic Mule Barney, in a grand programme every evening at 9 o'clock sharp.[16]

The Athenaeum and Daily News reported on one of the shows and was impressed by the performers' skills, especially "the infant prodigy Eva" who performed daring feats on a high trapeze.[17] Barney the Mule seems to have been popular, his forte being throwing into the dust any rider who tried to mount him, much to the hilarity of the audience. There were equestrian displays, acrobats, a comedian known as "Funny Bob", clowns and a Japanese contortionist by the name of May Kitchie. Interestingly, there were no animals in the show other than the horses for the equestrian displays and, of course, Barney.

Wilson's Circus moved on from Madras to Bangalore but, on its last night in Madras, hundreds of visitors had to be turned away even though they had bought tickets because the show was full to capacity. Refunds were given to the unlucky ones, but those who wanted to keep their tickets were offered seats at the circus' shows later in the month when the troupe would return to Madras from Bangalore.[18]

Performances of all kinds were staged at the College Hall, but one particular event is worth noting even though Wyvern would not have been able to attend because he was back in England on furlough at the time. In November 1876, an American entertainer, Dave Carson, brought his show to India and played the College Hall: it sold out and received a rave review in *The Athenaeum and Daily News*. The curious thing about Carson's show was that it was based on American minstrel shows where white entertainers "blacked up" to perform parodies of black

---

* Nowadays the Esplanade is the site of the High Court campus.

music. For his tour of India, Carson introduced a new character, "The Bengalee Babu", who would have been a recognisable stereotype to the local audience. In his book, *American Popular Music in Britain's Raj*, Bradley G. Shope tells us that:

> One of Carson's most popular characters was the "Bengalee Babu", an Anglicised Indian from Bengal who unsuccessfully attempted to imitate European manners and dress. Carson performed the character for years, including the 1878–79 season at the Royal Theatre in London. Audiences in India and London referred to his routine as the "Bengali-Minstrel Show" and he catered to the audience appetite for mockery of British refinement, or efforts by Bengali businessmen to achieve such refinement. The British used the term Babu to reference the social-climbing Bengali businessman.[19]

It all sounds completely unacceptable these days, but this type of show was hugely popular at the time. The reviewer for *The Athenaeum and Daily News* thought that Carson's Babu was "true to life" and that Carson had a "ready sparkling wit and quick repartee".[20] The rest of the show was essentially a variety performance with the cast singing, dancing and performing witty routines. A young woman named Etta "The Little Wonder" seems to have gone down particularly well with the audience when she performed her dance routines and her "characteristic impersonations". First-class seats were four rupees, and second class, two rupees. It was a late show (presumably to coincide with the cooler evening temperatures), with the doors opening at 8.15pm and the show starting at 9pm. According to a promotional flyer given out with *The Athenaeum and Daily News* "the agony terminates at the conclusion", which is Carson's jokey way of saying that he had no idea what time the show would end.

Shope informs us that:

> Amateur showmen performed the Bengalee Babu character at European ballroom dances and social clubs across India. Carson sold sheet music of the Bengalee Babu routine at his performances, disseminating his material to regimental bands and amateur variety troupes.[21]

So Wyvern may have seen the Bengalee Babu show after all once he returned to India from his furlough. Yet it would not have been performed by the maestro, Carson, but by his own regimental band or a local amateur dramatic society.

Carson's shows at the College Hall in November 1876 brought fun and jollity to the Anglo-Indians of Madras, but in the same month, a calamity of immense proportions was looming on the horizon for the peasant farmers and the poor of the Madras Presidency. The monsoon rains had failed, crops were drying up, cattle were beginning to die and a human catastrophe of epic proportions was about to unfold.

5

The Great Famine

There is one brief mention in *Culinary Jottings for Madras* about the Great Famine of 1876–78 which was particularly severe in the Madras Presidency. Wyvern writes in his chapter on "Roasting and Braising":

> Owing to the calamity which befell us in 1877, and the two previous seasons of scarcity, our market has, for the past few years, been hardly as well supplied as it formerly was; nevertheless, good meat is to be got.[1]

On the face of it, it seems that Wyvern is simply frustrated that he can no longer find the range of foodstuffs that he managed to get before the prolonged drought which caused the "calamity", but it is hard to imagine that anyone who lived through that terrible time would not have been affected by the deaths of millions of Indians who died in the famine. (And we should not forget that *Culinary Jottings for Madras* is a cookery book, and discussing famine in a cookery book is probably not a good way to sell copies.)

The Athenaeum and Daily News covered the developing drought and subsequent famine in some detail. There were regular editorials and many news items from all over the Madras Presidency. On 13 November 1876 there is a short but prescient report from Ooty. The newspaper's correspondent simply writes: "No rain yet and the standing crops have all withered. I fear we shall have a serious famine here soon."[2]

Two weeks earlier, an editorial in the newspaper urged for famine relief to be coordinated by each district in order to maximise the relief effort for the poor of Madras. It offers a "tough-love" solution:

> The great point in all these undertakings is just to keep pace with the progress of the famine, and nothing more. Any shortcomings would be attended with great misery, or even death. And excess, on the other hand, would encourage laziness and imposture, and pauperise the people. It is not the lavish hand that

is required, but the merciful and wise mind which knows to whom to give, and when.³

By early December, the famine was beginning to take hold. *The Athenaeum and Daily News* reported that large numbers of victims were migrating into the City of Madras, and that rice was being imported in large quantities to feed them. But, tragically, it notes that because the people were so poor, they did not have the means to buy fuel to cook the rice and were having to eat it raw.[4] This, in turn, was causing additional health problems for people who were already starving.

In January 1877 the correspondent in Mysore for *The Athenaeum and Daily News* wrote this tragic tale of what was happening in the province:

> Nearly all the green and verdant spots have dried up presenting everywhere the sombre footprint of drought. Almost all the water supplies have ceased to exist til next monsoon, and the face of the country is strewn with the skeletons of dead cattle. Deaths from starvation and exhaustion are now and then met with although they are yet few and far between thanks to the vigilant care of the local authorities. Ryots* and cattle are daily returning from the western Taluks whither they had gone in search of food and water. The coffee planters and other employers of labour can, it is said, no longer find work for the shoals of starving human beings who swarm the Malnad Taluks. The next few months will bring to our very doors the grim monster in all its terrors – May Heaven defend us.[5]

Late Victorian Holocausts: El Niño Famines and the Making of the Third World by Mike Davis is a hard book to read, not only for the complexity of its subject, but also for the human tragedy on a massive scale that it depicts. According to climate scientist Dr Michael Mann, the El Niño climate event is:

> An oscillation in the climate system that arises from the way atmospheric winds and ocean temperatures in the tropical Pacific influence each other. While El Niño's origins lie in the tropical Pacific, the phenomenon triggers, in turn, changes in wind patterns, temperature, rainfall, and drought around the world.[6]

In India, El Niño years are characterised by a weakening of the monsoon, and therefore the amount of rainfall that the monsoon delivers. The effects are

---

* peasant farmers

unpredictable and can range from almost normal rainfall to total failure. If the monsoon fails, drought inevitably follows – and the drought of 1876–77 was severe and catastrophic in its effect.

A contemporary journalist, William Digby, begins his book *The Famine Campaign in India* with the following contemporary exchange, which is not too dissimilar from the news from Ooty reported in *The Athenaeum and Daily News* at around the same time:

> "Here's the northeast monsoon at last," said Hon. Robert Ellis. C. B., junior member of the Governor's Council, Madras, as a heavy shower of rain fell at Coonoor, on a day towards the end of October 1876, when members of the Madras Government were returning from their summer sojourn on the hills. "I am afraid that is not the monsoon," said the gentleman to whom the remark was made. "Not the monsoon?" rejoined Mr Ellis. "Good God! It must be the monsoon. If it is not, and if the monsoon does not come, there will be an awful famine."[7]

As we now know, the monsoon did not come, and there was an awful famine. William Digby estimated that 10.3 million Indians died between 1876 and 1879 as a result.[8] Digby was outraged at the Indian government's refusal to provide comprehensive famine relief and published a critical report of their handling of the crisis.

The death toll was made far worse than it might have been by the lack of concerted government action to bring relief. As Davis tells us:

> The newly constructed railroads, lauded as institutional safeguards against famine, were instead used by merchants to ship grain inventories from drought-stricken districts to central depots for hoarding (as well as protection from rioters). Likewise the telegraph ensured that price hikes were coordinated in a thousand towns at once, regardless of local supply trends. Moreover, British antipathy to price control invited anyone who had the money to join in the frenzy of grain speculation.[9]

The historian Niall Ferguson, in his book *Empire*, writes: "When famine struck (in Ireland in the 1840s, in India in the 1870s) their response was negligent, in some measure positively culpable."[10]

Later in the book he concludes that the famine need not have been a disaster of such a magnitude, had the authorities pursued some of the policies which they had adopted during the famine in Bihar three years earlier:

> It is fashionable to allege that the British authorities did nothing to relieve the drought-induced famines of the period. But this is not so. In 1874 H. M. Kisch, an ICS magistrate of the Second Class, was sent to organize famine relief in an area of Behar covering 198 square miles and a population of around 100,000. "Since I came here" he wrote home proudly "I have erected 15 government grain store-houses, and opened about 22 relief works, I gave employment to about 15,000 men and women per day, and am feeding gratuitously about 3,000 more. I have full authority to do what I choose, and I do it". The calamity of 1877 was due to a failure to adopt the same methods.[11]

The authorities' failure to adopt widespread famine relief efforts was not accidental or due to incompetence. It was government policy. Historian Simon Schama tells us in *A History of Britain* that:

> [G]rain depots in Madras and Bombay were full of imported rice, heavily guarded by troops and police to prevent thefts or riot. The famished, as horrified journalists like William Digby (who published a two-volume history of the famine) testified, dropped dead in front of the fenced stockpiles. By a bitter irony, by the end of the century it was evident that it was those areas of India that had the most railway mileage and the most commercially developed economies that suffered most brutally in famine years, because of the ease of transporting grain to markets where it could be *hoarded* to maximise the profit from price rises.
>
> [...] Florence Nightingale, the most revered woman in Britain after the queen, read reports of missionaries and journalists like Digby and pronounced them a "hideous record of human suffering and destruction such as the world has never seen before".[12]

The Viceroy of India, Lord Lytton, could have prevented the profiteering – but he chose not to do so. Worse still, official relief efforts in the Madras Presidency were outlawed, and the governor was prevented from allocating tax revenues to the famine districts for the purpose of funding relief. Lytton railed against concerned voices back in England. He demanded: "Let the British public foot the bill for its 'cheap sentiment', if it wished to save life at a cost that would bankrupt India."[13]

The British people did indeed rise to Lytton's challenge. The famine was at its worst while Wyvern was home on furlough in England, and he writes about it in his weekly column for *The Athenaeum and Daily News*. The Lord Mayor of London had launched an appeal to raise money for famine relief in India, and Wyvern reports that after a slow start, donations were increasing rapidly, following an appeal from the Duke of Buckingham, the Governor of Madras.[14] He remarks that "wherever you go you are questioned by your friends about the Indian famine",[15] so it must have been an urgent and important topic of conversation in England at the time. By August 1877 the fund had grown considerably through donations from the general public and larger amounts from some of the major banks, such as Barings and Rothschild's.[16]

Lytton appointed Sir Richard Temple as Famine Commissioner,[17] and sent him to Madras to enforce his policies. Temple's appointment was not universally welcomed in Madras. An editorial in *The Athenaeum and Daily News* was direct and to the point:

> Regarding the telegrams announcing the appointment of Sir Richard Temple as a Famine Commissioner to Madras, we can only say that in our opinion the Supreme Government have seldom or never made a greater blunder, or one likely to lead to worse consequences.[18]

The editorial expresses resentment that a commissioner has been appointed when the Madras government was already making preparations for relief from the serious famine that was approaching. The Madras government's plan was to make sure that food was available to anyone with the means to buy it, to instigate numerous local infrastructure projects to employ those too poor to buy food but fit enough to work, and to feed without charge those who were too poor to buy food and too weak to work. The editorial concludes:

> And why, we ask, is a Government who are doing all this to be interrupted by the arrival of a fussy Commissioner who is noted for intense egoism, who wishes every thing to appear as if done by himself, and who may probably throw the whole previous organisation for famine relief into confusion and aggravate the evils he professes to cure a hundred fold.[19]

The answer was that Temple had no intention of continuing the Madras government's relief efforts – at least not in the form, or at the expense, in which they were already being carried out. Temple terminated the small local relief works, which were employing half a million people at that time. Instead, he forced the Madras government to insist that anyone requiring famine relief should be made to walk to dormitory camps at least ten miles from their local area, where they would be required to perform hard labour in return for a meagre ration of food. Many died walking to the camps, and many more died in the camps from a combination of starvation, exhaustion and disease.

Little did the British realise, but these callous policies would backfire in the long term. Later in 1877, starving villagers started walking out of the camps in what they called "relief strikes". Sympathy for the strike was taken up by Indian nationalist groups, and political unrest spread across Indian society. Mike Davis informs us that, ironically, it was Temple himself who coined the term "passive resistance" for the strike – a strategy which Gandhi would begin to use so effectively many years later in the struggle for Indian independence.[20]

There was great relief in the Madras Presidency when the north-east monsoon arrived as usual in 1877. By the middle of November, crops were starting to grow, and the price of rice and other staples started to fall. The number of people on work schemes and receiving famine rations were declining rapidly. In the Madras Presidency in one week alone the number of people carrying out famine works reduced by 54,000, and the number receiving free relief dropped by a massive 223,000.[21] But the total cost of the famine in human life and suffering had been catastrophic.

In stark contrast to the fate of the poor in the Madras Presidency, life for the Anglo-Indians went on much as normal during the Great Famine. Even the humblest civil servants or the lowest ranks in the army would not have suffered any great hardship. The famine certainly did not put the British off the idea of making a new life in India. An increasing number of British men were arriving in India to administer the government or serve in the army and, of course, the women of the "fishing fleet" (see Chapter 1) were not far behind. Their problem was not lack of food, but how to cope in an alien environment and run a household with no experience whatsoever and no mother at hand to offer guidance and advice.

Many books were written to try and help these young women settle into their new role, but none was more popular or as widely read as *The Complete Indian Housekeeper and Cook*.

6

Housekeeping and Life on the Move

An illuminating account of what everyday life was like for British housewives in late nineteenth-century India can be found in *The Complete Indian Housekeeper and Cook* by Flora Annie Steel and Grace Gardiner. Their book is dedicated to:

> THE ENGLISH GIRLS
>
> TO WHOM
>
> FATE MAY ASSIGN THE TASK OF BEING
>
> HOUSE-MOTHERS
>
> IN
>
> OUR EASTERN EMPIRE

Like *Culinary Jottings for Madras*, *The Complete Indian Housekeeper and Cook* was a highly successful book. It ran to ten editions, published between 1888 and 1921. In the introduction to their facsimile edition, Ralph Crane and Anna Johnston tell us that the book was initially self-published in India and then revised, corrected and brought up to date for each subsequent edition. Steel and Gardiner were *memsahibs** themselves, so were writing from personal experience. As Crane and Johnston put it in their introduction:

> From the moment they arrived in India – often newly married, inexperienced in both travel and housewifery, and suffering the culture shock that still confronts first-time visitors to India – these young women were on display as flag-bearers of Imperial British standards. Imagine their horror when, on entering their new home, they found "The kitchen is a black hole, the pantry a sink. The only servant who will condescend to tidy up is a skulking savage with

---

* married British women

a reed broom". What was an English girl to do?[1]

What the English girl would do is to fall back on her trusty copy of *The Complete Indian Housekeeper and Cook*. Steel and Gardiner would fulfil the role of the new housewife's mother, whereas Wyvern would have been her wise uncle offering sound advice on how to improve matters once she had established her household.

Grace Gardiner had arrived in India in the 1860s, a few years after Wyvern. She was in her early twenties at that time, and she and her husband went on to have a large family. Flora Annie Steel's husband was employed in the Indian Civil Service and had to travel extensively around his district. She often accompanied him on his travels, and began to get involved in life in India herself. The Steels were often on the move and Flora learned whatever language was local to where her husband was posted. She helped found several schools for Indian children, and eventually was appointed Inspectress of Schools for the Punjab. Together, Steel and Gardiner had a wealth of experience in the *memsahibs'* way of life in India, and they shared it with the English girls through their book.

The first chapter in *The Complete Indian Housekeeper and Cook* is "The Duties of the Mistress". It begins:

> Housekeeping in India, when once the first strangeness has worn off, is a far easier task in many ways than it is in England, though it none the less requires time, and, in this present transitional period, an almost phenomenal patience; for, while one mistress enforces cleanliness according to European methods, the next may belong to the opposite faction, who, so long as the dinner is nicely served, thinks nothing of it being cooked in a kitchen which is also a latrine.[2]

There are echoes of Wyvern's dire warnings about the state of the kitchens in India in the above passage (see Chapter 2). It is taken from the fourth edition of the book, published in 1898, so things do not seem to have improved much since Wyvern first wrote about them fifteen years earlier. Steel and Gardiner elaborate in graphic detail on those mistresses who are indifferent to the state of their kitchens:

> They never go into their kitchens, for the simple reason their appetite for breakfast might be marred by seeing the *khitmutgâr*[*] using his toes as an

---

[*] kitchen-hand or waiter

efficient toast-rack (*fact*); or their desire for dinner weakened by seeing the soup strained through a greasy *pugri**.³

Steel and Gardiner are as disgusted at the state of the kitchens in India as Wyvern was. They describe a sorry state of affairs where the kitchen floor is covered in the "refuse and offal of ages", and the drain water from the kitchen is spilling out onto the ground surrounding it.

Steel and Gardiner encourage their readers to adapt where necessary to the local conditions, but think that otherwise, the households in India should be run on exactly the same lines as in England. As Crane and Johnston observe:

> In this way British domestic practices were to be made universal, another component of the broader practice of 'raising up' other cultures to the high standards imperial proponents believed to be inherent in late Victorian culture.⁴

Wyvern's old friend "Mary-Jane", the archetypal plodding English cook, turns up here too. She is described as receiving suggestions for improvement with "sniffiness", and compared unfavourably to the Indian servants who are open to learning new skills. However, Steel and Gardiner caution the young mistress to be constantly vigilant because, in their estimation, the native servant will slip back into his old ways if not constantly watched and given instructions. As noted above, Steel herself learned many Indian languages, and she has no patience with a mistress who cannot even be bothered to learn the basics of the local language:

> The first duty of a mistress is, of course, to be able to give intelligible orders to her servants; therefore it is necessary she should learn to speak Hindustani. No sane Englishwoman would dream of living, say, for twenty years, in Germany, Italy, or France, without making the attempt, at any rate, to learn the language.⁵

It is a little unnerving to hear that they, just like Wyvern, consider that adult Indian servants should be treated like children: "The Indian servant is a child in everything save age, and should be treated as a child; that is to say, kindly, but with great firmness."⁶ They even set out a series of punishments which should be deployed if the servants disobey orders or do not follow instructions. The punishments consist of fines and, exactly as if the servant was a child,

---

* a kind of turban

administering castor oil as a "medicine" for forgetfulness. To Steel and Gardiner, it is essential that the mistress should "make a hold" on her household.

The Complete Indian Housekeeper and Cook tells us much more about everyday life for the English housewife than *Culinary Jottings for Madras*. Wyvern is preoccupied with producing fine dinners, while Steel and Gardiner are concerned with keeping the household running in all kinds of circumstances. Their book gives the impression that they are not altogether enamoured with Wyvern's passion for French-style dinners:

> As it is, one is often treated to a badly-cooked dinner in the style of a third-class French restaurant, even to the hors d'oeuvres. In regard to the latter, it is doubtful if they should ever be considered a legitimate part of the menu at private houses, though exceptions may be made occasionally in favour of fresh oysters.[7]

They far prefer simple English food, although they do agree that dinners have vastly improved in recent years in India. They note that by the time of writing, it was unusual to be served the old favourites of saddle of mutton, boiled chicken and almond soup.

The above quotes show that Steel and Gardiner's style of English is much more down to earth than Wyvern's florid prose and, as a result, their book is much easier to read, chapter by chapter, than *Culinary Jottings for Madras*. Their suggestions for holding dinner parties are also much more straightforward. Despite Wyvern's concerns about simplicity and economy, his dinners are designed to impress and are created under the "new régime". Steel and Gardiner advise the young mistress to keep things simple when entertaining – that formal dinners should not " rise too much beyond the daily level in cooking and serving".[8] They refuse to set out "imaginary menus" which they consider to be like a "swimming belt": once the belt is removed, the learner is still as helpless in the water as they were before.[9] In stark contrast, the second part of *Culinary Jottings for Madras* is wholly dedicated to listing the contents of thirty menus in considerable detail. Clearly, Wyvern is not concerned with swimming belts!

The debate about whether the *entrée* should precede the *relevé* or vice versa is still being waged in Steel and Gardiner's time (see Chapter 2). They firmly believe in serving a meal in the traditional order of *entrée* before *relevé*, and do not approve of the contemporary fashion for serving them the other way round (which Wyvern preferred, but which even he was not bold enough to recommend in his book). They become animated about the order of desserts too, and think that serving cold sweets before hot sweets amounts to "barbarism".

Steel and Gardiner had the tricky task of writing a book for the whole of British India with all its variations in geography, language, climate and costs, so in various chapters of the book they provide a comparison of the costs and availability of goods for the various presidencies. They explain that the Madras Presidency has a lower cost of living than other areas. Not only are houses cheaper to rent, but provisions are cheaper too. They suggest that the young housewife would need *at least* nine servants to run her household comfortably: butler, cook, matey,* *tunny ketch*,† waterman, sweeper, washerman and two servants to work the ceiling fans. They add an interesting footnote that a number of servants in the Madras Presidency are Christians.[10]

According to the 1901 census, and at the time of his highest reputation in England, Wyvern had only two servants: a parlour-maid and a cook. Our young housewife, starting her first home in the Madras Presidency in the late nineteenth century, would have been able to afford a minimum of *nine* servants, and had no domestic duties of her own to perform.

The Complete Indian Housekeeper and Cook contains a whole chapter about life at the hill stations, suitably titled "On the Hills" (see Chapter 7). The chapter begins:

When are you going to the hills? becomes the stereotyped question when April draws near, and people who have hitherto told you that they love heat begin to wonder what it will be like when it gets warmer. In India we launch from winter into summer, and the first experience of heat is a trying one.

And here is a word about the advantage of going to the hills. One of the authors‡ recommends it as a preventative measure, the yearly visit materially assisting in the maintenance of good health: her own experience of its benefits was that, having brought up a large family during a residence of twenty years in India, she was never once invalided, and only went to England twice during that

---

* kitchen-hand, waiter
† a female cook's assistant
‡ The author in question must be Gardiner, because she was the only one of the two to have a large family.

period, and then in the company of her husband and children.[11]

Steel and Gardiner explain to the young mistress how to choose a house (they were usually rented, and mostly unfurnished), and what to look for regarding its location and facilities. They advise that the servants' quarters will be smaller than she is used to, and she should enquire in advance how many servants the house will accommodate. They warn that the house may be dirty when the mistress arrives but give reassurance, in their condescending colonial voices, that "it is English people's dirt, not entirely natives'",[12] so the mistress should not worry unnecessarily.

There is a long section in the chapter on how to prepare for going to the Hills. Steel and Gardiner advise the young housewife on what to pack, and how to pack it. Most journeys to the hill stations could be started using the railways, but at that time, they would have to be finished by bullock cart or pack camel. The sheer quantity of goods and chattels they recommend taking is astonishing. For a journey made by a family comprising the mistress, three or four children and an English nurse, Steel and Gardiner require no less than *eleven* camels or *four* country carts for their steamer trunks.[13] The trunks contain clothing, furniture, ornaments, kitchen equipment, cutlery and crockery, books, bedding and carpets. That is, of course, not forgetting an additional cart if the mistress of the house wishes to take a piano with her! If camels are being used, an extra fourteen to sixteen labourers will be needed to carry the piano, if the lady cannot live without it. The servants have to manage as best they can, and must perch on the carts or camels while carrying their own belongings. Steel and Gardiner instruct the mistress to discourage the servants from bringing their own millstones and bedsteads. They warn that (unsurprisingly) the servants are likely to be quarrelsome, but the mistress should hold firm against allocating an additional cart for their sole use.

Steel and Gardiner conclude that in India, "happiness consists in carrying all kinds of creature comforts". They hardly need to include their final warning that:

> Going to the hills is not quite as simple a matter as going to the seaside in England, but then there are the delightfully hairbreadth risks and miraculous escapes as a pleasant excitement, and there is always something new and wonderful. Globe-trotters miss all these when they take good care to return home at the end of the cold season, to tell their friends that India has a most delightful climate.[14]

The next chapter brings the young housewife back down to earth with a bump, for she is now back "In the Plains". The unforgiving heat and dust of the plains of central India must have taken its toll on many a fair-skinned English exile. Once again, Steel and Gardiner are on hand to reassure the housewife that living on the plains can be accomplished "comfortably and healthfully", but only on the assumption that she decides to "set the claims of the husband above those of the children".[15] What they mean is that although they believe babies will happily acclimatise to the heat, once the children grow bigger they will become frustrated at being kept indoors all day, away from the heat of the sun. They recommend that older children should be sent back to school in England or, if that is too expensive, sent to boarding schools in the Hills.

Steel and Gardiner are not at all keen on the arrangement where the wife permanently lives on the Hills with the children, while the husband lives on his own on the plains and only sees his family occasionally when he gets leave to join them. Despite what some male doctors of the time had written, Steel and Gardiner "strenuously deny" that an Englishwoman cannot stand the heat as well as a man, and maintain that she can even fare better in the hot climate of India. They are made of sturdier stuff!

The first two-thirds of *The Complete Indian Housekeeper and Cook* are concerned with living in India: how to set up a home, keep accounts, manage servants, rear farm animals, bring up children and so on. The final third of the book is concerned with cookery, which Steel and Gardiner consider to be "the first duty of women".[16] The authors include many recipes in the book, but they work on the assumption that the housewife has no real experience of cooking other than in making fancy dishes such as ices and *nougâts*. As a result, the recipes are fairly straightforward. The advice on cooking often deals with how to instruct servants, and how to avoid common failures such as cloudy soups or lumpy sauces. Steel and Gardiner are in the business of teaching beginners, whereas Wyvern generally assumes some basic knowledge of cookery of his audience.

The treatment of curries in the two books is very different. Wyvern devotes two whole chapters to curries and mulligatawny soup in later editions of *Culinary Jottings for Madras*, whereas Steel and Gardiner stretch to only one-and-a-half pages on what they call "Native Dishes". The recipes seem to have been reluctantly included in the book, and only then "by request". They comment: "It may be mentioned incidentally that most native recipes are inordinately greasy and sweet, and that your native cooks invariably know how to make them fairly well."[17]

It appears that Steel and Gardiner are not great fans of curry, and do not even appreciate the Anglo-Indian curries which Wyvern is so proficient at making. They are far more interested in recipes for pickles and chutneys which include mango chutney, lime pickle and what they call *kasoundé*.[18] *Kasoundé* is a kind of mango pickle made by bottling green mangoes in mustard oil, flavoured with chillies, mustard seeds, salt, ginger, garlic and tamarind. Although Steel and Gardiner are not too keen on curries, they are certainly not averse to using spicy relishes to liven up the rather bland food that they are teaching their readers how to cook.

Once the new mistresses had settled into domestic life in India, it was often immediately disrupted by the need to travel around. Many jobs involved travel at that time, and the places they ended up with their husbands could be remote and inhospitable. But not to worry, Steel and Gardiner were on hand to offer useful advice to their English girls.

Food historian David Burton explains in his classic book *The Raj at Table: A Culinary History of the British in India*, that:

> In British India everybody's work involved travel at some time or other, whether as a magistrate, forestry officer, box-wallah,* missionary, or those in the police or army. Since government officials typically had jurisdiction over vast areas, many were obliged to spend the large part of the year on tour.[19]

We know this to be personally true both for Wyvern and Steel, as they wrote about life on the move in their respective books. There is a chapter in *Culinary Jottings for Madras* devoted to "Camp Cookery", and two chapters in *The Complete Indian Housekeeper and Cook* offering "Hints on Camp Life" and "Hints to Missionaries and Others Living in Camp and Jungles".

After he retired to England, Wyvern wrote an article in *Macmillan's Magazine*, "In the Days of John Company",[20] in which he recalls anecdotes from his travels across the Madras Presidency. As mentioned previously, many civil servants (and soldiers) were obliged to travel round their districts, and are likely to have ended up in some fairly isolated places. To that end, the authorities established lodging houses known as "*dak* bungalows" in outlying areas which could be used by travellers. David Burton describes a typical *dak*:

---

* travelling salesman

They were plainly furnished single-storeyed houses, usually surrounded by a verandah, unpretentious but sufficiently solid for many to have survived and still be in use today. [...] Indian butlers were installed to run the *dak* bungalows and offer meals. Known variously as peons, sepoys or mussalchees, they were paid only a token salary by the government, and were expected to make a profit as "licensed victuallers". While some enterprising butlers did indeed lay in stores of beer, brandy, and tinned meats, and sell them at a vast profit to travellers, at most *dak* bungalows the fare was dreadful.[21]

Wyvern seems to have had experience of many such *daks*, both good and bad. The journey up-country through rural areas, the *mofussil*, would have been made by means of an uncomfortable "bullock *dawk*" or cart. He would have taken tinned food with him as well as beer, wine and brandy, but that was only after he had learned the ropes from the old hands he had met on his travels.

On one occasion in his early days in the Madras Presidency, Wyvern arrived at a public bungalow and the native butler tricked him by saying that they were like hotels. What the butler did not tell him was that he was pocketing Wyvern's food money and serving him the native servants' food. One evening, Wyvern was unhappily waiting for "this parody of dinner" when he was asked by a fellow officer, who was using the bungalow, if he wanted to join him for dinner because he hated to eat alone. The officer had been long resident in India and, while they were enjoying a pre-dinner sherry, he describes what they are about to eat as "an old campaigner's dish".

Here is Wyvern's description of the large cooking pot which arrived at the table:

Its lid was sealed with paste, but when this was released a savoury odour steamed forth which would have tempted a "dying anchoret* to eat." "It is a sort of jugged stew," explained he, "of meat, soup, and vegetables combined, which I concoct myself, and send out to be cooked by my fellow." Never had I tasted anything more delicious. It was helped in soup-plates, and as it contained a fowl, four snipe, a partridge, some slices of bacon, a tin of hare soup, some onions, wine, and seasoning, it was as the captain had said both soup and stew, the very thing for a famished traveller. After this we had a teal apiece roasted to a turn, and then a sweet *omelette* baptised with brandy and set alight like a Christmas

---

* hermit

plum-pudding.[22]

The kindly captain then gave Wyvern some valuable advice on the best way to travel around India: "Make a rule, my boy, never to travel without a few necessities of life such as you see here."[23] Wyvern thought that the captain's "necessities" would have stocked a small shop – and, of course, included tinned food, beer and sherry. The old captain got up early in the morning to shoot game birds, took his dinner at 5pm, then moved on to the next bungalow in his itinerary, travelling in the evening and at night, as had been the custom before good roads and railways were established.

The *dak* bungalows were more socially relaxed than life in a military cantonment, and the normal rules of dressing formally for dinner did not necessarily apply. At one bungalow Wyvern was invited to dinner by an Irish colonel and his wife. First of all they sent round a servant to enquire about Wyvern's standing – his name, rank, regiment, etc. Then he received an invitation to dinner which noted cryptically: "You'll come in your comfortable things of course" and added "bring your own beer for we've run short". Wyvern wears his uniform to dinner, since he has no idea what else to do, and the colonel's wife teases him on his formal appearance when he arrives. She is wearing a loose-fitting cotton dress, and her husband is wearing a shirt and Indian-style pyjamas. Wyvern thinks they look like they are about to retire to bed rather than sit down for dinner, but their hospitality is welcoming and Wyvern enjoys a "pleasant little meal".[24]

We can see from the above exchange that all ranks, and men and women equally, enjoyed beer in the searing heat of the Madras Presidency. It was not simply wine for the officers and beer for the enlisted men. In 1877 alone, 136 million pints of beer were imported into India from Britain.[25] India Pale Ale (IPA) was brewed especially for the British in India as a beer that would travel the distance from England without spoiling.

By the time of the fourth edition of Steel and Gardiner's book in 1898, the development of the railways and establishment of the network of *dak* bungalows meant that extended periods of camp life were not as common as they had been in previous decades. For those who still had to make journeys into the *mofussil* and the jungles, Steel and Gardiner were on hand to make life as easy and as comfortable as possible. They remind their readers that a comfortable tent is no heavier than an uncomfortable one. Their second rule is that no box that has been used to carry household goods or supplies should be left unused when unpacked for camp. Everything should have a dual purpose and packing cases, for example, could be easily made into makeshift cupboards.

It was difficult to obtain regular supplies of bread, butter and vegetables, so Steel and Gardiner suggest suitable alternatives if resupply from their headquarters was impossible. The lack of butter and milk could be overcome by taking your own cow with you on the march to camp: that way, fresh supplies would be on hand from source. Bread could be made with baking powder rather than yeast, as bread made in this way kept longer than regular bread, which tended to become "a sour, almost putrid mass"[26] if left in the heat for more than a day. Alternatively, Steel and Gardiner suggest making native-style *chapattis* without any leavening agent.

Fresh vegetables (by which Steel and Gardiner mean English vegetables) appear to have been particularly difficult to obtain, although country vegetables could be bought from villages. Country carrots were popular, and a spinach substitute could be obtained using gram leaves or turnip tops. Steel and Gardiner give rather unappetising instructions on how to cook country turnips so that they lose their "paint-like" taste. They do not recommend carrying large quantities of tinned food, unlike Wyvern, but they maintain that the secret of camp life is to "not make yourself uncomfortable for want of things to which you are accustomed".[27]

Missionaries living in camps and jungles get a whole chapter to themselves in Steel and Gardiner. As yet another pillar of the colonial administration, it was increasingly common for missionaries to be dispatched to villages in remote areas to teach the natives about Christianity. Although life on the move was becoming less arduous for military and civil administrators at the time, missionaries were still existing for long periods under canvas. In Steel and Gardiner's eyes, missionaries were apt to forget about their own needs in pursuit of their higher calling. Food in particular seems to have been low on their list of priorities, which Steel and Gardiner consider to be very foolish. They maintain that not only does a good diet provide strength and stamina, but it also aids prevention of diseases such as malaria and fever. Newly-arrived missionaries who might be reading their brand new copy of *The Complete Indian Housekeeper and Cook* get a crash course in nutrition, cooking, obtaining supplies, living under canvas and how best to dress for work.

Of those things, food is the most important for Steel and Gardiner. They strongly disapprove of the common custom among men camping on their own of reheating a stew three or four times while adding new ingredients, such as a chicken, as they become available. They think it produces "biliousness, irritability, and a clogged brain". (I must say that eating a reheated stew for four days running in the heat of India would make me irritable and feeling a little sick too, so I am very much on Steel and Gardiner's side on this subject.) Finding fresh ingredients is not impossible at camp, and they explain that: "Rice flour, wheat, Indian corn, *dâl* (lentils), turnips and onions are to be found in most villages; fowl, eggs, lambs, kids in many".[28]

Wyvern, of course, has rather more grand ideas about living under canvas: the simple life of the missionary is not for him. Wyvern's mission is to explain to travellers, sportsmen and soldiers how they can "contrive to eat and drink in camp as luxuriously as in cantonment".[29] On one issue, Wyvern is in complete agreement with Steel and Gardiner – and that is bread making. He begins his chapter on "Camp Cookery" with a long discussion on the best methods of making bread under camp conditions. Like Steel and Gardiner, Wyvern favours making bread using baking powder as the raising agent rather than yeast, as it is "climate proof". Wyvern also strongly recommends the use of an Acmé Stove in camp. The Acmé Stove was a small portable cooking range fuelled by kerosene. It could be used as an oven, but also had facilities for boiling, frying and even grilling. Wyvern cannot sing its praises enough:

> In camp, the first thing the Acmé would do for you would be to boil the water for your tea; if a raw December, or January morning on the Deccan, or on the plateau of Mysore, you would not object to the operation being performed inside your tent, for the warmth would be very pleasant. It would then bake the bread for your breakfast, and warm up any *réchauffé* destined for that meal at the same time. During the day it would make the soup, and in the evening be available for work for dinner.[30]

Although the Acmé Stove performed many tasks, it excelled in bread making. Wyvern perfected a recipe using Yeatman's Baking Powder, American wheat flour, salt and water. He adds butter and milk to his tried and tested recipe if he wants to make "fancy rolls" (bread rolls). He spends some time explaining the bread recipe and the pitfalls which might occur, both under camp conditions and in India's climate.

Next, he turns his attention to making soups – one of his favourite themes – and explains that even when fresh meat is unavailable, good soups can made out of vegetables. If, say, a chicken is acquired, Wyvern recommends using tinned soup as the base for a stew with the addition of onions and other vegetables found locally.

He continues on this theme of tinned foodstuffs by suggesting ways of preparing tinned fish, but he also covers the cooking of fresh fish, if it can be caught near camp. Similarly, he suggests a number of ways for preparing tinned meat, which seems surprisingly versatile in its uses for cooking. Wyvern is not impressed with the quality of the meat itself because he finds it is invariably overcooked. The meat is of secondary importance to him; he much prefers the gravy that fills the tin, and uses it for making his favourite soups. He adds Bombay onions, vegetables, herbs, peppercorns, spices and maybe a little Marsala wine to the tin's gravy to make "an excellent consommé".

Wyvern's philosophy for living under canvas is as follows:

> If the pilgrim be blessed by the possession of an intelligent cook, and provided with a judicious assortment of culinary necessities and stores, his tent life should never fail to possess amongst its many attractions that indubitably important one – a really good dinner.[31]

There are a number of incidences of what today we might call product placement in the chapter on "Camp Cookery" – the Acmé Stove being one, and Yeatman's Baking Powder another. Whether Wyvern was commercially involved with these companies or whether he was merely recommending tried and tested products is unknown. However, we do know that there was a business relationship between Wyvern and John Moir & Son Ltd, a manufacturer of preserved foodstuffs. Moir's products are recommended on a number of occasions in the chapter of *Culinary Jottings for Madras* titled "In the Store-Room". We know too that Wyvern contributed to John Moir & Son's Export Catalogue for 1892 (see Chapter 9); there is also a note at the end of his chapter "Camp Cookery" pointing readers to the catalogue, recommending Wyvern's methods for preparing the company's products.

As we have seen, life in the Madras Presidency was not always hot and arduous. On occasion, the travellers' journey ended in the cooler climate of the hill stations, where it was possible to relax in comfort and imagine they were back home in England.

7

On the Hills

Wyvern would not have been able to take the Nilgiri Mountain Railway from Mettupalayam up to Ooty because, although construction started in 1891, it was not completed until 1902. It is a breathtaking journey, climbing 1877 m over a distance of 46 km, and takes nearly five hours.

Ooty is the popular name for the town known in Wyvern's day as Ootacamund, but which is now called Udhagamandalam. Wyvern penned the preface to the fifth edition of *Culinary Jottings* there on 1 July 1885. The time of year is significant, as Ooty was the summer residence for the Government of Madras in the same way as the more well-known Simla (now Shimla) was for the Viceroy of India and his officials.

The seasonal relocation of the whole machinery of government was made possible by construction of the railway, which dramatically reduced the journey time from Madras to the Nilgiri Hills. The historian Professor Dane Kennedy tells us in *The Magic Mountains: Hill Stations and the British Raj* that:

> In southern India, the railhead at Mettupalayam, at the foot of the Nilgiris, reduced travel from Madras to Ootacamund to little more than two days by the 1860s. The journey was shortened even further by the construction of a narrow-gauge line from Mettupalayam to Coonoor in 1899; it was extended to Ootacamund a few years later.[1]

Mrs Murray Mitchell spent three months at Coonoor in 1882. In her book, *Scenes in Southern India*, she describes her journey from Coimbatore up to Coonoor:

> The air grew cool and pure; the white-heat look died out of the sky, now a deep fathomless blue, absolutely without a cloud. The upland slopes were clothed with *shola**[*] of the freshest green. And, "What is that low, scrubby bush which

---

[*] clumps of trees

now covers the hillsides? That is surely tea?" we inquired of our intelligent driver. We were right; it was our old acquaintance, the lowly tea shrub. Next came coffee, a larger shrub, with larger, darker leaf, but trained to grow rather low for the better development of the berry. There was also the cinchona, with its large beautiful leaf. All these seemed to be extensively cultivated and covered vast reaches on the hillsides. Occasionally we passed the white bungalow of a planter and his little settlement, including the long line of huts for the coolies who work the estate, and then a few quaint little hamlets of curiously shaped huts, probably the villages of the wilder races who inhabit the hills.[2]

Wyvern mentions Ooty and the Nilgiri Hills many times in *Culinary Jottings for Madras*, although he usually refers to them as the "Neilgherries" or simply "the Hills".

The milder climate of the Hills allowed the British to cook in a way that was similar to how they would have done back in Britain. Wyvern notes that at the hill stations, the "never-empty stock pot of the English kitchen" could be maintained, whereas the stock would have spoiled in the heat of Madras. Pastry making would have been particularly difficult:

> In fact, without iced water at his elbow, the cook can scarcely hope to turn out really light puff pastry. I have heard a good many people speak in high praise of the pastry that they have eaten at certain hostelries on the Neilgherries, and express wonder that similarly excellent *feuilletage* is never placed before them here. Climate has a great deal to say to this, and without wishing to depreciate the talent of the Coonoor or Ooty *pâtissiers*, we must remember the advantages that they enjoy in the matter of temperature.[3]

Pies are another issue troubling Wyvern:

> On the Hills, at Bangalore, and at many of the stations of this Presidency during the cold months, every one of the pies I have described will be found when cold to contain firm jelly – not liquid gravy. If you desire to produce that cheerful effect at Madras, do not forget to place the pie upon ice for some little time before the meal at which it is to appear. The jelly is, of course, the united result of good gravy, and the juices of the various meats in the pie extracted by baking.[4]

Wyvern is especially keen on the vegetables grown in the cooler climate of the Hills (the area is still famous today for its market gardens). The town of Udhagamandalam is surrounded by terraced hillsides where what are known as "English vegetables" are grown on the rich terraces: peas, beans, spinach, Brussels sprouts, beetroot, carrots and all manner of non-native vegetables; what is more, the mild climate enables growers to produce as many as four crops a year by using modern varieties, whereas in Wyvern's day two crops a year were the norm.[5] Speciality vegetables were much appreciated in Wyvern's time. He writes: "There are several high class ways of serving globe artichokes which I, of course, dedicate to my readers who happen to be staying on the Hills", and he remarks that globe artichokes "are properly considered the choicest delicacies of the Neilgherry market by many people".[6]

Mitchell observes that:

> Every house has its garden, and the verandahs are bowery with trailers and creepers and beautiful orchids, while the avenues and drives are adorned with rare trees and evergreens and flowering shrubs in endless variety. [...] Fruit-trees also abound, especially the peach, and we have plenty of strawberries, and also home vegetables. The hotel garden is almost a peach orchard, the branches weighed down with the wealth of ripening fruit.[7]

Due to the length of time that government officials were stationed in Ooty, Wyvern had the opportunity to tend a vegetable garden of his own. He mentions it a number of times in *Culinary Jottings for Madras*, but it was not only private gardens that flourished there. Kennedy makes the following points:

> From the start, hill stations were centers of horticultural experimentation and emendation. The British were delighted to discover that many of the flowers, fruits, and vegetables popular in Britain flourished in the cool mountain climate.
>
> The fifty-four-acre Government Botanical Garden at Ootacamund was established in 1848 along the slopes of Dodabetta peak, the highest location in the area. The two gardens* played important roles in the development of tea, coffee, cinchona,† and other commercial crops, but they also served as pleasure

---

* Ooty and the botanical garden in Darjeeling
† Tree bark, from which quinine could be extracted for anti-malarial treatment.

parks for station residents and supplied them with flower and vegetable seeds, cuttings from ornamental shrubs, and shade and fruit trees. Only a few years after its founding, the government garden at Ootacamund was offering for sale fifty three varieties of apple trees.[8]

The botanical garden at Ooty still flourishes today. There are glasshouses, colourful flower borders and beautifully kept lawns – reminiscent of London's Kew Gardens – but all at 2,200 m (more than 7,000 feet) above sea level on the blue mountains of the Western Ghats of India.

It is interesting to observe that Wyvern considers the Nilgiri Hills to be almost an outlying area of England. For example, in a section on watercress, he notes that it is "common on our Hills, and frequently grown in private gardens".[9] The Nilgiris are considered by Wyvern to be *"our"* hills, not native land. Ooty was created *by* the British, *for* the British. These days, of course, it is a thriving Indian town but, before the British arrived in the 1820s, there was no major settlement on the site, although the native Toda and other tribes did inhabit the region, and still do in some rural areas.

In Wyvern's time, much of the natural landscape had been modified already by the British. They had dammed a stream in 1823 to create a reservoir which, after the planting of attractive shrubs and trees around the shore, doubled up as an ornamental lake. Most of the native trees had long ago been used for firewood or for building, so the British reforested the area with non-native trees – mainly Australian eucalyptus, blackwood and wattle. The whole landscape was transformed by the British and ended up, by design, resembling the familiar hill country of England or Scotland rather than the wild hills of the Western Ghats.

Kennedy explains how Ooty and the other hill stations were founded:

> It was above all as sanitaria, then, that the first hill stations had their origins and acquired their reputations. Most of the residents and visitors in the early years were civil and military officials from neighboring lowlands who sought a general restoration of spirits or recovery from specific infirmities. The founding fathers of highland settlements were invariably British East India Company servants, but they acted as often without as with the encouragement and support of the government. Soon, however, places like Simla, Mahabaleshwar, and Ootacamund received visits from governors and governors-general, and the development of hill stations became a matter of state policy. Roads were

cleared by labor corps or convicts, bungalows were built with official monies, convalescent depots were established for invalid troops, and medical data were collected by government physicians. Most civil and military authorities were soon convinced of the therapeutic value of hill stations.[10]

The hill stations may have started as sanitaria or convalescent homes where Europeans could gain some relief from the heat and diseases associated with living in India, but they did not stay that way for long. They became integral to the way that the British were governing the country. One of Kennedy's main conclusions in *The Magic Mountains* is that the British deliberately began to distance themselves from the native population, not just culturally but also physically. By the 1880s, the Government of Madras was spending up to eight months of the year in the Nilgiri Hills. However, the government back in Britain was not at all happy about this development, and ordered the Madras government to spend no more than three months of the year at Ooty. The order was quietly ignored.

An editorial in *The Athenaeum and Daily News* from March 1877 questions the wisdom of the Madras government's plans to move to Ooty for the hot season, when the presidency was in the grips of a catastrophic famine (see Chapter 5).[11] The editorial questions the government's ability to manage the effects of the famine properly from the safety and distance of the Nilgiri Hills. The government decamped to Ooty anyway – including the recently formed Famine Department – despite intense criticism in the newspapers and from many of the citizens of Madras.

The British had been shaken by what some British history books call the Indian Mutiny of 1857. Not only did the rebellion signal the end of the British East India Company's rule, to be replaced by direct rule by the British government, but it reinforced the idea that the uplands of India were much safer than the plains, especially for women and children. With the advent of the new railway system, which reduced journey times considerably, the hill stations looked even more desirable. On arriving in India in 1859, Wyvern would have been one of the first contingent of British soldiers sent there to secure direct rule.

(It should be noted that in India, what the British often call the "Indian Mutiny" is commonly referred to as the First War of Independence. In 2007, the Indian government organised an official celebration of the 150th anniversary of the uprising. The British quelled the uprising with as much violence as it had itself inflicted, but they could not stop the long, slow process of independence for India, which was finally achieved ninety years later in 1947.)

With the advent of direct British rule, it was not just soldiers who were sent to control India. The colonial population expanded exponentially, including civil servants, administrators, railway engineers, civil engineers, surveyors, tea, coffee and indigo planters, missionaries and all manner of entrepreneurs with an eye to making their fortune there. However, the colonial population did not reflect society back home. The British population of India had a proportion of men to women of about three to one in 1901, but even that unequal ratio had decreased from a high of about seven to one in 1861. It is intriguing to note that men and women were present in almost equal in numbers in the hill stations and, with the addition of young children, far more representative of normal society in England. But how could that be? The answer is, as so often in British society, class. Hill stations such as Ooty and Simla were the domain of military officers, government officials and senior civil servants. The female population were predominantly their wives (or widows), although a number of single women did run schools for the officers' children.

The rank-and-file soldiers (who were not allowed to marry) lived in all-male societies and, unsurprisingly, that caused problems of its own for the authorities in terms of alcoholism and prostitution. The Surgeon-General of Bengal estimated in 1881 that as many as 25% of the soldiers in his presidency were suffering from sexually-transmitted infections (STIs),[12] while other areas had even higher incidences of infections. The military authorities, desperately trying to reduce the incidence of STIs among the troops, set up official army brothels where the prostitutes could be regularly examined by doctors. Any women found to be infected were isolated in so-called "lock hospitals" for treatment. Religious groups such as the Gospel Purity Association thoroughly disapproved of this practice, and sent Alfred Dyer to India in 1887 to investigate. Dyer drew a fascinating map of the East Kent Regiment's encampment to illustrate his report, covering the army tents, tents of the general camp followers, the temperance tent and, in big bold letters, "tents of licensed harlots attached to the East Kent Regiment".[13] Needless to say, the military sanitaria – effectively hill stations for the common soldier – were located well apart from the hill stations proper.

Hill stations began to gain a reputation for relaxed living away from the responsibilities of colonial rule. Rudyard Kipling reflected on colonial society at Simla in books such as *Plain Tales from the Hills*, published in 1888. Thanks in part to Kipling's colourful characters such as Mrs Hauksbee, the "grass widows" – the wives of officers and officials who were away in post – gained a reputation for seducing single young officers. However, this is something of an exaggeration because society in the hill stations still strongly reflected nineteenth-century English society, with all its attendant taboos and constraints. In reality, there were dinner parties, balls, official functions, clubs, societies and everything that reflected English society at home.

English society was represented also by its class distinctions. Ooty had the nickname of "Snooty Ooty", while the hill station lower down the mountains at Coonoor was considered "vulgar". As we have seen, Ooty was, by and large, the preserve of the upper classes. Coonoor catered more for the middle classes such as civil servants, businesspeople and railway engineers. To complete the British social strata, there was a military sanitarium further down the hills at Wellington. Wellington later became a cantonment for the Madras Army, and today remains a military base for the Defence Services Staff College of the combined Indian armed forces.

Writing in June 1876, a correspondent for *The Athenaeum and Daily News* recommends Coonoor over Ooty to his readers, commenting caustically:

> Ootacamund, from being the summer residence of the Members of Government, considers itself, pre-eminently the fashionable hill station of this Presidency. To those, who cannot exist without indulging in a round of gaieties, this is the place where they should go, but it is a matter of doubt whether Ootacamund life of this sort is conducive either to the restoration or even the maintenance of health.[14]

I think we can pretty much guess to which social class our correspondent belongs. He maintains that the cost of living is Ooty is far too high and that Coonoor is much better value for money. Accommodation at Coonoor was considerably cheaper, as was buying food and supplies in the bazaar. In Wyvern's day, Coonoor was also much easier to get to than Ooty: the journey from the railway terminus at Mettupalayam took only four hours. We have seen from Mitchell's description that the journey by road was spectacular.

Kennedy describes the extensive clubs and facilities in Ooty:

> Ootacamund was renowned by the latter part of the nineteenth century as a center of sociality – a renown that rested on the presence of the venerable

Ootacamund Club, the later and less exclusive Nilgiri Club, the Gymkhana Club (which was preceded by separate clubs for boating, polo, cricket, golf, and trap, as well as archery, badminton, and croquet – the ABC Club), the Ootacamund Hunt Club (which hosted the largest gathering of horses and hounds in India), Hobart Park (the site of annual horse races), the Nilgiri Library (housed in a handsome Gothic building), the magnificent Botanical Gardens, the Assembly Rooms (for balls and amateur theatricals), and a Freemason lodge.[15]

Thus the hill stations became the focus of British cultural and family life in India. With men and women in roughly equal numbers, and with young children playing in their gardens, the British could imagine that for a few months of the year they were back in Britain, rather than "exiles" as Wyvern so often describes his situation.

It is important to note that the children were all relatively young. Very few British children spent their whole childhood in India, because most of them were sent away to boarding schools in Britain before they reached adolescence. Kennedy gives a telling explanation as to why the British considered this painful separation of children from their parents essential:

> Parents in the upper echelons of British Indian society seemed especially eager to provide their children with lavish entertainments; it is possible to view these actions as compensation for the wrenching separations that loomed ahead, for it was widely accepted that British children should be shipped back to Britain before they reached adolescence. Their removal from India was one of the most rigidly enforced customs of the British in India. Most medical men and other self-styled authorities agreed that it was essential for boys in particular to be gone by the age of six or seven; for girls an early departure was considered less imperative. The children's health was offered as the rationale for their removal, with warnings that prolonged presence in the tropics would make them feeble and "weedy". But their physical well-being was not as central a consideration as colonial rhetoric suggested. After all, the most precarious years in the lives of children occurred well before the age recommended for departure, and the natural dangers they faced were not peculiar to boys. The main motivation to ship children back to the motherland was concern about their social and cultural development and the role of this development in the perpetuation of the British imperial presence.[16]

In the final sentence above, Kennedy highlights a key issue surrounding the British colonial presence in India. British children born in India were sent back home not because they would grow "feeble" on account of their environment if they stayed, but because they would become nativised by their surroundings.

British parents of Wyvern's class contributed little to the day-to-day routine of bringing up their children. Their households were run by Indian servants at every level. They had servants to cook their meals, servants to clean their house and servants to look after their children. The servant who looked after the children was the *ayah*. She may also have been a general housekeeper or a lady's maid, but her principal duty was to make sure that the children of the house were washed, fed, entertained and put to bed. The closeness of the *ayah* to her young charges would have produced a strong emotional bond between them. If the presence of other servants in the house (cooks, cleaners, washermen, gardeners, etc.) with whom the children would have had day-to-day contact are factored into the situation, young British children might have easily begun to adopt Indian expressions and mannerisms. The British colonial authorities were extremely concerned that their progeny might be assimilated into Indian culture which, as a consequence, would dilute the unique Britishness that made them – in their eyes – racially superior.

Rudyard Kipling tells the tale of a boy called Tods in one of his short stories, "Tods' Amendment". Tods is "beyond his *ayah*'s control altogether" and wanders around the bazaars of Simla, talking to the locals. He is well liked by the family's servants and spends a great deal of time with them. He is only about six years old but already speaks the local language of Urdu. His English is peppered with native expressions and he even calls a government minister "*sahib*" rather than "sir".

One night Tods cannot sleep, so is allowed down into the room where his father is meeting with government officials. They have a problem with a legal bill which the natives are resisting, and they cannot understand why. Tods pipes up that he knows all about the bill and its problems from his friends in the bazaar. When asked what he knows, he has to translate what he has been told in Urdu into English. Kipling writes: "He spent a minute putting his ideas in order, and began very slowly, translating in his mind from the vernacular to English, as many Anglo-Indian children do."[17] The government officials now understand why the locals have taken against the bill, and they manage to find a way to amend it to everyone's satisfaction.

There is little doubt that poor Tods would soon be sent back to a boarding school in England, to have Britishness reasserted in his young mind.

Less well-off families, and those who could not bring themselves to send their children away at such a tender age, had another option. They could send their children to one of the many British boarding schools which had opened in the hill stations. Kennedy tells us that there were schools of this type in Ootacamund from as early as the 1830s, and many more opened in later years, They were used mainly by families where the father was in "the uncovenanted services (telegraph, mail, police, forestry, customs, opium), the railways, the army, and various commercial enterprises".[18] Some boarding schools later allowed mixed-race children to become students but, as Kennedy explains:

> Anglo-Indians were not welcome at most of the better schools, and Indians were almost entirely prohibited from enrolling in them until the interwar years. British parents often objected to their children rubbing shoulders with mixed-race students. M. M. Kaye and her sister were pulled out of Simla's Auckland House by their horrified mother when they began to acquire the so-called 'chi-chi' accent of Anglo-Indian classmates.[19]

Contrary to its use in the rest of this book, the term "Anglo-Indian" in the above quotation is used in the modern sense of meaning people who had, either directly or in a previous generation, an English father and an Indian mother (see Introduction). In Wyvern's time, such people were called "Eurasians". Wyvern uses the term "Anglo-Indian" throughout *Culinary Jottings for Madras* and *Furlough Reminiscences* but for him, Anglo-Indians are people like himself: white British nationals who are living in India. (I have adopted Wyvern's usage throughout this book in order to be consistent with his writing, despite it not being in current use in India.)

During the British Raj, Eurasians were not always accepted into British society as equals. Kipling includes a number of short stories in his book, *Plain Tales from the Hills*, in which Eurasians are rebuffed by white British society. Although Kipling was twenty-five years younger than Wyvern, *Plain Tales from the Hills* was published in 1888, therefore contemporary to Wyvern and representative of the social attitudes of his time in India. In Kipling's story, "Kidnapped", a young English officer by the name of Peythroppe falls in love with the beautiful Miss Castries. Peythroppe asks Miss Castries to marry him and she accepts, but his fellow Europeans are horrified. The narrator of the story explains:

> Understand clearly that there was not a breath of a word to be said against Miss

Castries – not a shadow of a breath. She was good and very lovely – possessed what innocent people at Home call a 'Spanish' complexion, with thick blue-black hair growing low down on the forehead, into a 'widow's peak', and big violet eyes under eyebrows as black and as straight as the borders of a Gazette Extraordinary when a big man dies. But – but – but – Well, she was a very sweet girl and very pious, but for many reasons she was 'impossible'. Quite so. All good Mammas know what 'impossible' means. It was obviously absurd that Peythroppe should marry her. The little opal-tinted onyx at the base of her finger-nails said this as plainly as print.[20]

Miss Castries, it seems, is not of pure European blood and everyone except Peythroppe understands what this means. The "opal-tinted onyx at the base of her finger-nails" was regarded by the British as a sure sign of "mixed blood", so it was out of the question for Peythroppe to marry her if he wanted to make a successful career and enjoy high social standing among his peers. To save him from his downfall, three of his fellow officers kidnap him, so as to miss his wedding day. On his return, Miss Castries breaks off the engagement. In his introduction to the Penguin edition of *Plain Tales from the Hills*, David Trotter explains how, for the British, it was important to keep themselves apart from Indians and to set fixed boundaries of social interaction:

> The most potent of all limits was that set between the races, between black and white. Necessary to the maintenance of power, it also became [...] the subject of many of Kipling's stories.
>
> Racial discrimination has become a habit of mind, almost an aesthetic. It seeks out signs of difference, pretending to measure even the consistency of blood. [...] Discrimination identifies both the observer and the observed; *they* have the manners and customs, *we* have the ability to measure and to grade.[21]

The British were rulers in a foreign country and obsessed with maintaining the mystique of cultural and racial superiority. Their numbers were tiny in comparison to the Indian population (see Introduction), so that mystique was essential in keeping control, especially after the Indian uprising of 1857.

The Kenney-Herberts conformed to the social norm in regard to their children's education. Their son Arthur, and daughter Enid, were born in Bangalore, but both were educated for the most part in England. Enid was certainly living in England when she was eleven years old. According to the census of 1881, she was living in Leamington Priors (now Leamington Spa) with five single sisters, aged fifty-nine to sixty-eight, by the name of Crane. We know that Kipling, who was born in Bombay and spent his early years there, was sent back to England by his parents at the tender age of five. Kipling confesses in his autobiography that he found the experience of being separated from his parents at such a young age highly traumatic, and it must surely have brought similar hardships to poor Arthur and Enid Kenney-Herbert.

For Wyvern, life in Ooty was anything but traumatic. He enjoyed participating in amateur dramatics, he tended his garden and cooked his home-grown vegetables. When he is stationed back in Madras, he thinks wistfully about his "fortunate friends on the Neilgherries", although he manages to comfort himself by undertaking one of his favourite pastimes – making curries.

8

Our Curries

Wyvern devotes two chapters in *Culinary Jottings for Madras* to the subject of curries. The chapters were incorporated into the fourth edition of the book in 1883, having been originally published as a series of articles in *The Pioneer* newspaper. They were omitted altogether from the seventh edition of the book, which was retitled *Wyvern's Indian Cookery Book* (although an Indian cookery book without any curry recipes seems to be something of a misnomer). The two chapters were merged into one for inclusion in Wyvern's later book, *Common-Sense Cookery*, but were partially rewritten with a British, rather than an Anglo-Indian, audience in mind.

"Our Curries" is the first chapter, and Wyvern is not talking about the sort of curries that his Indian servants would be making for themselves and their families. No, these are "our" curries. They are *British* curries.

The first paragraph is a classic example of Wyvern's prose:

> We are often told by men of old time, whose long connection with the country entitles them to speak with the confidence of "fellows who know, don't you know," that in inverse proportion, as it were, to the steady advance of civilization in India, the sublime art of curry-making has gradually passed away from the native cook. Elders at Madras – erst-while the acknowledged head-centre of the craft – shake their heads and say "Ichabod!"[*] and if encouraged to do so, paint beautiful mouthwatering "pictures in words" of succulent morsels cunningly dressed with all the savoury spices and condiments of Ind, the like of which, they say, we ne'er shall look upon again.[1]

It's an enjoyable quote but if you read it carefully, one part says something quite astonishing: "the sublime art of curry-making has gradually passed away from the

---

[*] "the glory has gone"

native cook".

What does this mean? Do the Indian servants of Wyvern's day not know how to make their own traditional dishes any more? Have they abandoned the culinary heritage of a thousand years and now eat only English food? No, that is clearly preposterous. What I think it means is by that time, Wyvern's "elders at Madras" were not eating traditional Indian food; rather, they were already eating a partially anglicised version of Indian food which better suited their western palates. To be sure, the food they were eating must have tasted uncomfortably pungent to the pale newcomers who had recently arrived from England, but it was almost certainly not the same as what their Indian servants enjoyed.

The art of making this type of curry was being lost because such dishes no longer formed a significant part of the Anglo-Indians' diet. In Wyvern's day, there were far greater numbers of British in India than in the days of the East India Company, and they were mostly eating European-style food. While curries or mulligatawny soup might still be served at breakfast or for lunch, no self-respecting Anglo-Indian lady at the time would serve a curry for guests at dinner. Only English – or even better, French – cooking would do if the hostess wanted to impress her guests.

In his chapter on "Our Kitchens in India", Wyvern mentions the old India hands who "chiefly preyed upon curry and rice, and lived to all intents and purposes *à la mode Indienne*".[2] He is referring here to an era even earlier than that of his predecessors in Madras. One such employee of the East India Company, John Henry Grose, was a "covenant servant and writer" who wrote *A Voyage to the East Indies* in 1772. He remarks:

> So much however is certainly true, that most of the Europeans soon reconcile themselves to the country-diet, and many at length prefer it to their own, even in point of taste or relish, independent of its being undoubtedly more wholesome, and more adapted to the climate, than the quantities of flesh to which we are used in these colder countries, where the heat being more concentered facilitates the digestion.[3]

Grose describes the "country-diet" of the native population, which the British were keen to adopt, as follows:

> They have likewise almost as many names for their dishes as the European

cookery; but the three most common ones all over India is, currees, kitcharee, and pilow. The currees are infinitely various, being a sort of fricacees, to eat with rice, made of any animals or vegetables; these last being chiefly used by the Bramins, who never eat what has had life in it; but the reigning ingredients are the pulp of the coconut for thickening, and turmeric for turning the sauce yellow, besides spices to heighten it.[4]

By the time that Dr R. Riddell had written his *Indian Domestic Economy and Receipt Book* in 1849, the British had already begun to adapt traditional Indian dishes to their own tastes. Riddell would certainly have qualified as one of Wyvern's "elders at Madras". He includes the recipes for as many as forty-four varieties of curry in his book, each with its own Indian name. He includes recipes for curries such as *quoormah, doepeaza* and *kulleah.* There are recipes for fifteen different types of *doepeaza* alone, including *doepeaza gheelanee, doepeaza jogooranth* and *doepeaza nargisse*, each with its own unique list of ingredients. It is clear that Riddell's curries are closer to the original Indian versions than Wyvern's, but the recipes have been modified, to a greater or lesser extent, to suit Anglo-Indian tastes.

In the introduction to his chapter on "Oriental Cookery", Riddell explains that some native ingredients

> would be disagreeable to a European palate, and are therefore omitted, though found in the receipts; and which, if copied, a literal translation would require. One or two are given, more as a curiosity than supposing they will ever be tried, however piquant they may be to an Asiatic palate.[5]

Wyvern was introduced to curry making shortly after his arrival in India. His guide was a "kind-hearted veteran who threw his doors open to me". Wyvern's mentor used to hold *tiffin* (lunch) parties where he would offer his guests eight or nine different varieties of curry, accompanied by a selection of freshly-made chutneys and other tasty morsels. The guests took pleasure in discussing each curry: it was good form to try every dish and then go back for seconds of the ones you liked the best. Wyvern explains, in a nostalgic mood:

> Now, this my friend was, I take it, a type of the last Anglo-Indian generation; a generation that fostered the art of curry-making, and bestowed as much attention to it as we, in these days of grace, do to copying the culinary triumphs

of the lively Gauls*.[6]

Wyvern's stated purpose in writing his first cookery book was to enable the British housewife to cook European-style food under Indian conditions. So he is possibly allowing himself a little indulgence by including in the book not just one but two chapters on making curries. In any case, Wyvern remarks that curries were still very much enjoyed in clubs, the army mess and, indeed, many private houses. So the "Ladies of Madras", to whom the book is dedicated, might still want help in making a nice curry for lunch (or even a quiet dinner – as long as no guests were expected!).

Wyvern is a firm believer in using pre-prepared curry powders and is scornful of the native cooks who want to "fabricate their 'curry-stuff,' on the spot, as it is required". He maintains that:

> The actual cooking of a curry presents no special difficulty. A cook who is an adept with the stew-pan, and who has mastered the art of slow, and very gentle simmering will, whether a Frenchman, an Englishman, or a mild Hindu, soon become familiar with the treatment of this particular dish.[7]

The irony of the implication that a Hindu servant would need to be taught how to make a dish which the British had appropriated from the Indians seems to be lost on Wyvern. But he is, of course, talking about making his very British curries. Wyvern discusses at length the making of curry powder, insisting that it should be made well in advance in large batches, and sealed in glass containers where it could mature and improve.

Wyvern was fortunate enough to have been given instructions in the art of curry making by others too. In particular, he was given a recipe for what would become his standard or "stock" curry powder as a parting gift from a British woman: he describes her as a *châtelaine* who had lived in India for some time, but was now returning home. The quantities in the recipe are enormous. Here it is verbatim, with Wyvern's spellings of English and local names:

4 lbs of turmeric	*huldi*
8 lbs of coriander-seed	*dhunnia*

---

* The French.

2 lbs of cummin-seed	*jeera*
1 lb of poppy-seed	*khush-khush*
2 lbs of fenugreek	*maythi*
1 lb of dry-ginger	*sont*
1 lb of mustard-seed	*rai*
1 lb of dried chillies	*sooka mirrch*
1 lb of black pepper corns	*kala mirrch*[8]

The total weight of the spices is an astonishing 21 lbs (about 9.5 kg)! That would make an awful lot of curries, so it's a good job that the powder kept well in sealed jars. Wyvern gives instructions to dry-roast the coriander and fenugreek seeds, as one would with coffee beans (in case his readers were not familiar with roasting spices). He adds a caveat that in order to make the full quantity of curry powder, the cook would need far greater quantities of whole seeds than the finished weight of ground spices. He takes coriander seed as an example, stating that it would be necessary to grind 24 oz of whole seeds to produce 8 oz of powder; the lost two-thirds of the original weight being the husks and coarser bits left over when the powder is sieved. He notes that turmeric loses half its weight, and cumin seed one-third. He adds salt to the curry powder while it is being poured into the jars.

When Wyvern's *châtelaine* gives him her precious recipe for curry powder, it comes with a warning from someone who has spent many years in India. She cautions Wyvern to make sure that he supervises the making of the curry powder, and instructs him to weigh the spices at each stage of the process. The British were convinced that their Indian servants would take every opportunity to steal from their employers, and this advice reinforces that view. The *châtelaine* urges Wyvern to weigh the spices when they are still whole, then to weigh the ground spices *and* the discarded husks again after the servant has ground the spices. She explains to Wyvern:

> In this way alone will you be able to guard against the disappearance of half an ounce of this, or an ounce of that – petty pilferings that take from the curry-powder that which it cannot get again, and leave it poor indeed.[9]

Wyvern recommends that if making their own curry powder is too much trouble, his readers should use the Madras curry powder and paste sold by Barrie and Co. He informs us that he had been using Barrie's condiments for more than twenty years, and has never found better products made by another company. He is also at pains to assure that:

> I am not employed as an advertising medium. My advice is not the advice of a "gent" travelling for Messrs. Barrie and Co., it is the honest exhortation of one, my friends, who has the success of your curries very closely at heart.[10]

If his readers happened to be on leave or retired to England, Wyvern directs them to the Oriental Depot in London's Leicester Square, where they would find "sundry casks of Barrie's curry-stuffs, chutneys, &c".[11] Wyvern had found the Oriental Depot by chance when he was on furlough in London, and had recognised the unmistakable smell of Barrie's curry powder while he was walking past the shop.

Once a good curry powder has been made (or bought from Barrie and Co.), the next thing Wyvern needs to make his curries is what he calls the "accessories". These are not the main ingredients per se, but the things that give the curry its "finish" or depth of flavour. Here are the most important, according to Wyvern.

1. The medium in which the onions are fried must be butter, despite its high price in the bazaars of Madras.
2. An ingredient which gives a "sweet-acid"* taste to a curry – his favourite is redcurrant jelly. He uses it as a substitute for the sweet and sour flavour of tamarind, which the natives of southern India would use, but he believes that redcurrant jelly is a major improvement over tamarind in terms of taste. (This is another good example of the British anglicising their curries.)
3. Fresh herbs, which will vary from curry to curry.
4. Coconut milk, which is indispensable when making a curry. He gives specific instructions of how to make coconut milk from fresh coconut and how – and just as importantly, when – to use it in making curries.
5. Good stock made from simmering meat trimmings, bones and vegetables in water.

Wyvern uses his "stock" curry powder in all his curries. In order to give each curry its own individual flavour, his recipes use additional aromatic spices together with

---

* What modern cooks would call "sweet and sour".

herbs, garlic, onion, green ginger, almonds and coconut in varying proportions. The aromatic spices he recommends are cloves, mace, cinnamon, nutmeg, cardamoms and allspice, but he cautions the cook to use only one, or at most two, for each curry. The herbs he recommends are fennel leaves, *maythi bajee* (fenugreek leaves), lemon grass, bay leaves, *karay-pauk* (curry leaves) and coriander leaves (cilantro).

The final component for Wyvern's "curry-stuff" is a paste made from a selection of the above ingredients, which he combines in equal measures with his stock curry powder when cooking his curries. Wyvern suggests a recipe for a "capital" curry paste containing the following ingredients:

 1 small onion
 1 clove garlic
 1 dessert-spoon turmeric
 1 dessert-spoon roasted coriander seed
 1 dessert-spoon poppy seed
 1 teaspoon "Nepaul" pepper (similar to Szechuan pepper)
 1 teaspoon sugar
 1 teaspoon salt
 1 teaspoon grated green ginger

The above ingredients are pounded to a paste with a little vegetable oil. Wyvern pounds together:

 12 almonds
 1 ounce fresh coconut
 a little lime juice

Next, he mixes the two pastes together and adds:

 1 salt-spoon of either ground cinnamon or ground cloves
 red chilli powder to taste – but only for "those who like very hot curries".

Wyvern then sets out the method for what was to become his famous recipe for Madras Chicken Curry. Here it is in his own words:

Choose a nice young chicken – and here let me point out that large chickens nearly full grown ought never to be used in curries – and having cut it up neatly as for a *fricassée*, place the pieces aside, and dredge over them a little flour. Next take all the trimmings, neck, pinions, leg bones, feet, head, &c., with any scraps of meat that can be spared, and cast them into a sauce-pan with an onion sliced, a carrot sliced, half a dozen pepper corns, a bit of celery, a pinch of salt and one of sugar, cover them with cold water and make the best broth you can. When ready, strain the contents of the sauce-pan into a bowl, and skim it clean. A good breakfast-cupful of weak stock should thus be obtained. Lastly, make a breakfast-cupful of milk of cocoanut, or almond.

Now take your stew-pan, and having sliced up six good shallots, or two small white onions, cast the rings into it, with two ounces of Denmark, Normandy, or other good tinned butter; add a finely-minced clove of garlic, and fry till the onions turn a nice yellow brown. Then add a heaped-up table-spoonful of the stock powder, and one of the paste, or, if you have not made the latter, two table-spoonfuls of the powder. Cook the curry-stuff with the onions and butter for a minute or two, slowly, adding by degrees a wine-glassful of the cocoanut milk, and then also by degrees the breakfast-cupful of broth. The effect of this when simmered for a quarter of an hour will be a rich, thick, curry gravy, or sauce. The stew-pan should now be placed *en bain-marie* while we proceed to prepare the chicken.

Take a frying-pan: melt in it an ounce of butter, or clarified beef suet, add a shallot cut up small, and fry for a couple of minutes. Next put the pieces of chicken into the *sauté*-pan, and lightly fry them. As soon as slightly coloured, the pieces of chicken should be transferred to the stew-pan in which they should rest for at least half an hour, marinading, as it were, in the curry gravy. After that, the stew-pan should be placed over a gentle fire, and if the liquid be found insufficient to cover the pieces of chicken, stock, if available, or water, should be added. A gentle simmering process should now be encouraged, during which the bay-leaf, chutney, and sweet-acid should be added. If powder without fresh paste has been used, the pounded almond and cocoanut must now be put in, with a little spice and grated green ginger. The curry gravy should at this period be tasted, and if a little more acid or sweet be found necessary, the proper correction should be made. As soon as the pieces of chicken have become tender, thoroughly stewed, that is to say, a coffee-cupful of cocoanut "milk," (the infusion I previously mentioned), should be stirred in, and in three minutes the operation will be complete.

If a semi-dry or dry curry be required, the gravy must be still further reduced by simmering with the lid off, the pieces of meat being continually stirred about with a wooden spoon to prevent their catching at the bottom of the pan. When the proper amount of absorption has been attained, remove the pan and serve.[12]

(I have created my own version of Wyvern's recipe which can be found in Appendix A, if you would like to try it. I have scaled down the quantities of spices needed to make the curry to a much more manageable level, so you will be relieved to know that making 9.5 kg of curry powder will not be necessary!)

Wyvern considers his method for making curries to be far superior to the "slipshod method of curry-making ordinarily followed by native cooks".[13] He recognises that some of his readers might find his method "needlessly troublesome", but he is unrepentant. He considers that he has created a dish that is on a par with his recipes for English and French dishes. He also believes that this extended method of cooking – making the stock, making and then frying off the curry powder and curry paste with onions and garlic, sautéing the chicken and then marinating the pieces in the curry gravy and, finally, making the coconut milk to be added near the end of the cooking – is completely worthwhile, if the objective is to "produce a dish of a superior class".

The second chapter on curries is mainly concerned with Malay or Ceylon curries and with mulligatawny soup which, as we have seen, he calls *mulligatunny*. (For my adaptations of Wyvern's recipes for Ceylon Curry, *Quoorma* (korma), Madras Chicken Curry and plain boiled rice, see Appendix A.)

As mentioned in Chapter 1, it was quite common for British "exiles" heading for southern India to make the sea passage from England to Ceylon (now Sri Lanka), cross the Palk Strait to India and finally make their way overland to Madras. Often, travellers' first experience of tasting authentic food from the Asian subcontinent would have been the cuisine of Ceylon, which became very popular with the British in southern India. Wyvern paints a dismal picture of the ersatz curries that the passengers may have endured on-board ship. He describes one such dish as "yellow Irish stew" which resembles

> a bright saffron-tinted swill, covering sundry knotty lumps of potato and a few bony atoms of mutton, with its surface beflecked, if I may so describe it, with glossy discs of molten grease.[14]

Not very appetising, especially if the traveller was already feeling a little sea-sick. Wyvern describes a Ceylon curry as follows:

> [T]he dish is quite a *spécialité*, peculiar originally to places where the cocoanut is extensively grown and appreciated. It is known by some as the "Malay curry," and it is closely allied to the *moli** of the Tamils of Southern India. Though best adapted for the treatment of shell-fish, ordinary fish, and vegetables of the *cucumis* or gourd family, it may be advantageously tried with chicken, or any nice white meat.[15]

Wyvern's Ceylon Curry is made with prawns (shrimp) and cucumbers. It is less spicy than his Madras Curry, and flavoured with coconut milk. The curry sauce is made with onions sautéed in butter but very little garlic, loosened with fish stock and flavoured with turmeric, salt, sugar, ground cloves and ground cinnamon. Slices of fresh ginger and thin strips of fresh chillies are added near the end of cooking. The coconut milk is added in two parts: first, while the sauce is cooking, and then at the end of the cooking, to give a more intense coconut flavour.

Wyvern takes great care in describing how to obtain the coconut milk. He reminds his readers that the liquid found inside a fresh coconut is coconut *water*, not *milk*. To obtain coconut milk, the coconut is broken in half and the flesh is grated with a coconut scraper. The flesh is then soaked in a little boiling water for a short while, and the resulting liquid strained off. This is Wyvern's "number one" infusion of coconut milk which is added in the final stages of his Ceylon Curry, because it has the fullest flavour. Not to waste any ingredients, the grated coconut is soaked for a second time in more boiling water, then transferred to a muslin bag from which the "number two" infusion is squeezed out. This second, less concentrated, coconut milk is added to the curry during the initial cooking of the sauce.

(I have used a traditional coconut scraper while on a cookery course in Chennai: it is not as easy to use as it may seem – my efforts greatly amused my cookery teachers. The scraper resembles a cowboy's spur, and sits on a wooden stand on the floor. You move a coconut half back and forth across the scraper to grate the flesh but must be careful not to grate the coconut too enthusiastically, or you can cut through to the woody exterior. Before you begin, the coconut is placed

---

* A dish from southern India with a coconut sauce.

over an open flame to burn off the fibrous exterior, so that the coarse brown fibres do not fall into the snowy-white coconut flesh. The coconut is then split in two with a sharp blow from a machete. The procedure is not for the faint hearted.)

Before Wyvern moves on to the subject of mulligatawny soup, he briefly refers to other styles of curry making. He explains that:

> Old Indian cookery books give a number of recipes for *kubáb* curries, for the most part of purely native design, and requiring condiments and ingredients which were perhaps appreciated by our forefathers who adopted an almost Oriental method of life.[16]

Riddell's *Indian Domestic Economy and Receipt Book* was one of those old cookery books. Riddell's volume includes a total of twenty-four recipes for *khubabs* (kebabs) in the chapter on "Oriental Cookery" in addition to his curry recipes, ten recipes for *brianee* (biryiani), twenty-five recipes for *pullow* (pilau) and fifteen recipes for *ash* – a dish made with meat, pulses, vegetables, fruit, sugar, milk and spices. As we have seen, Wyvern's curries and other Indian dishes have been considerably anglicised. His kebab recipe, for example, contains bacon – a meat which would not have been used by either the Hindus or Muslims of Madras.

Wyvern ends his feature on curries with a recipe for *quoorma*:

> The "*quoorma*," if well made, is undoubtedly an excellent curry. It used, I believe, to be one of the best at the Madras Club, in days when curries commanded closer attention than they do now.[17]

Wyvern's *quoorma* (korma) is made with mutton which is diced and marinated in pounded fresh ginger and salt. He fries some chopped onions and garlic in plenty of butter before adding ground spices – coriander, black pepper, cardamoms, and cloves. Next, he adds the meat and cooks the curry until the meat is browned and tender. He then removes the pan from the heat and adds almond milk, a cupful of cream, ground turmeric and sugar. The pan goes back on the heat to simmer and, finally, lime juice is added. The *quoorma* is very mild and contains no chillies or chilli powder whatsoever which for many people, Wyvern remarks, is its "chief attraction".

It was the custom to serve curries accompanied by a selection of chutneys.

Wyvern notes that:

> According to the ancient canons by which the service of curries was regulated, chutneys of various kinds were considered as essentially necessary as the lordly platter of rice which, of course, accompanied them. These may be divided into two distinct classes: the preserved or bottled chutneys, and those that are made of fresh materials on the spot.[18]

He advises that:

> Fresh chutneys should be served in saucers which should be tastefully arranged upon a tray. Four or five varieties can be presented together, so that there may be an opportunity of selection.[19]

Wyvern offers recipes for his favourite fresh chutneys – tomato, cucumber, *brinjal* (aubergine/eggplant), coconut, mint, mango, tamarind and – a most unusual inclusion – mashed potato flavoured with onions, green chillies and vinegar.

Wyvern's theme of the native cook no longer being an expert in making Anglo-Indian-style curries re-emerges in his section on "Mulligatunny". He believes a good *mulligatunny* may be "a thing of the past" but he still considers it to be an excellent and "invigorating" soup:

> This preparation, originally peculiar to Southern India, derives its name from two Tamil words – *molegoo* (pepper), and *tunnee* (water). In its simple form, as partaken of by the poorer natives of Madras, it is, as its name indicates, a "pepper-water" or *soupe maigre*.
>
> The English, taking their ideas from this simple composition, added other condiments, with chicken, mutton, &c., thickened the liquid with flour and butter, and by degrees succeeded in concocting a *soupe grasse* of a decidedly acceptable kind.[20]

Wyvern seems to have done his homework and is well acquainted with the traditional way of making the peasants' "pepper-water". He concludes – not surprisingly, given his views on the subject – that the English adaptation of the dish is much finer and more "acceptable". He also believes that some of the best mulligatawny soup could be found at that time not in India, but England. His explanation for this discrepancy is that the English version invariably uses a strong meat stock for its base, adding that this is "an important point that most Indian cooks slur over".[21]

Once again, Wyvern recommends the use of a product made by Messrs Barrie and Co. and he is confident that Barrie's Madras Mulligatunny Paste will give the best results in flavouring the soup. Wyvern tells the story of a fellow officer making *mulligatunny* for his old uncle, and thoroughly approves of his friend's method. He makes some strong meat stock the day before making the soup. On the following day, when the stock has been skimmed of fat, he fries some onions in butter and adds the Barrie's Madras Mulligatunny Paste and enough stock to thoroughly mix the ingredients. He then adds some "sub-acid" in the form of redcurrant jelly (as Wyvern does with his curries), a little lemon juice and some Madras chutney. Next, he pours in plenty of stock to make a thin soup and cooks the *mulligatunny* for fifteen minutes before adding some almond milk. The soup is taken off the heat and strained through a sieve. Finally, he thickens the soup with butter mixed with flour and garnishes the soup by pouring over some cream. Wyvern thinks his friend's recipe can be taken "as a very good guide".[22]

Wyvern does not approve of the common habit of his fellow Anglo-Indians of serving rice with mulligatawny soup. Why, he asks, would you serve rice with *mulligatunny* when you would not dream of serving it with a fine game or mock turtle soup? His explanation is that it is a custom handed down by the first Anglo-Indians who acquired the habit, and the soup itself, from the native Indians. When the natives' soup was merely flavoured water used to liven up a simple bowl of rice, the custom would have been acceptable. But Wyvern's soup is made with great care from the best ingredients, so he is adamant that it should be served on its own – just like any other high-class soup.

We have already seen that Wyvern was harsh in his criticism of "Ramasamy", his Indian cook, for his poor skills in cooking European food throughout the pages of *Culinary Jotting for Madras*. However, the cook more than redeems himself in Wyvern's eyes when it comes to cooking rice:

> The boiling of rice is, as I have said, a matter of no difficulty to us in India. The native cook thoroughly understands the process, and invariably, I may say, sends an inviting looking dish to the table in which each grain appears to have been cooked independently, snowy white in appearance, and free from impurities of all kinds. A sodden mass of "stodgy" rice as dressed by Mary-Jane in England is a thing unknown to the Anglo-Indian Exile.[23]

So now "Ramasamy" has got one up on "Mary-Jane". And the English exile is delighted with the Indian-style rice which accompanies his Anglo-Indian curry.

9

Later Life in India

An Irish newspaper, *The Freeman's Journal*, of 3 July 1879 tells us:

> Major A. R. Kenney-Herbert, Brigade Staff Deputy Assistant Quartermaster-General, Malabar and Canara, has obtained private leave for 60 days.[1]

The weather would have been searingly hot in Madras during July and August, so it is a safe bet that Major and Mrs Kenney-Herbert spent their holiday up in the cooler climate of the Nilgiri Hills. Shortly after their return to Madras there was good news: Wyvern was confirmed as a substantive major on 20 September 1879, on completion of twenty years' service.

Wyvern was not idle. His third book, *Sweet Dishes*, was published in 1881 and he considered it to be a companion volume to *Culinary Jottings for Madras*. He initially wrote a series of articles for publication in the *Madras Times* newspaper and later used them as the basis for the book. In his prologue, written on 1 June 1881, Wyvern writes:

> The highly gratifying reception accorded by the public to my little book upon savoury cookery, "*Culinary Jottings for Madras*," has induced me to endeavour to complete the work with a few chapters upon sweet dishes.
>
> I passed over this important branch of the cook's art when compiling my first *brochure*, being under the impression that advice concerning the preparation of soups, sauces, *entrées*, &c., was more generally required than about *entremets sucrés*.[2]

Wyvern acknowledges that Indian cooks are generally good at cooking sweet dishes, but in his view, they have too limited a repertoire; the mistress of the house would have had to wade through scores of recipe books herself in order to vary her menus. The purpose of Wyvern's book is to provide the mistress with a comprehensive selection of ideas for sweet dishes, and to set out straightforward instructions for making them which, in turn, the mistress can teach her Indian cook.

In an echo of his chapter on "Our Kitchens in India" from *Culinary Jottings for Madras*, Wyvern is appalled at the conditions in which many sweet dishes are made. He finds it astonishing that any at all are made in the dirty, smoky kitchens which were typical at the time. He insists that every utensil used should be scrupulously clean. He also recommends that the dishes should be made in the house itself, rather than in the kitchen (which normally would be situated in an outbuilding), as smoke from wood fires and savoury smells would ruin delicately flavoured recipes containing cream and fruit. Wyvern suggests using a small charcoal burner, which should be situated on the verandah of the house, to heat any dishes that require cooking. He reluctantly accepts that things such as cakes and puddings would have to be cooked in the kitchen, but only after they have been carefully mixed in the "sweet and airy" atmosphere of the house.

The suspicion of the Anglo-Indian community that their Indian servants were stealing from them at every opportunity re-emerges in *Sweet Dishes*. Wyvern recommends not sending wine, liqueurs, fruit or jam out to the kitchen because, in his experience, when the dishes they were intended for are sent over to the house, they are often found to be surprisingly lacking in the flavours of those special ingredients, despite the bottles coming back half-full. Wyvern warms to his theme when he discusses the amount of sugar used by the native cooks. According to Wyvern, not only do the cooks over-sweeten all the dishes they make, but there is often less sugar returned to the store cupboard than expected. Here is his solution to the problem:

> In order to prevent the mysterious evaporation of these dainty and expensive ingredients, the eye of the mistress is necessary. In the simple matter of sugar it is actually surprising to note how much nicer *entremets* are that a lady has superintended, than those that the butler and cook have concocted alone.[3]

Wyvern recommends that sugar should be kept under lock and key when not in use. He relates how "a charming *châtelaine*" had taken him to task about the cost of all the butter and cream in his recipes. She complained that her dairy bill had grown considerably since she had been following his recipes, and that her butler had assured her that (as Wyvern puts it in his approximation of the butler's accent): "That Wivn's cookree plenty yexpense for cream, butter, yeverything".[4]

Wyvern is stung by the criticism, and offers to inspect the *châtelaine*'s household accounts. He discovers that she is using far more than his recipes demand. She tackles her servants over the matter, and her *ayah* gives the game away by blurting out that the butler has been handing out rations to the other servants (except her). Wyvern recommends putting the butter and cream under lock and key along with the sugar and, when she does so, her dairy bills shrink back to an acceptable amount.

Back in his military life, Wyvern's tour of service as Deputy Assistant Quartermaster-General expired in April 1881, and he was replaced by a Captain Yule. Wyvern was given a temporary appointment as Military Secretary to the Governor of Madras, William Huddleston.[5] Huddleston had been appointed acting governor after the death of the previous incumbent, William Adam.[6] The new governor, coming in to replace Huddleston, was a man with the magnificent name of Mountstuart Elphinstone Grant Duff. As we saw in Chapter 1, Grant Duff had arrived at Bombay at the beginning of November 1881, and he writes in his diary for 5 November 1881 that when he reached Raichore (now Raichur) on the frontier of the Madras Presidency, he was met by "Major Kenney Herbert, Military Secretary to Mr. Huddleston, who has been Acting Governor since Adam's death, Colonel Shaw-Stewart, and others".[7] The party travelled on to Madras by train in special carriages belonging to the Governor of Madras. Grant Duff was sworn in as governor later that day.

It was not until 1883 that Wyvern's appointment was made permanent. The Naval and Military Intelligence section of *The Morning Post* announced on 15 March that "Maj. A.R. Kenney-Herbert, of the Madras Cavalry, has been appointed military secretary to the Governor of Madras, the Right Hon. M.E. Grant Duff".[8]

Promotion came with Wyvern's new appointment: on 19 March 1883 Wyvern was raised to the rank of brevet lieutenant-colonel but, unfortunately, bad news followed good. We can imagine Wyvern celebrating his promotion and enjoying his new role when he received the news from England that his father had died. Arthur Robert Kenney-Herbert senior died aged seventy-eight on 21 June 1883 at Bourton Rectory, where Wyvern had been born, and where he had been rector for the past forty-four years. We do not know whether Wyvern was able to travel back to England for his father's funeral, but the journey time would have made it highly unlikely. Indeed, 1883 was not a good year for the Kenney-Herberts, as Agnes' father, Lieutenant-General John Wheeler Cleveland, died in Bangalore on 1

November, aged ninety-two.

Wyvern is mentioned from time to time in Grant Duff's diaries. Grant Duff notes that they discussed the possibility of a war between France and Prussia over breakfast one morning; he calls Wyvern "Colonel K. Herbert", which sounds very formal. Grant Duff's diary entry for 18 January 1884 records: "With Colonel Herbert to inspect the military sanitarium* of Poonamallee, about which some questions have arisen."[9]

The writer and poet Wilfrid Scawen Blunt,[10] on a tour of India in November 1883, was not impressed with Grant Duff in his role as Governor of Madras. Blunt writes scathingly:

> He had come with a flourish of Liberal trumpets, but had proved a mere windbag, good at making speeches on generalities, but useless at administration. He had left all work to the permanent officials, who had thwarted Lord Ripon's good intentions everywhere.[11]

Whether Wyvern was one of those permanent officials is open to question. (Coincidentally, Blunt and Wyvern were exactly the same age and shared the same birthday.)

However, life was not all work for Wyvern. There was a lively social scene in Madras, and Wyvern was very much part of it. Grant Duff's diaries tell us that his wife held a "fancy ball" in the Banqueting Hall at Government House on 16 February 1885:

> Colonel Herbert [went] as Clive† – an admirable copy of the portrait (said to be the best of him existing) in the monsoon dining-room at Government House; [...] John Lubbock [went] in a very becoming dress arranged by Colonel Herbert;[12]

Wyvern seems to have many hidden talents! He was also active in the famous Madras Club and *The Asylum Press Almanac and Compendium of Intelligence for 1882* records that Major A. R. Kenney-Herbert was a member of the General Committee that year (for more on the Madras Club, see Chapter 4).[13]

---

* a convalescent home for soldiers (see Chapter 7)
† Robert Clive, also known as "Clive of India".

On 20 September 1885 Wyvern was promoted to substantive lieutenant-colonel, so he would now receive the pay for the rank which he had held as brevet for the last two-and-a-half years. Wyvern's rise in the military ranks is swift. Only 18 months later, on 19 March 1887, he was promoted to colonel but, confusingly, also holds the local rank of brigadier-general, which comes with his role as Secretary to the Government of Madras.

Grant Duff ended his tenure as Governor of Madras on 8 December 1886, and made his farewell speech to the presidency at large at a grand dinner given by the Maharajah of Vizianagram.[14] There is no mention in his diaries of a personal farewell to Wyvern, but that does not necessarily mean that he was not grateful to Wyvern for his services as his military secretary for the past five years. Wyvern was still Secretary to the Government of Madras on his promotion in March 1887, so he must then have reported to Grant Duff's successor as governor, Robert Bourke.[15]

Back in England, a local newspaper reports that Wyvern's daughter, Enid, attended a "Gentleman's Ball" held by the Tennis Court Club at Leamington Spa Town Hall in February 1888. Wyvern's son, Arthur, is also in England around that time. He is now a lieutenant in the Northamptonshire Regiment, and appointed as an Instructor at the Royal Military College in May 1890 (the College being the precursor to the present-day Royal Military Academy Sandhurst).

Meanwhile, Wyvern is still enjoying life in the Madras Presidency. In June 1891 he takes part in amateur dramatics at Ootacamund. According to reports in the English regional newspapers:

> Ootacamund is not likely to soon forget the appearance of General Kenney Herbert, who delivered his inimitable sketch of a native *khitmutgâr* with his face blacked and arrayed in orthodox costume.[16]

Clearly, there continued to be no social taboos about "blacking up" in Wyvern's day. Wyvern also takes part in "The Devil's Dance" at a ball in Ooty given by Sir James Dormer.[17] Eight men dressed in black as "devils" danced with eight women dressed in white as "angels". According to *The Homeward Mail*:

> The devils danced with the most wonderful fiendish grace and agility, dragging their partners, whirling them round and pirouetting round them. They finished up with a wild, rapid waltz, ended by giving yells of triumph and truly unearthly shrieks.[18]

Wyvern's partner was a Miss Galton, not his wife Agnes, and it sounds like he thoroughly enjoyed himself. Life was not all fun and games in Ooty though, and Wyvern still had to perform his official duties while stationed there. On one occasion, he is recorded as having read the Queen's Despatch at the investiture of Major Grant VC, who was known as "the hero of Thobal".[19]

After more than thirty years' service with the army in India, Wyvern retires. He handed over to his successor while still at the local rank of brigadier-general. Wyvern's length of service and periods of absence from duty, which were used to calculate his army pension, were calculated as at 30 November 1891. There is a note in Wyvern's military record that his pension will not be affected during his "current furlough", so he must have ceased his military duties at the end of November 1891 and taken leave until his official retirement on 20 April 1892.[20] There is a notice in *The London Gazette* which reads simply: "The Queen has approved of the retirement from the Service of the undermentioned Officers [...] Colonel A.R. Kenney-Herbert, Madras Cavalry."[21]

There is a retirement announcement in *The Homeward Mail* newspaper of 21 November 1891 which says "we believe he will stay among us for some little time longer".[22] While his exact date of departure for England is unknown, it would appear that Wyvern did not return straightaway.

After he had been back in England for a few months, Wyvern seems to have become a little nostalgic for his time in India. He wrote an article, "In the Days of John Company", published in December 1892 in *Macmillan's Magazine*.[23] "John Company" was the popular name for the East India Company which initially traded with and later ruled over much of India. In the aftermath of the Indian uprising of 1857, the East India Company's assets, including its army, were taken over by the British government in 1858. The article is written in the first person and supposedly tells of the experiences of a young officer in John Company in the 1850s, but Wyvern never served under the East India Company, and was only in India for the last two months of the 1850s.

The article paints a picture of the sort of characters that a young and inexperienced officer might meet on his travels around southern India. The anecdotes do have a ring of authenticity to them, and may well have been experienced by Wyvern himself. If so, the events most likely would have taken place in the early 1860s when he was a young lieutenant. It is possible that his intention, in exactly the same way as he deals with living characters in *Furlough Reminiscences*, is to disguise people's identities not only by changing their names, but also places and dates.

In an echo of his introduction to *Culinary Jottings for Madras*, Wyvern begins the article in a mood of wistful nostalgia for a long-lost time when every banquet (*burra khana*) included a course made up of curries, rice and chutneys:

> Curry certainly formed the *pièce de résistance* of our food at the time I speak of. It appeared at every meal, and, treated by the native cook according to his national traditions, the indifferent flesh and fowl of the country was thus rendered more acceptable than in any other method then known. It rejoiced the servants of honest John Company therefore to send round at their banquets, preceded by a great platter piled high with beautifully boiled rice, a large silver dish specially fashioned in compartments in each of which was placed a different sample of curry, together with trays of various chutneys freshly made and preserved, grilled ham, the roes of fishes, Bombay "ducks" and *paparum* or *paupad* biscuits.* The course was a meal in itself and occupied at least half an hour, for it was the correct thing to taste each sample and call for those that appealed to you pleasantly a second time.[24]

Wyvern describes one particular *burra khana* and the formalities of dining at that time. He arrives by bullock cart at 7pm at a major-general's bungalow on a military cantonment. He is introduced to the other guests and, although the temperature is 92ºF (33ºC), he is dressed in formal uniform with a high collar. When the meal is ready, the guests have to follow a strict procedure to enter the dining room – in order of rank, as specified by the local Civil and Military Lists – Wyvern is anxious not to offend his host by going in ahead of his rightful turn. The formalities take so long that once they sit down to dinner, the soup is no longer hot.

There are lines of large, covered silver dishes on each side of the table: the largest dish of all sits in the centre, surrounded by a garland of fresh flowers. Then two large plates holding joints of meat are brought to the table and placed before the junior officers, whose job it is to carve. First, there is a short course of heated, tinned salmon coated with tinned lobster sauce. Then the guests "attack the solids". The table groans under the weight of boiled turkey, roast saddle of mutton, boiled ham, roast beef, boiled chickens, roast duck, boiled leg of mutton and ox tongue. The meat is accompanied by various vegetables which, if English, are tinned or if

---

* papads or poppadums

local, fresh. The meal is washed down by chilled champagne. There was no ice available in those days, so the wine is cooled using saltpetre, which a servant has been chilling for hours in his cooler's godown.

Then, as if this huge selection of meats were not enough, comes the curry course, just as Wyvern describes it earlier in the article. The curries are followed by desserts including a "pineapple cheese". As the meal progresses the wine keeps on coming, and ends with a fine old Madeira. Wyvern leaves to go back to his quarters at midnight, even though he has a parade to attend first thing in the morning. Inevitably, he has to endure the parade while nursing "dire symptoms" through overindulgence of food and wine.[25]

Wyvern soon shakes off his nostalgia for his old life in Madras and seems to have quickly got down to business. We have seen in Chapter 6 that Wyvern was associated with a company called John Moir & Son Ltd. Wyvern adds a sentence (highlighted in italic below) to his chapter on "In the Store-Room" from the fifth edition of *Culinary Jottings* onwards:

> Messrs. Brand & Co.'s preparations for invalids, potted meats, soups, and strong essences of beef, chicken, &c., are *spécialités* in their way vastly superior to anything formerly in the market of a like description. *Messrs. Moir and Son have however taken up the subject recently with great success.*[26]

There is also an addition to the chapter on "Camp Cookery" for the fifth edition of *Culinary Jottings* which was published 1885. A footnote appears for the first time, which reads:

> Note. – For various methods of treating preserved food of all kinds, see Wyvern's annotated catalogue of Messrs. John Moir and Son's provisions.[27]

Wyvern and John Moir & Son Ltd renew their partnership in 1892. John Moir & Son was a manufacturer of preserved foods, and the title page for its export catalogue for 1893 reads *Tinned Food with Advice and Recipes for its Treatment; being John Moir & Son's (Limited) Export Catalogue – annotated by "Wyvern"*.[28] The cover of the book shows the slightly different title of:

MOIR'S PRESERVED FOOD
AND
HOW TO PREPARE IT FOR THE TABLE
BY "WYVERN"
AUTHOR OF CULINARY JOTTINGS
SWEET DISHES ETC.

Although the catalogue was nominally issued for trading in 1893, Wyvern's introduction to the book is signed "London, 1st May 1892". Therefore, it is probable that he wrote the bulk of his contribution to the catalogue before he officially retired, which would explain why he is using his pseudonym rather than his real name. His introduction states:

> The advice I give in this catalogue is more particularly addressed to Messrs J. Moir & Son's *clientèle* in India and the Colonies; nevertheless there is much of it quite practicable in England, and to be earnestly recommended to home consumers of preserved food.[29]

The distinction between India and the colonies of the British Empire comes up again later in the catalogue. Wyvern writes in his section on "Dried Herbs" that "Experience has led me to the conclusion that the majority of Indian exiles – I cannot speak of Colonists – fail to appreciate the value of these flavouring agents".[30] So, to Wyvern's way of thinking, the British were "exiles" in India but "colonists" elsewhere in the empire.

The first part of the of the book contains a catalogue of 119 numbered entries for Moir's products, with Wyvern's suggestions for use. The section is full of useful advice on how to treat the products in a hot climate. Tinned butter, for example, should be chilled with ice and washed in milk before use. Wyvern thoroughly recommends Moir's Danish butter which, he advises, should be used for all types of cooking and is "altogether superior to the best butter procurable in the Native market in tropical climates".[31]

The remarkable feature of Moir's catalogue is the huge variety of foodstuffs that were available preserved either in tins or glass jars in the late nineteenth century.

Not only were there the sort of items one might expect such as soups, vegetables and jam, but the catalogue also contains entries for such things as tinned sausages, roast beef and a variety of cheeses.

There are numerous references in the catalogue to Wyvern's book, *Culinary Jottings*, to which he directs readers who wish to read further on specific topics of cooking. For example, under the entry for "Curry Powders", he writes:

> Messrs. Moir & Son have been at some pains to get some sound stock Curry Powders and Pastes, and they have been successful. The public should, however, be warned that, although a good powder or paste, or both, are important points gained on the line of advance to a good curry, the dish will never reach perfection unless properly cooked, and unless all the laws which govern curry-making are carried out. Wyvern's *"Culinary Jottings"* (Higginbotham & Co., Madras), contains the fullest directions for curry and mulligatunny-making. It must suffice here to give a brief *resumé* on the subject.[32]

The second part of the catalogue features Wyvern's recipes for using Moir's products, and primarily addresses Moir's customers living in England. In his Introduction, Wyvern assures the mistress of the house that he understands some of the treatments he recommends for tinned goods may sound "a little troublesome", but explains that cooks in India and the colonies have achieved great success in preparing them. However, he does accept that their success may be due to having more time on their hands and, as a result, the native cook is able to watch over his stew pan with "the patience of a monument". If the mistress of the house and her cook cannot find the time, then Wyvern assures her that Moir's products are good enough to be used just as they are, without further embellishment.

Wyvern is, of course, now living in England too – and a new chapter in his life is just beginning.

10

Home to England

Wyvern was now officially retired from the Madras Cavalry. He had served in the British Army in India for almost thirty-three years. He had started off, like so many young men of his class, as an officer-cadet and had ended up as a colonel.

As we have seen in Chapter 9, Wyvern's military duties finished on 30 November 1891, and he was on furlough until his official retirement on 20 April 1892. Wyvern was not in retirement for long. His first months back in England saw him writing numerous magazine articles which had the effect of raising his public profile considerably. In particular, he wrote a trilogy of articles in a journal, *The Nineteenth Century*, which stirred up quite a controversy. First came "The Art of Dining" (August 1892), then "The Art of Cooking" (November 1892), and finally "The Art of Household Management" (August 1893).

However, Wyvern did not solely write articles on the philosophy of cooking; some were intended purely for entertainment. As we have seen in previous chapters, "In the Days of John Company" was published in *Macmillan's Magazine* for December 1892. Unlike Wyvern's more serious articles, it is wittily written and entertaining to read. I can imagine quite a few retired military men and their wives nodding in fond recognition at the scenes Wyvern is describing, nostalgically remembering their own time in India. The reaction to his articles in *The Nineteenth Century* was considerably different.

The contrast between the chatty anecdotes and gossipy stories recounted in "In the Days of John Company" and the wordy intellectualism of "The Art of Dining" is stark indeed. In many ways it is hard to believe that the same author wrote both articles. Here is a sample from the latter:

> To dine tastefully both in regard to our food and surroundings is now a consummation devoutly wished for by all, and inasmuch as good dinners demand skilful preparation, an impetus has thus been given to scientific cookery.[1]

The article is primarily about formal dining and the changes in fashion towards a strict code of dining "in accordance with French gastronomical laws".[2] What seems to have happened, at least in Wyvern's estimation, is that the English had adopted the new French style but were regularly getting it wrong and not following those unforgiving "laws".

The French had long ago abandoned their traditional style of formal dining – *service à la Française* – and had adopted a new style imported from the Russian royal court which became known as *service à la Russe* (see Chapter 2). According to Ian Kelly in his book *Cooking for Kings*, the French master-chef Antonin Carême[3] was a pioneer of this new form of service for banquets, but even he was still using *service à la Française* for a dinner held in 1829 by James and Betty de Rothschild, the richest couple in France at that time. Kelly explains:

> Carême still catered for the tastes of his French employers for *service à la Française*, where nearly all the food was presented on the table at the start of the meal, with only the soups and the *entrées* literally 'making an entrance' hot. *Service à la Russe* (the style that Carême helped to import from Russia of serving plated courses in sequence as we might expect today) was a fashion too daring in 1829 for the socially ambitious Rothschilds.[4]

In *service à la Française* the host (including Rothschild himself) would stand and carve the roast meats which were on display when the guests entered the dining room. In the new *service à la Russe* the courses were brought to the table one at a time. When each course was finished, the plates would be cleared away and the next course would be brought out hot from the kitchen and placed before the diners. In Carême's feast for the Rothschilds, Kelly informs us that:

> The roasts and highly dressed "*grosses pièces*" would adorn the table as the guests arrived, along with the side-dishes (*entremets*) including the centre-piece dessert.
>
> Twice, the table would be completely reset with plates and cutlery. After the soup there would be a re-lay or *relevés* of hot fish, and after the roasts and *entrées* a new re-lay of cold desserts.[5]

So not all the food was presented on the table at the start of the meal, but the most impressive pieces were clearly on show to impress the guests when they entered the dining room.

The upper classes in London had adopted the new *service à la Russe* style of formal dining some time after the French, but it was well established by the time Wyvern retired to England. The courses all had specific names, and convention dictated that they should be served in a specific order. However, the English seem to have got a bit confused about the different courses and their French names. The stated purpose of Wyvern's article is to put them right. It is not hard to imagine how some high-society noses might have been put out of joint by this relatively unknown newcomer coming along and criticising their knowledge of fine dining. To be sure, it does not help matters that the French names for each of the courses were often the same ones as those used in the old *service à la Française*, but their original function (to relay the table with hot food – the *relevés*) was now obsolete.

Wyvern provocatively claims that:

> Taking first of all the composition of some London dinners of to-day, modelled, it is to be presumed, in accordance with French gastronomical laws, we find, to be sure, a fine parade of terms: *potages, poissons, relevés, entrées, rôts* and so forth; but if we look into the *menus* themselves 'tis odds [sic] that we discover that the majority of English dinner-givers who work on these lines still misunderstand or misapply the classification they have adopted. Few, at least, seem to appreciate what manner of thing a *relevé* really is, and the proper place in the meal for its introduction; while the *raison d'être* of the unfortunate *rôt* is ignored, and its name continually taken in vain.[6]

He declares:

> If the *Code Français* and the teaching of Brillat-Savarin are to be followed, the *relevé* must follow the fish, and the *rôt,* as the term plainly indicates, be 'a roast' served after the *entrées*: that the former is by no means the piece of plainly roasted meat called by Anglo-Saxons a 'joint,' and that the latter is not a savoury *plat* or *entremets*, but if possible a spitted bird*.[7]

After Wyvern has shown the English where they are going wrong, he suggests a simplified version, based on a more authentic version of the *Code Français*, without

---

* spit-roasted bird

the English tendency to serve too much over-elaborate food in too many courses and containing too many joints of roasted meat. He is a recommending a renaissance in English formal dining.

The article continues in this manner and is, frankly, almost impenetrable at times – but it seems to have achieved its object. Wyvern touched a nerve. He got noticed. The newspapers commented on his article and their letters columns were filled with replies.

A scathing review of the article in *Tatler* shows how at that time, Wyvern was not anywhere near as well known in England as he was in India. The reviewer writes:

> [N]ow let me tell you what Colonel What's-his-name says. Before I read the article I thought dining was a thing I understood thoroughly. Now I am quite sure that I don't, and that you don't either. When you dine and when I dine, we dine like barbarians. We don't understand the Art of the thing, and I gather that it is the Art we want. Never mind a cent about the victuals, so long as you get the Art.
>
> No man dines artistically until indigestion has killed him.[8]

The review includes quite a good joke at Wyvern's expense:

> And if you don't happen to know what a *rôt* is, or what the other things are, why then you pretty soon come to the conclusion that it is all "rot," and in nine cases of ten you won't be far wrong either.[9]

The second article in the trilogy, "The Art of Cooking",[10] is a little more accessible than "The Art of Dining" because it is talking about practical matters in the kitchen rather than the finer points of the French menu. However, the article is just as critical of English cooks as it was of the English experience of formal dining.

Poor old "Mary-Jane", the stereotypical English cook, does not get a good write-up. It starts well enough for her, because she is considered by Wyvern to be more skilful and reliable than the recent crop of French cooks who were masquerading as chefs in England at that time. Wyvern laments that once upon a time any household which employed a French chef could enjoy "immunity from all trouble in regard to their table", but no longer. He then moves on to his favourite theme of a renaissance of English cuisine for which he coins the title "the Anglo-French

School of Cookery". He considers the new movement to be in its infancy and in need of careful nurturing. Wyvern reflects on English cuisine and thinks that:

> England seems to have been absolutely handicapped by her goodly heritage of fish, flesh, and game; things so excellent in themselves, indeed, that even ignorant treatment could hardly rob them of their virtues. The national taste, never of a very fastidious type, was easily gratified with simple fare provided that the quality of the meat was beyond question, that it was plainly cooked, and that there was enough of it. Sowers who attempted to sow the good seed of French gastronomy in English soil found that it fell on stony ground.[11]

Wyvern lays the blame at the door of "Mary-Jane", whom he considers to have little interest in cooking other than as a chore which must be accomplished as quickly as possible, and with the minimum of fuss. He accepts that there are exceptions but complains that "This diabolical hatred of trouble is the cardinal sin of the English kitchen".[12]

He tells the story of a fellow officer in India, a general, who brought his cook from Madras home with him when he retired. The cook had worked for him since he was young, so the general, being a culinary expert himself, had schooled him in European cooking until he was highly proficient. Once the general was back in England he stayed with his sister, whose cook produced a clear soup that was nowhere near up the quality to which the general was accustomed; so he arranged for his cook to show his sister's "Mary-Jane" how to make a really good *consommé*. The following day, the general's sister enjoys the best soup she has ever tasted, and goes to thank "Mary-Jane", who is outraged: the general's cook had made the soup. She would never have had time to make that soup with all her other work to do. She tells her mistress the Indian cook had spent all morning making only the soup and nothing else. Wyvern maintains that this a gross exaggeration and that "Mary-Jane" is a "self-satisfied ignoramus" who resents having someone in her own kitchen that knows more than her.

So, Wyvern's advice is to train your own cook from an early age before she (and he bemoans the fact that it is almost always a she – in India the cooks were always men) gets into bad habits. "Mary-Jane" then would be able make some delicious sauces to go with what would otherwise be her usual plain boiled fish. She would be able to roast a chicken on a spit over charcoal the "proper" way, rather than the modern way of cooking the chicken in a "ventilated oven" which, if left to her own devices, she would use to cook almost everything, because it took so little time and effort.

His condescension towards "Mary-Jane" is unbounded. He maintains that even with the best training, she is never going to be able to manage the complexities of haute cuisine. He concludes: "All that we can hope to do is to raise her from the level she has at present reached to that of a very sound well-taught *cook*."[13]

It is doubtful that many "Mary-Janes" actually read Wyvern's article in *The Nineteenth Century*, so he was probably safe from their anger at his criticism. That would not be true for the subject of Wyvern's next and final article in the trilogy, "The Art of Household Management", which concerns the shortcomings of the lady of the house.[14]

Wyvern begins the article by back-pedalling a little on his criticism of the cook. He admits that he may have "sketched poor Mary-Jane at her worst perhaps". He accepts that not every household can employ "skilled artists" to cook for them on account of the cost, and that an ordinary cook is not wholly to blame if the dinners she makes are disappointing:

> To begin with, if you want to gallicise* your *cuisine* to a moderate extent, and put nice little dinners upon your table, you must be prepared to take upon yourself a fair share of the trouble necessary to attain your object; and not only must you show personal interest in the undertaking, but you must really make a friend of your cook.[15]

Despite the fact that Wyvern is about to open his own cookery school, he considers sending "Mary-Jane" on an advanced cookery course to be a waste of time. He thinks the best way to educate her in the art of cookery is for the lady of the house to teach her, step-by-step, in her own kitchen, but admits that the process will need a great deal of "tact, good temper, and discretion" on the mistress's part.

Wyvern now warms to his controversial theme:

> It is an unfortunate that out of the many English ladies who personally control their households but very few have any practical knowledge of the art of cooking. Am I exaggerating when I say that hardly one in fifty can design a

---

* make in the French style

really artistic little dinner, and fewer still explain in detail with necessary accuracy the dishes that compose it?[16]

As we have seen, his theme of the art of management begins with proper training for the cook and, if necessary, the mistress herself. Wyvern suggests that the mistress acquaints herself with a cookery book that is "concise, readable, and free from clap-trap" (Wyvern's *Common-Sense Cookery* perhaps?), and then, when she is ready, the mistress might "attend a course of lectures at an advanced academy of cookery" (Wyvern's Common-Sense Cookery Association maybe?). Only then will the lady of the house be able to instruct her cook satisfactorily.

Next, Wyvern tackles the issue of buying food and dealing with tradespeople. Wyvern does not recommend sending a note to, say, the butcher, simply setting out what is required and letting the butcher make the final choice on the cuts of meat. Neither does he recommend using the newly established Co-operative Stores which, although they sell high-quality products, are unable to give the mistress sufficient attention for her to buy exactly what she needs. No, Wyvern – like many of his modern-day counterparts – prefers to deal directly with an independent supplier who has his own shop: "Mr Judkins" he calls him. Wyvern recommends walking into Judkins' shop, passing the time of day, then listening to his advice on what excellent things he has in store today. That way, not only can the lady get exactly what she needs, but also she may come across some delicacy that she had not even thought about while making her shopping list.

On a more negative note, Wyvern emphasises that by dealing with suppliers directly, there is less chance of getting a short weight, or of having meat or fish trimmings – which the mistress paid for when she purchased a whole joint of meat or a whole fish – slyly being put aside to be sold later to another customer. (As we have seen in *Culinary Jotting for Madras*, trimmings are essential to his preoccupation with economy, because they can be used to make stock for soups or gravy, and so improve the flavour of the finished dish at no added expense.)

Finally, Wyvern comes to the art of giving the day's meal orders to the cook. He says that all too often, he hears of a cook's despair that she has not been given them early enough to make the best of them. The result is that if the food she needs is delivered too late, inevitably its preparation and cooking will be rushed, and the meal spoiled. He relates a story about discussing his own requirements for the day with Judkins in his shop when:

A breathless woman hurried into the shop and ordered a piece of beef for boiling to be sent up at once for lunch. The joint was despatched almost immediately, and as the messenger hurried off with it the good butcher observed "There you are, sir," raising his eyes to the clock, "eleven gone; well, it'll be 'arf parst nearly before that meat's put on the fire: it'll be boiled ever so much too farst, and come to the table as 'ard as a brick. To-morrow probably the lady herself will call and complain of my supplying her with such tough inferior meat! Believe me, sir, that isn't so much the fault of the cooks as these hurried orders."[17]

Wyvern concludes that so much unhappiness with the quality of the finished dish is brought about by "incompetent management rather than incompetent cooks". We can but wonder how the good ladies of London reacted to his conclusion. One reaction came from a review of the article in the *Nottingham Evening Post*, under the heading of "A Man's Idea of Cookery" – which rather puts Wyvern in his place.[18]

Wyvern's next career move is to branch out from writing about cooking to giving practical demonstrations of his methods and ideas. There is a brief notice in *The Morning Post* of 7 December 1893 which states, in the section on "Arrangements for this Day": "Common-sense Cookery Association – Lecture by Colonel A. Kenney-Herbert, Queen's-gate Hall, 3[pm]."[19] We do not know precisely what Wyvern said in his lecture on that day in London's South Kensington, but it was the start of his journey towards becoming a celebrity chef of his day.

"Common-Sense Cookery" is about to become Wyvern's brand name. His first step was to launch the Common-Sense Cookery Association in December 1893. With the name established, Edward Arnold (an important publisher of the day, and publisher to the India Office) published Wyvern's *Common-Sense Cookery for English Households, Based upon Modern English and Continental Principles, with Twenty Menus for Little Dinners Worked Out in Detail*, in 1894.[20] The title is almost as long as the preface, which Wyvern wrote in October of that year. Edward Arnold did not print a publication date for the second edition of *Common-Sense Cookery*, but there are advertisements for their latest books in the back pages, dated March 1898. The book was highly successful and in continuous publication for at least eleven years, with the second edition alone running to five impressions.

At first glance, it appears that Wyvern had been working on two books simultaneously since he had retired from the army in April 1892. *Common-Sense Cookery* and *Fifty Breakfasts* were published only months apart. However, a closer look at *Common-Sense Cookery* reveals that it is not entirely a new book. There is a chapter in *Culinary Jottings* titled "Réchauffés". It turns out that *Common-Sense Cookery* is actually a *réchauffé* of *Culinary Jottings*. However, to be fair, Wyvern made major revisions to the book and had updated the recipes and the menus. He also edited out all references relating specifically to India, and omitted the chapters on Indian kitchens, servants and conditions. There is some new content in *Common-Sense Cookery*: for example, he weaves into the book the contents of his trilogy of articles for *The Nineteenth Century*. In an echo from "The Art of Household Management" (see above) he writes:

> If you want to be well fed, and to put nice little dinners before your friends, you must not only be prepared to take considerable personal interest in food and feeding, but you must make a *friend* of your cook.[21]

Despite Wyvern's revisions, *Common-Sense Cookery* still uses a great deal of content taken directly from *Culinary Jottings*, as shown in this example.

Culinary Jottings for Madras	**Common-Sense Cookery**
Chapter I – The Menu	*Chapter III – The Menu*
All who have studied the <u>reformed system of dinner-giving</u>	All who have studied the <u>art of dining from the standpoint of modern good taste</u>
will, I think, agree with me when I say that the *menu* <u>of a dinner anywhere, but in India especially,</u> should be reduced to the smallest compass possible. An hour at the outside should suffice for the discussion of the daintiest of bills of fare, so to ensure this, we should <u>strike out of it all unnecessary encumbrances.</u>	will, I think, agree with me when I say that the *menu* should be reduced to the smallest compass possible. An hour at the outside should suffice for the discussion of the daintiest of bills of fare, so to ensure this, we should <u>compose our dinner with deliberation.</u>

The book goes on in much the same way. Wyvern has rearranged the chapters a little, but they cover the same territory. "The Cook and his Management" becomes "To Housekeepers" and has been completely rewritten. "Kitchen Requisites" has a totally different slant, as one would expect, and "In the Store-Room" has been omitted altogether.

Wyvern is now writing for a more sophisticated audience with higher expectations of their approach to dining, compared with the British in India. In *Common-Sense Cookery*, the trials and tribulations of the Madras housewife who was valiantly trying to instruct her servants on how to cook European food without all the necessary ingredients and under sometimes very basic conditions, have evaporated. Wyvern's English readers will have all the foodstuffs they need to make European dishes and a range cooker with a modern oven.

When we get to the chapters on cookery, we can see that they have been extensively rewritten; but if the two books had been published by different authors, the author of *Culinary Jottings* would certainly have a strong claim that the author of *Common-Sense Cookery* had plagiarised his work.

The two chapters on curries and mulligatawny soup in *Culinary Jottings* have been condensed to one single chapter for *Common-Sense Cookery*. When explaining how to cook curries, Wyvern now has the opposite problem: all the exotic ingredients which were so common in India are now more difficult to find, and are relatively expensive in England. It is also "Mary-Jane's" turn to be at a disadvantage, much as "Ramasamy" was when he was required to cook European dishes. She is likely to struggle to cook Indian-style dishes incorporating spice blends and curry pastes because, unlike him, she does not have the experience.

In his usual thorough style, Wyvern gives detailed instructions on how to cook his curry recipes. The recipes are essentially the same as in *Culinary Jotting*s, but there are some interesting differences in his approach. The method for making curries is much easier to follow in *Common-Sense Cookery* because Wyvern has numbered the steps of the cooking process. In *Culinary Jottings* the cooking method is written as continuous text, with added information and comments. Gone are the long, detailed instructions on how to make 21 lbs (9.5 kg) of home-made curry powder, as are those on how to make your own curry paste. Instead, Wyvern recommends using bottles of commercially-made curry powder and curry paste.

Wyvern seems to have changed his mind about the best way to add what he calls "the sweet-acid" taste to his curries. As we have seen previously, in *Culinary Jottings* he maintains that using redcurrant jelly is an improvement over the Indian method of using tamarind paste. In *Common-Sense Cookery*, he changes his mind and says that although redcurrant jelly can be used to good effect:

> The natives of Southern India use a conserve of tamarind worked with a little coarse sugar, and there can be no doubt that tamarind is the best of all acid ingredients. Chopped apples are unnecessary; at all events they are not used in curry-land* itself. Some of the liquid, say a teaspoonful, out of a bottle of Madras made lime pickle is to be commended for both flavour and acid.[22]

Using chopped apples in curries was a very British addition, as recommended by none other than Mrs Beeton in her famous *Book of Household Management* from 1861,[23] and so followed by a great many British cooks. As we can see above, Wyvern is dismissive. He assures his readers that apples are not used in "curry-land".

The menus in *Common-Sense Cookery* have been reduced from the thirty listed in *Culinary Jottings* down to twenty. There are still ten menus for a dinner party of eight people, and another ten for a dinner party of six people, but there are no menus for Wyvern's "little home dinners". The menus are not the same as the ones in *Culinary Jottings*, and they have been completely revised for his British readers.

Wyvern remarks on his menus:

> To some of my readers these *menus* may seem to provide an insufficient amount of food. All I ask is a fair trial before judgement. Although the exaggerated feast with two or more *entrées* and as many sweets, with two of everything as well as an English "joint," is fortunately no longer met with at the tables of people of taste, many are still inclined to be too generous in regard to the quantity of good things they offer to their friends. Now I venture to say that the little dinners I propose will, if courageously tried as they are, be found ample. They should be served well within the hour, and the giver of the small feast may rest assured that the absence of the joint will not be noticed.
>
> Those who dissent from my views on this subject can obviously add a joint of meat to any of the *menus*, according to the English custom, after the *entrée*,

---

* India

but such a thing is never to be seen in a correct French dinner.[24]

So the object of the menus in *Common-Sense Cookery* is to create "a correct French dinner" reflecting "modern good taste", rather than the traditional English dinners of old which consisted of "a procession of meats".

Here is one of Wyvern's spring menus for eight people:[25]

Consommé aux pâtes d'Italie	Clear soup with Italian paste
Filets de soles aux fines herbes	Fillets of sole with herbs
Côtelettes à la Soyer	Cutlets à la Soyer
Quenelles de volaille fourrées aux truffes	Chicken quenelles with truffles
Canetons rôtis à la Dubois	Ducklings roasted
Salade	Salad
Petits pois à l'Anglaise	Green peas the English way
Crème au praline	Vacherin with burnt almond cream
Croustades de merluche fumée	Cases with smoked haddock

He has dispensed with using the French terminology for the names of the courses for a formal meal although, in practice, he still follows it. The above menu follows the classic sequence of *potage, poisson, relevé, entrée, rôt, salade, entremet, dessert* and *hors d'oeuvre*, just as he was recommending in his article on "The Art of Dining". However, he does mention that it is becoming the custom in Paris to serve the hors d'oeuvres between the soup and the fish.

The cookery writer, Elizabeth David, hits the nail on the head in her book *Spices, Salt and Aromatics in the English Kitchen*, when she is discussing Wyvern's menus:

His menu planning, modest though it was for his own times, is over elaborate for ours, and many of his dishes now appear fussy and over-sauced; and, in the style of the period, his pages are peppered with italicized kitchen French.[26]

In Wyvern's preface to *Common-Sense Cookery*, he thanks Sir Henry Thompson[27] for the assistance he has given him in his writings. Thompson returns the compliment in his own book, *Food and Feeding*. He includes in the eleventh edition a recipe for boiling rice to accompany curry, for which he gives credit to Wyvern in a footnote:

> The above receipt is based on the instructions given in one of the best practical cook's guides I know, a work written by an accomplished officer of her Majesty's service in India, "Culinary Jottings: a Treatise in Thirty Chapters," etc., by Wyvern. Fifth Edition. Madras: Higginbotham & Co. 1885. A most interesting and suggestive work to the European, although designed for Anglo-Indians. In my opinion no culinary library, even of modest pretensions, is complete without it.
>
> The foregoing note, which has appeared in two or three previous editions, I purposely retain in this also, for Colonel Kenney-Herbert, the author, known at that date as "Wyvern," has returned to this country; and still devoting his leisure to the improvement of culinary art, has written various interesting and useful small works, e.g. "Fifty Breakfasts," "Fifty Lunches," "Fifty Dinners," and "Fifty Suppers." But his chief and most complete volume, entitled "Common Sense Cookery for English Households," pp. 504, 1894: E. Arnold, London, is admirably adapted for heads of families, as well as to cooks of the present day who take interest in their duties and desire to improve.[28]

Thompson's endorsement of Wyvern's books must have been very satisfying for Wyvern. Being cited in such a popular book (*Food and Feeding* ran to twelve editions, from 1880 to 1910) must have enhanced Wyvern's reputation no end.

There are some press reviews of *Common-Sense Cookery* printed in the back of later editions. *The Times* is quoted as saying it is:

> A book which is sure to have a large circulation, since the author, the well-known "Wyvern," has been for some time generally accepted as perhaps the chief English authority on the art of cookery.[29]

The Morning Post's opinion was that the book was:

> An elaborate treatise on the culinary art. The rules are laid down simply and clearly, and the recipes are given with such precision as to quantities that

mistakes can scarcely occur if proper attention is paid to the instructions.[30]

And finally, the *Manchester Guardian*'s view:

> We are very glad to see that Colonel Kenney Herbert has at last put his unrivalled combination of practical experience with theoretical enthusiasm and study at the service of readers in a more elaborate and comprehensive form than his "Jottings." His book is very comprehensive; it embodies the most elaborate systems of French cookery as well as the simplest of English; it shows an excellent conception of a dish, and a still better one of a dinner, and above all it is practical from end to end.[31]

Fifty Breakfasts, mentioned in Thompson's footnote, was Wyvern's first complete cookery book written after he had returned to England. Published in March 1894, it was to be the first part of a trilogy dedicated to specific meals of the day (the companion volumes are *Fifty Dinners*, published in 1895, and *Fifty Luncheons*, published in 1896). However, I think that Thompson's reference to a book written by Wyvern entitled "Fifty Suppers" is an error, and can only assume he is referring to Wyvern's *Picnics and Suppers*, published in January 1901.

The reviews of *Fifty Breakfasts* were rather mixed. The *Pall Mall Gazette* of 24 March carries a long and extensive review of the book. Here is the reviewer's conclusion:

> To sum up: to the art of breakfasting, Mr. Herbert's book may not be accepted as an infallible guide. But in it the artist will find hints innumerable to aid him in the creation of many a masterpiece. The pupil may often surpass the teacher. If from these "Fifty Breakfasts" of mediocre merit is evolved one of supreme accomplishment, Mr. Herbert could ask for no greater profit of his labours. His volume may be placed on the shelf below Mrs. Glass and Dumas and Brillat-Savarin, and the giants, but side by side with the "St. James's Cookery Book" and many other of modern manufacture, and there prove itself. Distinctly, it is a book to be read and studied, preserved for reference, but not as an authority.[32]

The publishers used the above quote in an advertisement for *Fifty Breakfasts* contained in the back pages of the second edition of *Common-Sense Cookery* but slyly condensed the review to "Distinctly it is a book to be read and studied"[33] – which does not sound anything like as critical as the full review.

Others were kinder. *The Cheltenham Looker-On* wrote:

> Let me give a word of commendation to a new cookery book which has lately appeared.
> A careful and intelligent study of this volume would enable a housewife to set before her family something a little more varied than the bacon, poached eggs and kidneys, which often form the whole *repertoire* of an English "plain cook".[34]

The Manchester Guardian's view of *Fifty Breakfasts* read:

> The craftsmanship and precision of his directions for the actual composition of his dishes are beyond praise. The vagueness which is the curse of cookery books entirely disappears here, and there is not only a distinct indication of quantities and times, but the minutest description, without verbiage, of processes implements, and the like. It is really a very good book.[35]

In the back pages of the second edition of *Fifty Breakfasts* there is an advertisement for the Common-Sense Cookery Association. The managing director of the Association is identified as "Colonel Kenney-Herbert", and its objects are described in full:

1. To provide Lectures in which the rules of good, refined, and economical Cookery will be explained and practically demonstrated.
2. To afford opportunities of systematic instruction at moderate cost to Students, Cooks, and others, who are desirous of attaining to efficiency and to qualify for good situations.
3. To establish a Registry for Cooks whose antecedents have been ascertained and qualifications tested, and who can, accordingly, be with confidence recommended.[36]

The advertisement goes on to explain that:

> The Registry has been opened at 13, Sloane Street, and the Lectures are delivered on Mondays at the Queen's Gate Hall. Particulars obtainable at Gastrell's Library, 15, Sussex Place, South Kensington.[37]

The Epicure magazine ran a monthly feature titled "Notes from Cookery Schools", and in the edition for February 1894 a notice appears for the Common-Sense Cookery Association.[38] It confirms that at the time, the Association was housed at 13 Sloane Street, and that Colonel A. Kenney-Herbert was "the managing director and guiding spirit" whose articles "in current periodicals are well known". The notice announces that Wyvern intends to make a series of ten lectures on Mondays in January, February and March of that year at Queen's Gate Hall. The lectures were intended for "lady students and cooks", and the topics were to be soups, fish, *entrées*, roasting and browning, boiling and steaming, stewing and frying, vegetables, savouries and sweets. It was also announced that the Association would establish a "Registry Office", or employment agency, for housekeepers, cooks, skilled waitresses and kitchen maids.

Wyvern's lectures and cooking demonstrations at Queen's Gate Hall seem to have been quite successful.[39] There are numerous adverts for his lectures in the London newspapers of the time. The titles of his lectures and demonstrations include "Vegetables", "Sweets" (meaning desserts) and "Oriental Cookery", in which he shows his students how to cook curries, mulligatawnies, rice, pilaus and chutneys. The "Oriental Cookery" classes took place every Tuesday at 3pm and, not surprisingly given Wyvern's expertise, seem to have been very popular. The general cooking demonstrations were on Mondays at 11am and 3pm. Each session cost two shillings and sixpence, or £1 and one shilling for a course of ten classes.

In *The Cheltenham Looker-On* of 14 April 1894, its "A Woman's Chit-Chat" feature notes how the Common-Sense Cookery Association had recently started its second course of lectures at Queen's Gate Hall, and explains that although there are already several cookery schools operating in London:

> scarcely one has hit the happy medium of giving lessons in really refined yet not extravagant *cuisine*. With this special type of instruction does the C.S.C. Association chiefly concern itself and so far its efforts have been attended with success, much interest having been aroused in those who have already attended Col. Kenney-Herbert's ("Wyvern") excellent lectures. On Tuesdays Oriental cookery – curries, pilaus and the like – will be specially dealt with, and with this subject Col. Kenney-Herbert is particularly well qualified to deal.[40]

The fact that a provincial newspaper such as *The Cheltenham Looker-On* is reporting on the Association's classes gives us an indication of how Wyvern's stock is beginning to rise. At the other end of the country, an article in *The Glasgow Herald* of 27 June 1894 confirms Wyvern's growing reputation. Its London correspondent writes:

> Colonel Kenney-Herbert whose newly opened school of cookery in Sloane Street is just now attracting a good deal of the attention of society, won a reputation long ago in this direction in India.[41]

The next phase of Wyvern's business venture was to formalise the cooking classes and establish a permanent cookery school for the Association. Its premises were located at 17 Sloane Street, just along the road from the Association's Registry, and the cooking classes and demonstrations moved there from Queen's Gate Hall in early June 1894. The July edition of *The Epicure* has a notice for the Association in its "Notes from Cookery Schools" section, announcing the school's move to 17 Sloane Street, and explaining that its object is:

> To supply at reasonable rates practical instruction in good, refined and economical cookery. It is invaluable for ladies desirous of instruction, and for cooks who wish either to qualify for situations in which thorough proficiency is essential, or to improve themselves in any particular branch of cookery. The school is under the personal superintendence of Colonel Kenney-Herbert, who himself conducts the demonstrations, and assists and instructs the students. The course of 24 days is arranged to embrace every branch of cookery; but every demonstration is complete in itself.[42]

It is interesting to see that the students were not only professional cooks, but also ladies who wished to improve their own knowledge of cookery. What a lady would think of being taught alongside her or someone else's cook, we do not know. The cookery classes grew ever more popular, and Wyvern increased the frequency of classes to twice a day, five days a week. According to the *Pall Mall Gazette*:

> The new school, invested with a formidable *batterie de cuisine*, and equipped with all the modern appliances of refined cookery, will, no doubt, be highly appreciated by many aspirants to a higher standard of excellence than their means and knowledge now render attainable.[43]

The original building at 17 Sloane Street has since been demolished. The site was redeveloped in the 1970s, and No. 17 is now the address of the Millennium Hotel. The hotel's website tells us that it is: "Perfectly positioned in the heart of one of London's most prestigious districts [...] with an exclusive Sloane Street location."[44] The area was just as well-to-do in Wyvern's day.

Not only did Wyvern's cooking classes prove popular but the dishes he created, especially the curries, mulligatawnies, pilaus, and other Indian dishes, were now being sold to the public at the end of the day. Wyvern was starting to sell complete meals too. An advertisement in the *Pall Mall Gazette* of 16 July 1894 announces: "dishes cooked in the school on sale daily. Complete dinners or single dishes supplied".[45] So, Wyvern is pioneering a Victorian version of the Indian takeaway!

We know from *Furlough Reminiscences* that London society was very quiet during the month of August. Wyvern is still in town though, and an advertisement in *The Morning Post* announces a "Special Holiday Course, every Tuesday and Thursday in August. Subjects next week on both days: Pastry, Cakes, and Sweets".[46] When the summer season was over, Wyvern was back in business on a more regular basis. The Association's advertisements for the last week of October 1894 announce that "classes at the above School have recommenced. Three days weekly". The subjects for the week were:

Monday, Oct. 29 – Entrées, Mousseline of game, Grilled Fillets de Boeuf &c., with sauces.

Tuesday, Oct. 30 – Savouries, suitable for Luncheon, Afternoon teas, and Dinners

Thursday, Nov. 1 – Soups, Games Purées, Clear Mock Turtle, &c.[47]

Wyvern was working hard to build up the Association. He would have needed to, because rival cookery schools were also placing advertisements in the London daily newspapers. Two schools in particular, Marshall's School of Cookery and The National Training School for Cookery, already had a firm footing in town, so the Association had some catching up to do.

We will look at what became known as the "servant problem" in the next chapter, and see how the various cookery schools made attempts to solve it.

11

The Servant Problem

If you browse through late Victorian and Edwardian newspapers and periodicals, you cannot help but notice a recurring reference to what was called "the servant problem" in England. Put simply, it was not just a shortage of servants, but a lack of training and experience among the servant population. Cooks, housemaids and nursemaids were all in high demand, and this was an issue that preyed on the mind of every upper-class lady of the house. These were not just the big country houses of the aristocracy, but the homes of the wealthy social elite: Wyvern's "Upper Ten" (see Chapter 3). The growing number of affluent middle-class households wanting servants made the problem even worse.

A book published in 1899, appropriately titled *The Servant Problem: An Attempt at Its Solution*, explains the issue in some detail. The author, known only by her pseudonym of "Amara Veritas" (which roughly translates from the Latin as "harsh reality"), describes herself as "an Experienced Mistress". The statistical validity of her sample of correspondents is somewhat in question because she seems to have canvassed her friends, but she does provide some graphic examples of people's unfortunate experiences with their servants. One of her correspondents replies:

> You used to say "I did not know I was born" in regard to the "Servant Question". I do now. I have a cook who sometimes sends up part of the dinner and forgets the other half; one day she forgot it altogether. When gently remonstrated with, she said: "I didn't come 'ere to kill myself with your work. I came becos I 'eard it was an easy place, and plenty of good livin'." My house is just filthy […] and I dare not say a word, else they will just rise and walk out.[1]

Another reported:

> I dare not say anything is wrong, in case I receive notice on the spot – and I might get worse, or none at all; I therefore put up with an otherwise almost

intolerable state of matters.[2]

And yet another: "We live in a state of perpetual fermentation and unrest through them, not knowing what the next minute may bring forth."[3] One lamented: "They have been more than anything else the cause of angry words between my husband and myself in our married life."[4]

The servant problem even caught Wyvern off guard on his return to England on furlough. There is a chapter in *Furlough Reminiscences* (see Chapter 3) which deals with Wyvern's trials and tribulations in the matter of hiring servants while in England, but he first tackles the topic in 1877, in one of his articles for *The Athenaeum and Daily News*. Before he left India, Wyvern had been told by a female friend who had just returned from London: "Wait till you have had a little experience of London servants." He soon gains some unwelcome personal experience of what she means:

> I little thought at the moment that my experience would, in a short space of time, be so extensive, and so bitter. In a year we have had a deaf cook, a cook blind of one eye, two drunken cooks, an eccentric cook, and a very amorous cook. All these persons started satisfactorily; their failings were discovered as acquaintance ripened into intimacy. We have only had one utterly incompetent cook whose method of cooking macaroni with cheese deserves to be recorded; she put it, without any previous soaking or boiling, hard and dry into the oven on the top of some thick slices of cheese. Have you ever tried to bite a pipe of macaroni *au natural*, and found it a little harder than wood? Well, if you bake it you can get it still harder – a capital thing to snap a tooth upon. This unhappy woman once made a pie the paste of which looked like the cover of an old parish register, and so hard that no knife could penetrate it.[5]

In another story, also repeated later in *Furlough Reminiscences*, Wyvern asserts that the most reliable servant he employed during his stay in England was an *ayah* from Madras whom he describes as a "jewel without price".[6] The contrast between the abundance of servants in Madras and their relative scarcity in London must have come as quite a shock to Wyvern and his fellow exiles returning home from India.

Drunken cooks, like the one in Wyvern's example, seem to have been all too common. However, Amara Veritas does have some sympathy with their plight:

> Have ladies and gentlemen, who have their refreshing baths every morning,

their round of outdoor exercises and pleasures daily, ever thought what it must mean to stand all day in a hot kitchen, over a broiling fire, and this, week in, week out, with hardly any intermission?

Certainly it must be a most trying life, and one that entails a strain on the worker's vitality. It can scarcely, then, be a matter of wonder that so many cooks fall victims to that terrible craving for strong drink – a failing that has caused their name and their profession to be quite a byword.[7]

Amara Veritas speaks from personal experience, telling of a cook in her employ who would often be drunk by midday and who would boast to her fellow servants about how much she could consume. The servants begged Amara Veritas to sack the cook because they could not stand the disruption any longer, having to do extra work to cover for her when she was incapacitated. When the cook was finally dismissed, the housemaid found little bottles of spirits stashed around the house in the most unlikely of places, including up the chimney!

Amara Veritas claims that the servant problem was one that affected nearly every home (by which she means upper-class homes). She explains that the demand for servants was far greater than the supply: this created a situation where servants could almost do as they pleased or, if checked, walk out and easily find another job. She points out that the newspapers were full of advertisements for vacancies for domestic servants, and complains that if her husband had a vacancy for a clerk, he would be inundated with applications. He would have the pick of the applicants, whereas she would have to take whomever she could get – and on whatever terms they demanded.

Apart from placing advertisements in the newspapers, the other common way to find cooks and housemaids was through registry offices, which were what we would now call employment agencies. There seems to have been a quite a few agencies which engaged in dubious practices, at least in Amara Veritas and her acquaintances' experience. She explains that the registry office would demand a fee from the prospective employer before they would even consider suggesting suitable servants. The fee was non-returnable and did not guarantee that the agency would find appropriate staff for them, let alone whether they might have any servants at all on their books at that time.

Amara Veritas gives examples of popular scams undertaken by the less scrupulous agencies. One of the registry office's tricks was to place an advertisement in the newspapers claiming that it had, say, experienced cooks on its books with glowing references from previous employers, who were seeking suitable employment. The response was that numerous ladies, desperate to find a reliable cook, would visit the agency, each pay it a fee just to be "on the books", then have the opportunity to interview the cook. The problem was that in reality, the cook (for there was only one) was interviewing the ladies rather than vice versa, working out which prospective mistress would agree to the most advantageous benefits. The lucky lady who reluctantly gave in to the cook's demands then had the honour of paying the agency a second fee, once she employed the cook. All the other disappointed ladies would go home, having not successfully engaged anyone, but still having paid the initial fee.[8]

Another scam was where the servant was in collusion with the registry office. A lady looking for a cook would turn up at the registry office, pay her fee and be introduced to someone who sounded like the ideal cook. The cook would claim experience in all aspects of cookery and answer the lady's questions satisfactorily. The lady would engage the cook, subject to references, and they would leave the agency together, but only after the lady had paid the customary second fee. Even though the reference was minimal, since the cook had only been employed for a short time by her previous employer, a desperate lady might decide to engage the cook anyway. However, on the cook's first day at work, she would pretend to object to having to do all sorts of normally acceptable work, such as cleaning the kitchen, and immediately walk out. The cook, of course, ends up back with the agency and the lady, despite having paid the two non-refundable fees, still has no cook.[9]

Wyvern had his own bad experiences of the registry offices that he had to use while looking for servants during his furlough in London:

> There can be no doubt that there is the utmost difficulty experienced by people whose stay in London is limited to a year or so, in procuring servants of a superior class, for the riff-raff one has to select from at the Registry Offices is, as a rule quite worthless.[10]

Perhaps that was one of the reasons why, on his retirement back to England, Wyvern thought it would be a good idea to start a reliable registry office of his own.

However, not all the registry offices engaged in sharp practices, and even Amara Veritas concedes that some of the agencies, especially the smaller ones, provided a good service. She remarks on an advertisement that she has seen in a newspaper for the sale of a registry office, which reads:

Agency to be disposed of.

Easily worked.

Handsome profits.

Best principles.[11]

She is outraged that if an agency working on the best principles can still make a handsome profit, then those who use the underhand methods she describes must be making enormous amounts of money at the expense of desperate ladies. (As we will see in the next chapter, the servants' registry of the Common-Sense Cookery Association was still thriving when Amara Veritas published her book – which endorses how profitable the registry offices could be. She may even have used the Association's services!)

The "servant problem" not only involved staff shortages, but the lack of training for a majority of cooks meant that the quality of their work was also a significant issue. Many cooks received what limited training they had as a kitchen maid, under the guidance of a cook who might have been poorly trained herself. Others, especially those migrating to the large cites from the countryside, went straight from helping their mothers in the home kitchen to working as a cook for a family, with no formal training whatsoever. Wyvern identifies the problem in an article he wrote for *The Nineteenth Century* in May 1906 titled, appropriately enough, "The Teaching of Cookery". He confesses that since he wrote his series of articles for the same magazine in 1892 and 1893, cookery teaching in England has been carried out "if not with great enthusiasm" then certainly "with some degree of perseverance".[12]

Wyvern identifies the opening of The National Training School for Cookery in 1874 as a landmark in the history of cookery teaching. Prior to that, there had been no significant cookery schools in London, let alone around the country. "The National", as it was fondly known to its alumni, emerged out of the organisation for the Great Exhibition of 1851. The huge success of the Great Exhibition led to a series of smaller exhibitions in South Kensington, held on what is now Exhibition Road. Henry Cole – later Sir Henry Cole[13] – was asked to organise the 1873 exhibition and he thought it would be a good idea to include cooking as one of the subjects. Little did he know when he first started planning it just how successful the cookery demonstrations would be. In her seminal work, *The National: The*

Story of a Pioneer College, Dorothy Stone tells us that the exhibition committee chose a flamboyant character named John Charles Buckmaster[14] to give the cookery demonstrations. They could not have chosen a better person. The exhibition drew in half a million visitors, and Buckmaster's lectures proved to be a particular hit with the public. Wyvern notes in his article that Buckmaster gave a running commentary while a team of cooks made the dishes in front of the audience – even Queen Victoria attended one of the demonstrations.

Not only was the exhibition successful, it also made a profit. Entrance to the cookery exhibition was free (except for the seats in the front row, whose occupants were allowed to taste the dishes), but the committee had wisely taken the decision to sell recipes of the dishes being demonstrated. The audiences could not buy the recipes fast enough and the cookery exhibition made an astonishing profit of £1,765 (about £140,000 in today's money).

When the exhibition closed, Cole persuaded the committee to establish a permanent training school for cookery. As Dorothy Stone writes of Cole's aims:

> The school was not to fill any purely local need; it was not to be a 'South Kensington', nor even a 'London' school. It was to be a 'National' school in the sense that it was designed to pioneer a national effort for the recognition and teaching of cookery (and incidentally hygiene) as being vital to the interests and the well being of the whole country.[15]

No doubt many ladies were equally happy that graduates of the school would add eventually to the well-being of their households too.

The National opened in March 1874 using the same premises as the previous year's exhibition. The premises and all the equipment from the exhibition were provided free of charge, but the corrugated iron buildings were only designed for temporary use and inevitably caused problems of their own. They were cold in winter, unbearably hot in summer and lacked adequate light and ventilation. The school had to wait until 1889 before it could move into a purpose-built building in Buckingham Palace Road, where it remained for the rest of its existence.

Edith Nicolls, soon to become Mrs Charles Clarke,[16] was appointed Lady Superintendent of The National in 1875. She remained in that position for forty-five years, guiding the school through good times and bad. In many ways it was ahead of its time, since not only did it have a female principal, but it also catered for all abilities and social classes. The learners' classes were very popular: ladies were encouraged to bring their cooks with them to the school and to take written and practical exams to obtain a certificate of competence. In The National's first year, a total of 176 students passed the examination, twenty-seven of whom were cooks who had been taken along by their mistresses. New classes were soon introduced, in line with the school's objectives, to train cookery teachers. Edith Clarke took one of these courses herself a year before she was appointed superintendent and, of course, passed with flying colours. By 1876, the graduates of The National had spread out around the country and were working in newly-opened cookery schools. Schools had already started up in eight cities, and six more were in the process of opening.

It is interesting to note that The National was not restricted by social class or race. Stone refers to a report by Eliza Youmans, who trained at The National and wrote the American edition of the school's handbook. Youmans wrote:

> I was a pupil there for several weeks and carefully observed its operations. The classes showed the most extraordinary mental and social diversity. There were cultivated ladies, the daughters of country gentlemen, old housekeepers, servants, cooks, and coloured girls from South Africa, together with a large proportion of intelligent young women who were preparing to become teachers.[17]

As soon as The National had moved into its permanent home in Buckingham Palace Road, Edith Clarke redesigned the curriculum in line with the enhanced facilities of the new training kitchens and the educational needs of the time. The classes were divided into two categories: plain cookery and high-class cookery. Plain cookery was further subdivided into household cookery, for cooks hoping to gain employment in upper and middle-class households, and artisan cookery, for the wives of manual workers and for working-class schoolchildren. Students who wanted to become cookery teachers and gain The National's full Teaching Diploma had to study and pass exams in both categories.

A new character appears on the scene in 1892: a renowned Swiss chef, Charles Herman Senn.[18] Senn had founded the Universal Cookery and Food Association in 1885, and the committee of The National approached him with an offer to become its Lecturer and Inspecting Chief in an attempt to establish the school's credentials as a leading culinary authority. Senn's appointment resulted in important advances in prestige for The National, and not a little professional friction with Clarke. Senn basically tried to take over The National in 1905. The school was suffering one of its periodic financial crises, and he submitted plans to stabilise its income by concentrating solely on high-class cookery. Senn also promised that, if his plans for The National were accepted, he would abandon his own plans to establish a rival cookery school allied to his Cookery and Food Association. Clarke, with the help of sympathetic committee members, succeeded in rebuffing Senn's plans, and he withdrew.

The principal players in London's cookery scene seem to have been well acquainted with each other. We will see in the following chapter that Wyvern was involved with Senn's Universal Cookery and Food Association. Even Edith Clarke is listed as a governor of the Association in an advertisement in *The Epicure* magazine from December 1894, although this was a few years before Senn made his abortive attempt to take over The National. Others on the Association's management committee included the famous Auguste Escoffier,[19] head chef at the Savoy Hotel, and Mr A. F. Feltham, who was Queen Victoria's chef.[20]

Senn did eventually launch his International College of Cookery in 1909, but The National had already been in competition with numerous rival cookery schools for some years previously – not least of which was Wyvern's Common-Sense Cookery Association. Advertisements for The National in the London newspapers of 1894 sit right alongside advertisements for the Common-Sense Cookery Association and Marshall's School of Cookery. The three cookery schools seem to have been in competition to outdo each other with a record of their accomplishments and expertise, but in terms of column inches for the advertisements, Marshall's Cookery School wins hands down. Its principal, Agnes Marshall, was not overly modest about the achievements of her school, claiming that it was "the largest and most successful of its kind in the world".[21]

Agnes Marshall was a highly successful businesswoman. Not only did she run her eponymous cookery school, but she diversified into selling her own branded kitchen equipment and kitchen supplies. She also established her own publishing company to publish a weekly magazine entitled *The Table: A weekly paper of cookery, gastronomy, food, amusements, &c.,* published between 1886 and (posthumously by her husband) 1918. Marshall became famous as the "Queen of Ices". Her first book was entitled *Ices Plain and Fancy: The Book of Ices* (1885); she even patented her own design for an ice cream-making machine. Her second book, *Mrs A. B. Marshall's Cookery Book,* was first published in 1888, and ran to numerous revised editions until 1926, long after her death.

Marshall's book reflects the style of "high class French and English cookery"[22] which was taught in her school. She personally conducted lessons at the school every weekday between 10.30am and 4pm. Marshall's School of Cookery also acted as an employment agency for cooks and as a supplier of temporary cooks who could be hired for large, one-off events such as balls, grand dinners and weddings. The school hired out catering equipment for events, and sold its own brands of kitchen equipment, including her famous ice cream machine. Marshall sold foodstuffs, including her own imported Madras curry powder, branded with the name of her cookery school. The entrepreneurial Agnes Marshall could even design a kitchen and supply all the new equipment "in accordance with the requirements of modern cookery".[23] All a lady had to do was ask for a free estimate. Tragically, Marshall's flourishing career was cut short by a riding accident, and she died at the age of forty-nine in 1905.

It is possible that Wyvern used Marshall's School of Cookery as his template when he launched the Common-Sense Cookery Association in 1893. Marshall had founded her cookery school in Mortimer Street, London a decade earlier, while Wyvern was still serving in India. By 1893, Marshall's School of Cookery had become a successful business and was being feted in the top society magazines as *the* place to go to learn high-class cooking. Wyvern followed Marshall's lead by conducting demonstrations, teaching classes and by establishing an employment agency for domestic servants. When interviewed by *The Epicure* magazine in 1894,[24] Wyvern explains how he intends to start selling his own line of imported Indian spices (just like Marshall's), although there is no evidence that this particular plan ever came to fruition.

By the 1890s "the servant problem" was being addressed by The National and other cookery schools through their efforts to reduce the skills shortage. The other element of the problem, the shortage of domestic labour, was being tackled by the more reputable employment agencies, such as Wyvern's and Marshall's. A completely different solution was suggested by Elizabeth Lewis in an article for *The Nineteenth Century* in January 1893. "A Reformation of Domestic Service" argues that it might be possible, even desirable, to do away with live-in servants altogether. Lewis gives us her view of servants:

> If we keep a number of servants, the more we keep the less they do for us, and the more certainly the bulk of the rougher work is thrown upon the oppressed shoulders of some poor little 'scrubbie' or 'tweenie', or Jack-of-all-work. The

scale of their diet is always rising, and the smaller the amount of work they perform the less they are contented, and the more holidays, outings, and exciting pleasures they demand, finding little pleasure in the work they do.[25]

Lewis argues that services such as brewing, baking and laundry had already been done away with in large country houses, in favour of outsourcing them to specialist companies. She does not see any reason why domestic service in urban households should not be treated similarly. Her vision is that there would be a "culinary depot" on every street in London which would supply meals to the neighbouring households. If there were enough kitchens in an area, there would be sufficient competition to ensure that the quality of the ingredients and variety of meals did not suffer. Each kitchen would send round its menu every morning, and the lady of the house could place her order by return. Her order would then be delivered, meal by meal, throughout the day. She thinks the meals might be delivered by hand or tricycle, and transported in insulated containers.

Next, Lewis moves on to servants other than the cook. A housemaid could come in daily to perform her chores, but would be employed by an agency rather than directly by the household. That way, there would be no need for live-in servants at all, and the mistress would be freed from the stresses and strains of employing servants in order to spend her time on more intellectual pursuits; an added bonus also being that another room in her house would become free.

Wyvern refers to Lewis' article in his own article, "Distributing Kitchens", for *The National Review* in January 1902,[26] by which time he had already launched his own business on the lines that Lewis had suggested some nine years earlier. We take a look at Wyvern's plans in the next chapter.

12

Victorian Celebrity Chef

Elizabeth David mentions in her book, *Spices, Salt and Aromatics in the English Kitchen*, that Wyvern was interviewed for an article in *The Epicure* magazine. The interview was published in the September 1894 edition, titled "The Colonel and His Cookery School". I managed to find the article while browsing through copies of the magazine in the British Library, and was thrilled to find that it is illustrated with a fetching portrait of Wyvern himself. He would have been fifty-four at the time and looks very dapper in his high-collared shirt, sporting a bushy moustache. (The portrait is featured on the cover of this book.)

The Epicure's (unnamed) reporter went to interview Wyvern at the Association's new premises at 17 Sloane Street. He starts out by remarking on the considerable attention attracted by the articles that Wyvern had written for *The Nineteenth Century*:

> There was a certain novelty about the publication which, apart from the merit of the articles, may have had something to do with assuring their popularity. It was unusual, for one thing, to find the pages of *The Nineteenth Century* devoted to such a subject at all, and it was still more unusual to find a Colonel of cavalry speaking as one having authority on matters connected with the cuisine.[1]

The Nineteenth Century was a sober magazine containing articles such as "Why I Voted for Mr Gladstone", so the appearance of Wyvern's trilogy of articles on cuisine is likely to have caught the attention of some influential people. Although Wyvern was well known to the British in India as an authority on cooking, back in England he was, as the reporter puts it, "making his debut as a culinary expert". Announcements on the progress of setting up the Common-Sense Cookery Association had been featured in *The Epicure* over the previous months, and its reporter remarks that Wyvern's intention to open a cookery school of his own had "created no small amount of active curiosity".[2]

The reporter remarks on how busy Wyvern is, and has to interview him while he is "struggling into his working coat" and his assistants were preparing for that day's cookery lesson. His first question is to ask Wyvern what had brought him into cookery in the first place. Wyvern replies that he had always been interested in the art of cookery and that, eighteen years ago, when he was home on furlough, he had made a special study of it with the intention of starting the Association on retiring from the army. Wyvern felt that his age would bar him from continuing in public service, so he needed to be independent. The success of his books, *Culinary Jottings For Madras* and *Sweet Dishes*, had persuaded Wyvern to build on his cookery experience when he returned to England. Wyvern tells his interviewer that the articles published in *The Nineteenth Century* had caught the eye of a London publisher (Edward Arnold), who had persuaded him to write *Common-Sense Cookery* for an English audience.

While he was writing *Common-Sense Cookery*, Wyvern became convinced that:

> There was a field wide open in London for the spread of education in cookery, that the demand for betterment in the treatment of food was daily increasing, and that independently of the good schools already established there was room for many more.[3]

Wyvern explains that he founded the Association "with a friend interested in the subject to help me", but one can only guess who this friend might be because Wyvern does not name them. The reporter then asks about the guiding principles of the Association. Wyvern replies:

> Briefly sketched the principles we advocate are economy in conjunction with thoroughly good cooking, no waste, and the production of effects without the employment of ready-made sauces and flavourings. We are strongly opposed to over-ornamentation, the use of fancy colours in savoury cookery, and 'poaching' on the confectioners 'preserves' by using forcing-bags with pipe, etc., etc., in this branch. Finikin decoration – the making of 'pretty-pretty' dishes at the cost of flavour and much valuable time – is a mistake in private houses where the kitchen staff consists of two or three persons. Besides, people of taste have declared against this practice. Simplicity in cookery, simplicity in materials, and simplicity in dishing up are consequently a feature in my teaching.[4]

At the end of the interview, Wyvern talks about the "Oriental branch" of the Association where he teaches the skills of making Indian dishes which, he maintains, are not well known in England. He discloses that the Association is intending to import spices directly from Madras, "the head-quarters of curry making", but it is not clear whether that venture ever got off the ground. There the article ends because Wyvern has to begin his teaching for the day.

The new year of 1895 brings a new line of business to the Common-Sense Cookery Association, in line with the third object of the Association: "To establish a Registry for Cooks whose antecedents have been ascertained and qualifications tested, and who can, accordingly, be with confidence recommended."[5]

Advertisements begin to appear in the London newspapers for the Association acting as a recruitment agency. They are aimed at employers looking to recruit suitable domestic staff. For example:

Registry for Servants. – Managing Director, Colonel A. Kenney Herbert.– The Association has several Good COOKS, £30–£40; also MENSERVANTS, with excellent characters.– Apply 17, Sloane-street.[6]

By now the Association is well established, and appears in the *Post Office London Directory* for 1895, showing Col. Arthur Kenney Herbert as Managing Director, with premises at 17 Sloane Street, SW.

Wyvern continues to write magazine articles. In *The National Review* for January 1895, he writes on "The Literature of Cookery".[7] He is showing off his academic credentials in the article, discussing the merits of literature on the subject of cookery from as far back as the ancient Greeks through to the end of the seventeenth century.

By this time, Wyvern had become involved with the Universal Cookery and Food Association (see Chapter 11). The Association's ninth annual banquet was held on 31 October 1895 and chaired by Wyvern himself. One of the speakers at the dinner was the Honorary Secretary, Herman Senn, who is reported as saying that "the extension of the knowledge of homely cookery among the poor was absolutely necessary".[8] Although the Association was primarily a culinary association with links to L'Art Culinaire in France, it was also involved in charitable outreach work in the poorest areas of London. Senn announced that it had started giving cookery lessons in the Walworth area, and that 150 men and women had benefited already.

There were happy events in Wyvern's personal life. On 17 August 1895 his daughter, Enid, married Reginald Childers Culling Carr, who was employed by the Indian Civil Service and one of the under-secretaries to the Government of Madras. The wedding was held at St Mary Abbotts Church in Kensington, London. Presiding over the ceremony was the Reverend Humberston Skipwith, Wyvern's brother-in-law. So Enid, who was born in Madras and who had spent her early years in India, would now return there with her new husband. Her first child, Herbert, would be born in Madras a year later and baptised there at St George's Church.

The second part of Wyvern's "Fifty" trilogy, *Fifty Dinners*, was published in November 1895. The reviewer for the *Pall Mall Gazette*, once again, gives grudging praise. He writes:

> On the whole Colonel Herbert, here, as in his "Fifty Breakfasts", has done his work well. He has been amused in the making of his menus; as a consequence he amuses others. He has some respect for the art of eating, and is an enemy to the slovenly and the heedless. He has, however, one foolish scruple; never forgetting that he is, as he himself has proclaimed, the Common-Sense Cook, the necessity of economy haunts him.[9]

The *Leeds Mercury*, like the reviews in the provincial newspapers for *Common-Sense Cookery*, is more enthusiastic:

> Although of the making of cookery books there appears to be no end, yet any work bearing upon this subject from the pen of Colonel Kenney Herbert (Wyvern) at once attracts attention, and can be taken up by any one interested in the art and practice of cookery with a certainty of finding many new and tempting dishes clearly explained. "Fifty Dinners" will prove invaluable in households where the family is small, and the mistress – with a moderately long purse – either through disinclination or lack of time and knowledge finds it irksome to think out and arrange tempting dinners for daily home consumption.[10]

Wyvern is certainly keeping himself busy. Not only is he writing his own books and articles for magazines, he is also writing contributory chapters to publishers' themed books. He writes a section on cooking for a book called *The Hare*, which was the latest volume in Longmans' "Fur and Feather" series.[11] Other sections include "Shooting", "Coursing" and "Natural History", each with its own contributor.

It is possible that Wyvern was so busy with his writing and other endeavours that he began to take a lesser role at the Common-Sense Cookery Association. In the Association's advertisement in *The Morning Post* of 14 March 1896, Wyvern is described as usual as the managing director, but the classes are no longer recorded as being under his personal supervision. The advertisement says that the Tuesday class is "Mrs Seaton's Practice Class for Ladies".[12] Mrs Seaton appears to be deputising for Wyvern, and even may have been the business associate whom Wyvern mentions in his interview for *The Epicure* magazine. In another advertisement, it is clear that Wyvern's curries are still just as popular as ever. It proclaims: "Speciality – Curries of a quality and in a variety unobtainable elsewhere in London."[13] Another says: "Dishes on sale at four o'clock. Curries every day."[14]

Curiously, the advertisements for the cookery classes disappear altogether in the second half of 1896, but the ones for the recruitment agency carry on as before. It seems likely that the cookery school stopped giving classes, but we do not know why. In an article from November 1900, Wyvern writes about the "school of cookery with which I was at the time associated",[15] so his involvement is definitely in the past at the time of writing that article. We do know that he is still the managing director of the Association until at least September 1896. An advertisement in *The Standard* declares:

> Ladies requiring thoroughly reliable servants should apply to the Common-sense Cookery Association for cooks, parlourmaids, housemaids, and men servants; the Association can recommend their servants as having excellent personal characters; also job cooks who can be well recommended. – Apply Servants' Registry. 17, Sloane-street. Hours 10.0 to 4.30. Managing Director, Colonel Kenney Herbert.[16]

Advertisements placed in *The Morning Post* of 8 September 1896 announce:

> THE COMMON-SENSE COOKERY ASSOCIATION REQUIRE (for town) Good COOK. £35; LADY'S MAID, French. £35: BUTLER, £45; PARLOURMAID. £24; KITCHEN-MAID, £20; and CHEF. £70–£80. — Apply immediately to the Secretary, Servants Registry, 17, Sloane-street, SW. Ten to 4.30.

ALL SERVANTS with good characters can obtain SITUATIONS by applying at the Registry Office, 17, Sloane-street. Managing Director, Colonel Kenney Herbert.[17]

By the end of 1896, Wyvern's name had ceased to appear even in the Association's recruitment agency advertisements. However, he is still writing magazine articles, and continues to write books. The final instalment in his "Fifty" trilogy, *Fifty Luncheons*, was published in October 1896.

Wyvern was busy with public engagements throughout that year. He gave a lecture on the development of cookery in England at the ninth Universal Cookery and Food Exhibition, which opened at the Imperial Institute (now part of Imperial College London) on 27 April 1896. The exhibition sounds magnificent, and was open for a week. It was opened by Princess Louise, the daughter of Queen Victoria, and many dignitaries attended including Herman Senn.

The exhibition drew a large crowd and, by all accounts, they were thrilled by the exhibits. There were stalls lining the exhibition hall, and it sounds rather like today's RHS Chelsea Flower Show, with each of the stallholders trying to outdo the others. There was a wedding cake on display adorned with real pearls, spun-sugar sculptures and even a large architectural piece made from mutton fat and wax (let's hope the exhibition hall didn't get too hot!). The Italian Club of Culinary Art provided a display made out of ortolans, quail, fish, confectionery and fruit. There was a raised game pie on another stall which was decorated all over with pheasant feathers.

However, not all of the stalls were designed to show off the exhibitors' skills. One section of the hall displayed examples of good household cookery, which turned out to be very popular with the crowds. It showed beef olives, lamb cutlets, tomato soup, curries, vegetarian rissoles and puddings, chicken creams, stuffed eggs, cheesecakes, raspberry buns, Scotch soda scones, cherry cake and blancmanges of various kinds.

Although some of the displays sound rather frivolous, the exhibition was in fact a charitable event to raise money for teachers in poor neighbourhoods to give free cookery lessons and distribute free recipes. Their aim was to instruct people how to make the most out of the small amount of food available on a tight budget, but they also provided meals for destitute children. In addition, the Association awarded scholarships to promising but poor students, so they could attend approved courses leading to a recognised qualification. We do not know how well

Wyvern's evening lecture was received, but he is certainly mixing in the right circles.

In *The National Review* of October 1896, Wyvern follows up his earlier article in the same magazine on the literature of cookery. The new article is titled "The Aesthetics of the Dining Table". It is another academic article, studded with long French quotations, which brings his discourse on the literature of cookery up to date. He makes reference to Antonin Carême and his period of cooking for the Baron de Rothschild (see also Chapter 10). Carême is clearly one of Wyvern's culinary inspirations. Wyvern's all-time culinary hero, Brillat-Savarin, whom he eulogises in *Culinary Jottings for Madras*, is of course discussed at length in the article in the most favourable terms.[18]

By this time, Wyvern's reputation as a culinary expert had grown sufficiently for him to be in demand as a consultant. One of his early engagements is very interesting because it brought him in touch with the Garrett family. Agnes Garrett[19] and her cousin, Rhoda Garrett,[20] had established the first interior design company in England to be run by women. Agnes' sister, Millicent Fawcett,[21] was a leader of the suffrage campaign to enfranchise women, and another sister, Elizabeth Garrett Anderson,[22] was the first woman to qualify as a doctor in England.

In her paper for the University College London Bloomsbury Project, "Spirited Women of Gower Street: The Garretts and their Circle", historian Elizabeth Crawford writes:

> For during the last quarter of the 19th century – and well into the 20th – from two Gower Street houses Agnes Garrett, her cousin, Rhoda, her sister, Millicent Fawcett, and their friend, and later sister-in-law, Fanny Wilkinson, worked to transform not only the political and educational status of women, but also the home surroundings of Britain's burgeoning middle class, the nature of the accommodation available to middle-class working women, and last – but by no means least – the physical geography of London.[23]

Agnes Garrett's ambition to change the nature of accommodation available to educated working women had led her to establish a company called Ladies' Residential Chambers Ltd. The company built the Chenies Street Chambers in Bloomsbury, London, which were officially opened by Millicent Fawcett in 1889. The success of the chambers encouraged the company to build a second block of chambers in York Street in 1891, and to extend the Chenies Street Chambers in

1896. The Chambers provided apartments for working single women who wished to live independently and included writers, artists, musicians and academics among its residents. Each apartment had a small kitchen, but there was also a large communal dining room in the basement of the building. Meals were prepared in the chambers' own kitchen by a qualified cook.

All did not go smoothly with the catering arrangements. The minutes of the meeting of the chambers' management committee on 9 March 1896, recorded in the very neat handwriting of Agnes Garrett herself, tell the story. There had been numerous complaints from the residents about the quality of the food being served in the dining room. Under the heading "Cooking" is the following minute:

> The Secretary reported that she had arranged with Colonel Kenney Herbert to give some instruction in cooking to the cook at the York St. Chambers and later to the Chenies St. Chambers cook.[24]

So Wyvern is now offering his services to catering establishments in need of improvement. His tuition seems to have improved matters, at least at first. By the time of the management committee's meeting of 11 December 1896, the following minute appeared under the heading "Complaint as to catering at York St.":

> Letters were read complaining of the catering during August and further letters dated Dec. 8. 1896 saying that the food served was satisfactory. The Committee went into the matter, examined the menus and came to the conclusion that there was no longer cause of reasonable complaint. The Secretary was accordingly instructed to write letters in reply to this effect.[25]

Three years later, Wyvern's services were needed again. At the management committee's meeting of 9 January 1900, the following minute appeared under the heading "Dining-rooms Chenies St.": "Col. Kenney-Herbert. It was agreed that Col. Kenney-Herbert should give a course of instruction to the cook".[26] A final reference to Wyvern appears in the minutes of 6 February 1900, and follows up on Wyvern's instruction to the Chenies Street Chambers' cook: "Col. Kenney-Herbert. The kitchen utensils suggested by Col. Kenney-Herbert were authorised to be bought".[27]

Ladies' Residential Chambers was not the only consultancy assignment that Wyvern undertook. In April 1898, an article in *The Morning Post* describes a new building development in London's Kensington called Campden House Residential Chambers, for whom "Colonel Kenney-Herbert ("Wyvern") has agreed to assist in superintending the cuisine and dining room arrangements, which is hoped to bring as near perfection as possible".[28]

The apartments in Campden House Chambers (the building still exists today, but is now called simply Campden House) had living rooms, bedrooms, a pantry and a bathroom but no proper kitchen. To compensate for the lack of kitchen space, there was a large dining room in the basement of the building which served meals to residents at their own tables. There were also a number of private dining rooms where residents could entertain visitors. The apartments were sold unfurnished, but there was electric lighting, a lift and a "noble dining room" with "excellent cuisine, supervised by Colonel Kenny-Herbert", according to the many advertisements placed in the London newspapers.[29] So by now, Wyvern was sufficiently famous to be used as a selling point for the apartments.

Campden House Chambers organised an open day where prospective residents could go along and view the apartments. One visitor going by the name of "Penelope", a columnist for "Letter to the Ladies" for the regional newspapers, thought that the apartments were "in absolutely good taste". It does not appear that she met Wyvern that day, but he must surely have been in attendance after all the advance publicity. She was aware though that "the services of a first-rate *chef* with many underlings have been secured", and describes the dining room as "magnificent, with a vaulted roof and lordly decorations".[30]

The promise of "Cookery under personal superintendence of Colonel Kenney-Herbert" continued to appear in the newspaper advertisements for Campden House Chambers until the end of 1898 when, presumably, his work was done and he could move on to his next project. An advertisement from September 1899 merely states "catering under French chef".[31]

Advertisements for the Common-Sense Cookery Association's servants' registry continue until the summer of 1898, then the name disappears. Advertisements still appear for a servants' registry at 17 Sloane Street, but they do not mention Wyvern or the Association. Servants looking for positions are now urged to "Apply Miss Dodwell, Servants' Registry, 17. Sloane-street".[32] In the *Post Office London Directory* for 1899 there is an entry under "Cookery Schools" for the Association at 17 Sloane Street, and the manageress is indeed named as "Miss Lizzie Dodwell". So the name of the Association is still in use, but there is no mention of Wyvern. By 1907 the recruitment agency has changed its name to "Miss

Dodwell's Agency", and is still at 17 Sloane Street. In 1914 the agency remains at 17 Sloane Street, but the principal is now Miss Dorothy Dodwell. So, the recruitment business which Wyvern started must have thrived. According to the 1901 census of England, there was a Mrs Elizabeth Dodwell living in Paddington with her husband, a furniture warehouse porter, and her daughter Dorothy. Elizabeth Dodwell was forty-one at the time of the census and Dorothy was six, making her nineteen in 1914, so the ages fit – this may well be our Dodwell family.

Wyvern continues to write for magazines during this time. A new weekly, *The Onlooker*, was launched in October 1900 and Wyvern was one of its first contributors. *The Onlooker* was a kind of society magazine containing articles on subjects such as society gossip, politics, cooking and handicrafts, and some humorous columns such as "Tapping the Telephone" (similar to modern articles on texting embarrassments, but rather about mishaps using the newly-available telephone system).

In the third issue of *The Onlooker*, published on 3 November 1900, Wyvern is invited to guest-write a weekly column on "The Business of Pleasure". His particular pleasure is, of course, cookery, but later editions include subjects such as needlecraft from other guest writers. Wyvern's theme is "Journalistic Cookery", in which he relates how cooking is being covered in contemporary publications. He is not overly impressed. He recounts the tale of a charming young lady who comes to visit him at his cookery school and wants to learn about cooking. Wyvern is astonished to discover that she does not want instruction in actually learning how to cook, but instead wants to learn enough to become a cookery correspondent for a newspaper. Wyvern explains to her that it might take some three years to fully understand the fundamentals of cookery, but that he himself has still not learned every aspect of cooking, even with his twenty years' experience. His young visitor is sceptical and retorts:

> Really! I think you are mistaken, for a friend of mine manages capitally, and she knows nothing about cookery. She has books, you know, out of which she picks things – not *copying*, exactly – but guiding herself by them.[33]

Wyvern is outraged, spluttering that it is "very unfair to the authors whose work she makes use of without acknowledgement"[34] and prematurely terminates the interview. It seems that plagiarism in cookery writing is not a modern phenomenon, and appears to have been widespread even at that time. Agnes

Marshall (see Chapter 11) was clearly concerned about her copyright being abused, because she adds a notice to the title page of *Mrs A. B. Marshall's Cookery Book* stating that "Infringements of copyright will be prosecuted".[35]

Three weeks after his first guest appearance on "The Business of Pleasure" column, Wyvern is invited to write another. This time his theme is "Plain Cooking". For him, there are only two kinds of cookery: good and bad. To Wyvern, plain cookery is perfectly good and the current fashion for "smart cookery" with excessive decoration and embellishment is undoubtedly bad. He goes on to describe a meal he has recently enjoyed which he thinks is an example of good, plain cooking. The meal started with smelts* "fried to perfection", followed by *noisettes* of mutton with a Milanaise sauce, then roast pheasant with bread sauce. The smelts came with *beurre fondu*† and brown bread, the noisettes of mutton with *spaghetti à l'Italienne*, and the pheasant with *sauté* potatoes and an endive salad (made by the host himself). Wyvern declares that the bread sauce was very well made and nothing like the "liquefied bread poultice" which some people are in the habit of serving. Dessert was an omelette with apricot and rum *confiture*, served coated with rum which was set alight. A plain meal indeed! Wyvern's point is that a well-trained domestic cook would have been capable enough to make such a delightful meal. He adds that the mistress of the house must have known a good deal about cooking to have created such a successful menu and that, in order to achieve success, she undoubtedly "makes a friend of her cook" (to coin a well-worn phrase of Wyvern's).[36]

Wyvern concludes 1900 by writing the Christmas cookery column for *The Onlooker*. He gives a number of Christmas-themed recipes and then ends with a helpful recipe for using up the inevitable leftover cold turkey.[37] The new year sees Wyvern signing to a new publisher, Swan Sonnenschein, and the publication of his new book, *Picnics and Suppers*, in January.

The 1901 census, taken on Sunday 31 March, reveals that Wyvern is living at Overstrand Mansions, Prince of Wales Road, Battersea with his wife Agnes and two young female servants, a parlour-maid and a cook. The magnetic pull of London seems to have been as strong then as it is now: the cook was born in Manchester, and the parlour-maid in Birmingham. What is curious about their census entry is that Agnes Kenney-Herbert is a little loose about her age. Wyvern gives his

---

* small fish
† Emulsified butter, made by melting butter in water.

occupation as "Colonel in the Army, Retired" and his age as sixty, which is correct. However, Agnes is recorded as being fifty-seven – but we know from the India Office records that she was two months older than Wyvern, so also sixty at the time.[38] Perhaps she felt it was impertinent to ask a lady her age, even in a census! Wyvern's younger brother, Edward, was reaching the peak of his career at around this time. The 1901 census informs us that his occupation is "His Majesty's Inspector of Schools". He is living in the London suburb of Ealing with his wife Lady Jane, son Aubrey, daughter Doreen and a total of five servants: cook, lady's maid, parlour-maid, housemaid and kitchen maid.

Wyvern's own career as a catering consultant was about to take a new direction. In May 1901, a company called Distributing Kitchens Ltd published a prospectus for the issue of shares in the company. The prospectus lists the directors of the company and also notes (misspelling Wyvern's name): "Advisory Expert: Colonel Kenny Herbert ('Wyvern')".[39]

The company had been formed in February 1900 under the name of The Reformed Food (Vegetarian) Company Limited, but changed its name in November that year. The managing director of the company was John Ablett. His fellow directors were Oscar Klein, a coffee merchant, and Miss Kate Warburton, a gentlewoman. An article in the *Northern Daily Telegraph* states that the kitchens of The Reformed Food (Vegetarian) Company were under Wyvern's supervision, and that he started teaching the cooks employed by the company in August 1900.[40]

The prospectus tells us that Ablett was a major shareholder in the company, and that his shareholding was gained "as consideration for the purchase of goodwill, stock, &c., of a School of Cookery carried on by him".[41] The prospectus does not tell us the name of Ablett's cookery school, but he describes himself as a "food expert" and was also the editor of a magazine called *The Vegetarian*.

The directors had acquired the rights to a "Patent Carrier" which was being used already by the business: the issue of new shares was intended to raise capital in the company to buy more carriers and extend its premises. The business is described in the prospectus:

Premises were rented, fitted and stocked at Westminster Palace Gardens, and the carrier commenced running in January 1901. In less than a month the Kitchen was sending out over a hundred portions daily, and the carrier will soon be working up to its full capacity in Victoria Street and its immediate neighbourhood. Scores of orders and enquiries from various other parts of

London are being received, and a very great interest is being displayed on all sides of the undertaking.[42]

The company was making vegetarian meals in its kitchen and using insulated containers (carriers) to keep the food warm while delivered to its customers' premises. The new capital would allow for the development and purchase of improved carriers, also for the food to be delivered by motor vehicle instead of the horse-drawn carts the company was currently using. The improved carriers and transport would enable it to extend the range of its deliveries beyond the current four-mile radius from the kitchen.

Wyvern did not confine himself to advising Distributing Kitchens Ltd. In May 1901, the Manchester Ladies Domestic Association formed a company which it called Manchester Distributive Kitchens. The purpose of the company was to cook hot meals in a central kitchen and deliver them in insulated containers to busy housewives and sick people who could not cater for themselves. It also planned to deliver to businesses and produce a line of high-quality dishes. The Committee of Manchester Distributive Kitchens arranged for Wyvern, "the well-known authority on cooking", to act as advisor for the purchase of its kitchen equipment. Meals were to be transported to customers in insulating "thermaphors" by means of a "tricycle van". A thermaphor is a canister (imported from Berlin, where it was invented) of double walls separated by a layer of a crystalline substance which dissolves when the container is immersed in boiling water, and retains its heat for some time afterwards.

In September 1901, according to the *Manchester Courier and Lancashire General Advertiser*:

> Col. Kenney-Herbert, the well-known authority on cooking, gave a cookery demonstration at the Manchester Distributive Kitchens, which were opened in Oxford-road on Tuesday, the object of which is to supplement household cooking by the supply of well cooked food, served hot, within a given radius.[43]

In June 1901, Distributing Kitchens Ltd spawned a new company, which it called (somewhat unadventurously) London Distributing Kitchens Ltd. The new company had the same three directors as the parent company. The prospectus for the issue of shares explains that the company is in the same business as Distributing Kitchens, but will not confine itself to vegetarian meals. The new company shares

Distributing Kitchens' patent carriers and its motor delivery vans to deliver meals to its customers' residences. The new company had already secured an agreement to supply the catering for a number of mansion blocks: St James' Court, Buckingham Gate Gardens, Westminster Palace Gardens, Iverna Gardens and 25 Victoria Street being those listed. Wyvern is not named as the advisory expert this time, but the new company does have a "consulting expert" in the person of G. M. de Saint Lèger, who is described as "The Organiser of the Carlton and Savoy Hotels".[44]

In January 1902, Wyvern wrote an article for *The National Review* titled, appropriately enough, "Distributing Kitchens". The concept obviously had been discussed at some length in contemporary newspapers and magazines, but Wyvern's article is concerned with practical application of the idea. Unlike the social enterprise in Manchester, Wyvern's aim was to alleviate what was commonly called "the servant problem" (see Chapter 11). As we saw in Chapter 11, an 1893 article in *The Nineteenth Century* by Elizabeth Lewis had discussed the "decay of the English cook",[45] and how it might become necessary to buy in meals rather than have servants cook them at home (Lewis does not seem to have considered the idea of cooking her meals herself). Wyvern does not fully subscribe to Lewis' doomsday scenario, and does not believe that people who live in larger houses necessarily need such a service.

Wyvern believes that demand for the services of a distributing kitchen would come from the ever-expanding occupants of flats (echoing the prospectus for London Distributing Kitchens). There had been a building boom in residential mansion blocks in London in recent years. Many of the new flats in those mansion blocks had very little accommodation for servants, and the kitchens were small and poorly equipped. Wyvern thinks that "Too often the architect seems to have thought that the darkest and least well ventilated room in the tenement would do for the preparation of food".[46]

Many kitchens were poorly designed, with the food larder having no outside ventilation and being located right next to the kitchen fire grate, which would mean that food would be stored at too high a temperature and spoil quickly (of course, these being the days before refrigeration). Wyvern complains that he personally knows tenants living in large, expensive flats who are unable to employ a high-quality cook because the apartment has no room for a kitchen maid. He mentions other problems with the new mansion blocks, such as no tradesman's entrance for deliveries – they would have to come through the main hall door (fancy having to pass a tradesperson in the hallway of your expensive apartment block!). A more realistic objection was that the lack of decent ventilation meant that cooking smells would not only linger in each apartment, but spread round the communal areas as well.

Wyvern's conclusion is that all these inconveniences would encourage flat-dwellers to make use of the services of a distributing kitchen. He suggests that the builders of new mansion blocks should even encourage a distributing kitchen to use the basement of the block as a service to its residents. No doubt his experiences with Chenies Street Chambers and Campden House Chambers led him to this conclusion, although he is not proposing a communal dining room for the mansion blocks; rather, merely locating kitchens in the basement, at a modest rent, to conveniently deliver prepared meals to the upstairs flats. The distributing kitchens would not be able to provide a complete range of meals. Wyvern believes that such things as soups, *ragoûts* and *fricassées* would ideally suit this style of catering, and that roast meats – "the best joints, certainly not cut in slices" – would be very popular. What would not be suitable are dishes that could not be transported successfully. Under this heading he lists anything which should be served crisp, such as fried fish, and dishes that should be served immediately after cooking, such as omelettes and soufflés.

Wyvern suggests that a new enterprise should start in a small way, and build up custom once its reputation has increased. His reasoning is that the concept of the distributing kitchen is new in England, and that people need to be convinced that buying in meals is a practical and economical proposition. Once the company has made its name and householders can see their neighbours successfully using the service, only then would it be time for expansion. Wyvern discusses the physical means of delivering the meals at some length, because he considers it to be "the crux of the whole scheme".[47] He prefers the thermaphor arrangement pioneered by Manchester Distributive Kitchens where the prepared dishes are placed inside the heated thermaphor, which is then sealed. Wyvern recommends that tricycle carts be used to carry the sealed containers to the customers' homes, where the food inside would arrive just as hot as when it was cooked.

Wyvern is not listed as one of the original directors of London Distributing Kitchens, but we can safely assume that he was involved with the company because, after Kate Warburton resigned as a director to return to New York, he was appointed in her place in September 1902. Not only is Wyvern now a director, but he also seems to be running the business. An article in the *Yorkshire Evening Post* on 7 April 1903, quoting a London correspondent, describes how:

> That famous authority on gastronomy, Colonel Kenney-Herbert, has gone on from his success with the distributing kitchen in Westminster to open one in Belgravia. You only have to send a postcard to the gallant Colonel and a dinner of eight courses, including all the luxuries of the season, arrives like magic on a tricycle.[48]

However, all did not go entirely smoothly for every transaction. The correspondent reports that a lady from Eaton Square accidentally sent her order to the wrong colonel: the recipient, one Colonel Slaney, thought it was a practical joke and replied as such to the lady concerned. We do not know whether she ever received her dinner.

In August 1903 London Distributing Kitchens moved its registered office to the St James' Court Restaurant. St James' Court had been mentioned in the company's prospectus as one of its confirmed customers. In the same month, full-page advertisements appear in the St James' Gazette for "residential flats and bachelors' suites" at St James' Court in Buckingham Gate, London. The accommodation is described as being "of the highest order".[49] Buckingham Gate is a prime location, close to Buckingham Palace and the Houses of Parliament. The rents were between £90 and £500 per year for apartments of between two and ten rooms. The building had every modern convenience of the time: lifts (passenger and tradespeople's), electric light, bells, telephone and a "speaking tube". The residents did not even have to operate the lifts themselves, there was a lift attendant to do that and page boys in the lobbies. Every need was catered for – the premises also had a doctor, a hairdresser (who would visit a lady's flat if required), and a "messengers' call office" where residents could order tickets for theatres and race meetings. The advertisements describe St James' Court as having its own catering facilities with a restaurant where residents had separate tables. There were also private dining rooms. The kitchen is declared to be under the control of an "experienced cook" who, presumably, was employed by London Distributing Kitchens.

Intriguingly, anyone wishing to make enquiries with regard to renting one of the flats is encouraged to get in touch with the general manager, who is declared to be a certain Col. A. Kenney-Herbert. So is Wyvern now working directly for St James' Court as well as being a director of London Distributing Kitchens, which held the catering franchise? The picture becomes clearer later in the year. On 12

December 1903 an extraordinary general meeting of London Distributing Kitchens Ltd was held at the Hotel Windsor in Victoria, London. The meeting passed the following resolution:

> That it has been proved to the satisfaction of this Meeting, that the Company cannot, by reason of its liabilities, continue its business, and that it is advisable to wind up the same, and that the Company be wound up voluntarily.[50]

A liquidator was appointed and the resolution was signed by the chairman of the company: A. Kenney-Herbert. Unfortunately, the parent company, Distributing Kitchens Ltd, suffered the same fate, although the company was wound up in January 1904 on the orders of the Official Receiver, on behalf of the creditors, rather than going into voluntary liquidation.[51]

St James' Court took out full-page advertisements in the London newspapers during the summer of 1903 and large two-column advertisements throughout the rest of the year, into the first few months of 1904. Wyvern is still described as being the general manager during August and September. Towards the end of October 1903 his role changes to resident manager, which presumably coincides with London Distributing Kitchens ceasing to trade.

So Wyvern, being the *resident* manager, not only has a new occupation but also a new place to live. It sounds a very responsible job. He must have had several hundred staff under his control, and the residents of such exclusive apartments would have been some of the wealthiest and most influential in the country. It sounds like just the job for an military man. (St James' Court is now the St James' Court Hotel, owned by Taj Hotels, and it still boasts of its proximity to Buckingham Palace and the Houses of Parliament.)

Wyvern's final book, *Vegetarian and Simple Diet*, was published by Swan Sonnenschein in October 1904. It is possible that working with John Ablett, editor of *The Vegetarian* magazine, and acting as the advisory expert for Distributing Kitchens, sparked an interest in vegetarian cooking for Wyvern. The book is extensive and runs to 450 pages, almost as long as *Common-Sense Cookery*. A review in *The Scotsman* said:

> "Vegetarian and Simple Diet" […] may claim some pretension to being one of the leading guides to the housekeeper who has to prepare savoury dishes without fish, flesh, or fowl. It has been compiled by Colonel A. R. Kenney-

Herbert (Wyvern), whose aim has been to show that "vegetarian diet need not be marked by ascetic plainness, nor restricted to a few uninteresting dishes,"* and this at least is clearly demonstrated that there need be no lack of variety. It seems a pity that so many French technical terms have been used in the work when English would have served the purpose just as well.[52]

Wyvern's original publisher, Edward Arnold, published a new edition of *Common-Sense Cookery* in 1905. The publisher describes the book as being a revised and enlarged edition with illustrations. Wyvern's preface is dated June 1905, and he claims that the new edition has been updated and corrected to such an extent that it is "practically speaking a new book".[53] Wyvern notes that fashions in dining have changed since the publication of the first edition of *Common-Sense Cookery*, more than ten years previously. He maintains that his original book had already pre-empted the ensuing changes in dining habits but, even so, he explains that he has removed some of the more old-fashioned and unnecessary details from the new edition. The illustrations are typical of cookery books of the time: drawings of cooking equipment and serving dishes; although they brighten up the text a little, they do not really add much to the book.

Wyvern turned sixty-five on 17 August 1905, but he does not appear to have fully retired. He is still writing cookery articles for *The Onlooker* magazine and, in the Christmas 1905 edition, his column includes a number of recipes for savoury Christmas pies. He continues to write for *The Onlooker* throughout 1906. In January and February he writes two articles on "Winter Vegetables", in March and April he writes a trio of articles on "Dishes of Eggs", in August he gives recipes for "Picnic Dishes" and rounds off the year with an article entitled "Christmas in the Kitchen". He starts his Christmas column with the following declaration: "According to my rule, I leave the customary Christmas dishes of old time to good English cooks, who need but little advice about them."[54]

Despite his rule, he continues by offering some tips on how to cook the turkey. He suggests placing the turkey's liver in the cavity of the bird along with some onions wrapped in bacon, which gives "a marked effect upon the flavour of the meat". Somehow, Wyvern manages to include the word "lissom" (previously used on a number of occasions in *Furlough Reminiscences* to describe attractive young women) in the article. He is describing making pastry and the instruction is to

---

* A quote from Wyvern's preface to the book.

knead it lightly into a "lissom paste".[55]

In May 1906, Wyvern wrote an article which was, once again, published in *The Nineteenth Century*. In "The Teaching of Cookery" (see also Chapter 11) he attempts to chart the history of culinary instruction in England, and assess its current state. It is mostly another of Wyvern's wordy academic articles, apart from a little *réchauffé* of one of his articles in *The Onlooker* from six years previously. The story of the attractive young woman turning up at Wyvern's cookery school, wanting to be taught how to write about cookery without actually learning how to cook, gets another airing. Wyvern is still just as indignant at her presumptuousness as he was before – and still just as contemptuous of newspaper editors who publish articles in their cookery columns written by such inexperienced authors.

By this time, Wyvern is not featured in the newspapers as often as he used to be; however, in June 1907 his name reappears, not just in England but also in Australia, India, South Africa and other parts of the British Empire. A large advertisement in the *Army and Navy Gazette* appeared, showing a prospectus for the issue of 207,000 ordinary shares of £1 each in the United Services Co-operative Hotel Company Limited. The company's aim was to acquire land in South Kensington and build a "first-class" hotel which would be run on cooperative principles. The directors' aim was to run the hotel on the same lines as the Co-operative Stores, where shareholders are given rights and privileges when they are also customers. The directors' target market was members of parliament, the Indian and colonial legislative councils, commissioned officers in the Navy, Army and auxiliary forces, and members in the "superior" grades of the home, Indian and colonial civil service. Those who were employed in such occupations would be given preference when shares were allocated, but the directors intended to reserve a significant number of shares for sale to the general public. Shareholders owning ten shares or more would be entitled to discounted rates at the hotel for accommodation and meals.

The directors of the United Services Co-operative Hotel Company are listed in the prospectus, and include one Colonel Arthur Robert Kenney-Herbert of 8 Castlebar Road, Ealing who is described as "late Secretary to Government Military Department, Madras". There is a special note in the prospectus which reads as follows:

> The Directors fully recognise the great importance of securing capable management to ensure the success of the undertaking. They have, therefore,

secured the services on the Board of Colonel Kenney-Herbert, who opened and controlled the restaurants at Wellington Court and St. James' Court, and who is well known under the *nom de plume* "Wyvern".[56]

The prospectus itself displays an artist's impression of the grand hotel which the company hoped to build near the Brompton Oratory in London. The Oratory dome is shown in the background, while well-dressed ladies and gentleman parade in the foreground and an elegant motor car draws up at the entrance. There is also a map showing the proposed location of the hotel on the corner of Brompton Road and Alexander Place.

Company records show that Wyvern was a director right from the company's incorporation on 13 May 1907. His fellow directors were Sir Charles Layard, ex-Chief Justice of Ceylon, Edgar Money, a merchant, William Saunders, managing director of the Grand Oriental Hotel, Colombo, Ceylon, and Jacques Hoffer, formerly manager of the Cecil Hotel, London. Each of the directors agreed to take and pay for 250 shares of £1 each, as required by the articles of the company to qualify as a director. So Wyvern had a financial interest in the company as well as being a director.

Take-up of the shares seems to have been rather slow because they are still on sale in early November 1909, despite the original cut-off dates being 27 June for London and 1 July for the countries of the empire. According to a notice from the *Naval and Military Record*, applications from the more remote parts of the empire and from ships had been a problem, and so the deadline for the application for shares had to be extended.[57] The notice is not over-optimistic about the possibility of reaching the minimum share capital required by the time of the revised deadline, and warns its readers that the opportunity to buy shares would soon be lost. Wyvern is mentioned in the notice, which tells us that he is intending to make arrangements for "Oriental" dishes to be served at the hotel's restaurant.

The warning in the *Naval and Military Record* about the possibility of insufficient capital being raised turns out to have been prophetic. The company secretary wrote to the Registrar of Joint Stock Companies on 30 November 1909:

> This company was formed in May 1907, but owing to insufficient applications did not proceed to allotment. All monies paid on application were returned to the subscribers. The company never had any funds, it never carried on business.[58]

The London Gazette of 10 March 1911 records a list of joint stock companies which have been dissolved, and the United Services Co-operative Hotel Company Limited is among them. The elegant hotel shown in the prospectus was never built.[59]

The prospectus for United Services Co-operative Hotel Company confirms that Wyvern was no longer living at St James' Court in 1907, and that he was now living in Ealing, the "Queen of the Suburbs". Wyvern's brother, Edward, was still living in Ealing at that time so they would have been close neighbours.

Wyvern wrote another controversial article for *The Nineteenth Century* in September 1910. Like his articles for the same publication in 1892 and 1893, "The Prominence of Pastime" caused quite a stir, but this time it was not about cookery – rather, popular sports in general, and football in particular. The article starts harmlessly enough by identifying cricket as the British national game (after all, he was captain of the first eleven at Rugby School). He goes on to lament the current state of English cricket and remarks that "modern 'first class' cricket has ceased to be a game and has become a business".[60] His disappointment over the developments in cricket soon make way for his obvious disgust at the ever-increasing popularity of football. Playing football, he despairs, had "spread to the lower classes". The spectators at the increasingly popular professional football matches were "of the roughest classes" and "among such people betting is in these days epidemic" while, as the match progresses, they become "inflamed with drink". He describes the rowdiness of football matches where: "Even the neighbourhood of the ground where one of these matches has taken place is, we are told, often rendered unendurable for hours afterwards by lingering hooligans."[61]

Maybe Wyvern should have remembered the betting scandals of the Madras Club and his own story from his article, "In the Days of John Company", where he is nursing his "dire symptoms" from the previous night's heavy drinking while on military parade the following morning. It seems that such behaviour is acceptable for people of his class, yet frowned upon for those in the lower classes. Wyvern is coming to his point, and it turns out that football is just a peg on which to hang his real theme:

> Is it not true that of late years we have allowed our indulgence in pastimes to exceed all reasonable limits? And is not this becoming especially grave when we consider seriously the signs of the times in which we are living? I have tried to show that many thousands of our male population give up the greater part of

their time either to playing games or to watching them. Is it exaggeration to say that not one of these men realises that his country has a claim upon a part at least of the time that he thus wastes?[62]

Wyvern cannot help having a dig at the press too. His disdain for the sports photographer is clear. "Pictorial art is outraged by these productions" is Wyvern's considered view of the sports photographs published in the popular illustrated newspapers. It might have been wiser not to attack the press, because it came back at him with a vengeance. The *Athletic News* does not pull its punches: "Has Our King Blundered?" asks its headline. King George V had been recently appointed patron of the Football Association, and the newspaper craftily sets up Wyvern as being in opposition to the monarch himself:

> His Majesty will probably repent him of his hasty decision – especially when he is confronted with the conclusion that our love of sport is undermining our love of country and our duties as citizens and patriots.[63]

The article continues:

> Colonel Herbert gains his boldness in making such ill-founded charges from ignorance. He must have relied on his imagination for his facts, and on the tales of some soured folk who have never paid sixpence to see a game of football.[64]

It is sad to think that Wyvern had turned into the stereotype of a crusty old colonel, preferring the past to the present and military service to peaceful recreation. However, as a military man, it is clear that Wyvern viewed the recent military escalation in Europe with some alarm and was trying to warn the British nation that they were unprepared for war. "Procrastination may even bring us to our downfall"[65] he declares, and concludes that some form of universal military training should be adopted in England without delay. Four years later, of course, England was at war with Germany and, in 1916, the British government introduced conscription.

The census of England, taken on the night of Sunday 2 April 1911, shows that Arthur and Agnes Kenney-Herbert were now living at 19a Sinclair Gardens, Kensington, so they must have moved back to London from Ealing. Wyvern's occupation is stated as "Colonel in the Army, Retired". There was one female servant living in their household. The census records that Wyvern was seventy at the time, and Agnes was sixty-nine. As we know, The India Office records confirm that she was two months older than Wyvern, so it appears that Agnes Kenney-Herbert is still playing fast and loose with her age for the purpose of the census; however, this time she is claiming to be only one year younger than she really is, rather than the three years she previously deducted for the 1901 census.

A final recognition for Wyvern's service in the Indian Army is announced in *The London Gazette*.[66] He is to be granted the honorary rank of brigadier-general with effect from 24 August 1912.

Arthur Robert Kenney-Herbert died on 5 March 1916 at the age of seventy-five. His obituary in the *Coventry Standard* (a newspaper local to his place of birth) tells us a little about his final years:

> Most of us have heard of a cook-general, but a general who is an authority on cooking is decidedly rarer. Yet such a one was Brigadier-General A. R. Kenney-Herbert, whose death occurred this week. The deceased gentleman, who was the son of the late Rev. A. Kenney-Herbert, of Bourton, near Rugby, knew all about the preparation of food for the table, and his published works on the subject under the pen-name of "Wyvern" – "Culinary Jottings", "Common Sense Cookery", and others – were regarded as classics of housekeeping all over India, and also in this country. He was also an amateur actor of some distinction and a clever sketcher.
>
> One of his chief hobbies after his retirement was the minute study of the Waterloo campaign; he seemed to know the hourly position and disposition of every regiment, both French and English, and had himself carefully been over every bit of ground from Charleroi, Namur, Louvain, and through Quatre Bras to Brussels, and examined every road and bridge. His abstemiousness and his constant observances of all the Church's services were so rigidly severe in the last years of his life that there can be little doubt that they affected his health and hastened his end. General Kenney-Herbert was an old Rugby boy, where he was captain of the school eleven.[67]

H. R. C. Carr, Wyvern's grandson, wrote an article about him, "The Man Who Taught the Raj to Cook" in the November 1968 edition of *Country Life* magazine. His commentary on Wyvern's final years is as follows:

> Wyvern lived for most of his retirement in London, except for a period in Brussels when he made an intensive study of the field of Waterloo with a view

to publishing a defence of Marshal Ney in the centenary year, but in 1915 other battles occupied the mind of the nation and he failed to find a publisher.[68]

13

Wyvern's Legacy

Wyvern's influence on the cooking of the British in India was profound. *Culinary Jottings for Madras* was still being published in India even after Wyvern had long since retired to England. Another essential book for housewives in India, *The Complete Indian Housekeeper and Cook* by Flora Annie Steel and Grace Gardiner, came a little later, but it was clearly influenced by Wyvern's popular book and even includes one of his recipes, which they rename "Wyvern Soup" in honour of the man himself (see Chapter 6).

When Wyvern retired from the army in India a colonial newspaper, *The Homeward Mail*, summed up his time there. After relating his military career and its successes, the article moves on to describe him:

> In General Kenney Herbert we have a writer of charming *vers de société*, of piquant stories, and of those light fragments of fiction which run so easily as you read but not so as you write; we have a character actor of exceptional strength, and a painter who possesses talents far beyond those of the usual amateur. As Wyvern he is of the company of Brillat-Savarin. In the cricket-field the services of the old Rugby captain will be missed. He was an excellent tactician, and keen to the last. When Ceylon comes, the Madras Eleven will not seem complete without the well-known form umpiring in a dressing gown. When he departs, India loses a man of vast popularity, of infinite variety, and of a versatility of genius.[1]

The article concludes:

> When he takes his farewell, he will leave behind him widespread regrets, and we hope that the memory of the many happy hours which he has created for his fellow exiles in Madras will be kept green for us by hearing of fresh laurels gathered in wider fields, either as a diplomat – for which he is so eminently fitted – or in the social and literary circles of the modern Babylon.[2]

Wyvern was obviously well liked and respected by his fellow "exiles" in India, and it does seem that those who had met him remembered him fondly.

The three provocative articles in *The Nineteenth Century* and the publication of *Common-Sense Cookery* established Wyvern as a force in British culinary circles, and he used the opportunity to write further books and articles, give lectures and act as a catering consultant.

However, as we have seen, the evidence suggests that Wyvern was not necessarily a successful businessman. The Common-Sense Cookery Association lasted for less than three years, and London Distributing Kitchens Ltd had an even shorter lifespan of just over two years. His considerable talents for writing about and demonstrating cooking, and his natural flair for teaching brought him considerable fame, although probably not great fortune. Wyvern's association with United Services Co-operative Hotels might have turned out to be lucrative for him but the project never got off the ground due to lack of capital.

Leslie Forbes believes that writing *Culinary Jottings for Madras* might have used up too much of Wyvern's creative energy. She thinks that his later cookery books displayed none of the "magic" of his famous work. She reflects on Wyvern's later books, the ones published in England:

> After his death in March 1916, this collection joined all the other diaries, letters, curry recipes and reminiscences of military gentlemen whose retirement from active service in India to cottages in Sevenoaks or Guildford left them too much time to reflect on their more colourful past. It seemed to me a sadly anticlimactic ending for the Colonel.[3]

She may be right. *Common-Sense Cookery* sold many copies but it was, fundamentally, a revision of *Culinary Jottings for Madras* rewritten to appeal to a British audience. The books that followed never caused quite such a stir, although they were still given good reviews in most of the newspapers.

In his chapters on curries, Wyvern laments the fact that the art of curry making was dying out among the British. He takes it upon himself to keep the flame alive, including several recipes for different types of curry in *Culinary Jottings for Madras*. So the households which subsequently used Wyvern's book as a guide would become the next generation to continue the tradition of British curry making. Many Anglo-Indians who returned home to Britain at the end of their time in India took their favourite recipes with them, and it is quite likely that many of those lovingly crafted "family recipes" were in fact adaptations of Wyvern's own recipes. *Culinary Jottings for Madras* was extremely popular among the British in India; his curry recipes, in particular, gained an impressive reputation back in Britain too, first among repatriated Anglo-Indians, then later with the general public.

Good Things in England, a nice little cookery book from 1932 by Florence White, describes Wyvern as follows:

> The greatest modern authority on curries and curry-making is Colonel Kenney Herbert. The following directions are condensed from his chapter on curries in *Commonsense Cookery*, published about thirty years ago.[4]

White provides recipes for her own adaptations of Wyvern's Madras Chicken Curry, Ceylon Curry and Prawn Curry, and adds some of his cooking notes for clarity. She also includes, verbatim, Wyvern's recipe for cooking rice to accompany the curries. So even in the 1930s, Wyvern was still being cited as an authority on curry and rice.

Wyvern's reputation was revived once again in 1970 when Elizabeth David wrote about him in *Spices, Salt and Aromatics in the English Kitchen*. David was an influential cookery writer between 1950 and the 1970s: her books, such as *A Book of Mediterranean Food* and *French Country Cooking*,[5] were classics of their time. She had lived in and wrote about several Mediterranean countries, but she had also lived in Egypt and India and was fascinated by what she called "the English preoccupation with the spices and the scents, the fruit, the flavourings, the sauces and condiments of the orient, near and far".[6]

Wyvern has his very own section in David's chapter, "Meat Dishes", in *Spices, Salt and Aromatics in the English Kitchen*: "Officer of the Kitchen". Here is her introduction:

> Writing in the British India of the nineties, under the pen name of Wyvern, Colonel Kenney-Herbert's cookery books were directed at the bewildered mem-sahibs who often found themselves transported from cosy suburban or small country houses into an unfathomable situation as ruler of a whole hierarchy of Indian servants, incomprehensible in their ways and highly erratic in the performance of their duties.[7]

David had first-hand knowledge of being a *memsahib* during the time that her husband was stationed in India in the mid-1940s. She observes despondently that seventy years on, the kitchens she encountered in New Delhi were still "unbelievably primitive", despite Wyvern's attempts to shame his contemporaries into upgrading them (see Chapter 2). She welcomes his military approach to cooking, and writes:

> Several good cookery books have been written by professional soldiers, and this is perhaps no coincidence. On the whole the most successful books of technical instruction, and this applies as much to cookery as to other subjects, are those in which the author expresses his views with soldierly precision and authority and is prepared to got to some lengths to defend them.
>
> Colonel Kenney-Herbert's parade ground voice is lowered in his books to lecture-room pitch, but commands no less attention for that.[8]

David's enthusiasm for Wyvern's cookery books was almost certainly a significant factor in his being introduced to a new generation of food lovers (myself included). One of my favourite contemporary cookery writers, Simon Hopkinson, is also an admirer of Wyvern. Hopkinson recreates one of his curries in *The Conran Cookbook*, for which he wrote the recipes, and calls the recipe "Wyvern's Chicken Curry with Coconut".[9] Hopkinson introduces his version of Wyvern's signature curry by saying: "This delicious curry recipe exemplifies his straightforward approach", echoing David's remarks from thirty years previously. (See Appendix A for my own versions of Wyvern's curry recipes from 135 years ago.)

Arthur Robert Kenney-Herbert is buried in Margravine Cemetery (also known as Hammersmith Old Cemetery) in West London. His headstone reads:

IN

LOVING MEMORY

OF

BRIG GENERAL ARTHUR ROBERT KENNEY-HERBERT

LATE MADRAS CAVALRY

ENTERED INTO REST 5TH MARCH 1916

AGED 75

LOOKING UNTO JESUS THE AUTHOR AND

[FINISHER] OF OUR FAITH [*HEBREWS 12:2*][*]

There is an inscription at ground level which is very difficult to read, as soil and grass have almost fully covered it over and it is badly eroded. When I paid a visit to the grave, I managed (with the help of two very kind passers-by whose young eyes are keener than mine) to decipher what it says. It is the inscription for Agnes Kenney-Herbert, who must be buried alongside Wyvern. It reads:

AGNES EMILY, HIS WIFE,

DAUGHTER OF GENERAL CLEVELAND

That is it. No mention of being a good mother to their son and daughter. No mention of her making a home for her family for fifty-odd years. There is not even a record that she died on 20 January 1920. Agnes Emily's life is solely defined as being one man's wife, and another man's daughter.

Arthur Herbert Cleveland Kenney-Herbert was Wyvern and Agnes' only son. As we have seen, he was born in Bangalore in 1863 and would have been sent away to boarding school in England at the age of about six or seven (see Chapter 7). Arthur became a military man like his father and joined the Northamptonshire Regiment in 1883. He was appointed as an Instructor at the Royal Military College in May 1890 at the rank of lieutenant, a post which he held for five years. From

---

[*] The square brackets indicate the likely content of the inscription which has badly worn away in places.

there he was posted to India, which must have pleased his parents, and became an expert in military drawing. Next, he was posted to South Africa in 1899 at the onset of the Second Anglo-Boer War (of 1899–1902). Now promoted to captain, he worked for the army's Intelligence Department as a military surveyor. An article in the *Leamington Spa Courier* tells us that while the Northamptonshire Regiment was marching to the battlefront in March 1900, they came under fire and Arthur was nearly killed.[10] Tragically, having survived the attack, he was involved in a serious accident the very next day. While Arthur was crossing a bridge over the Tugela River, he was knocked over by the oxen pulling a cart, and the cartwheel ran over his arm. He was rushed to hospital in Pietermaritzburg but the surgeons were not able to save his hand, which had to be amputated. After the accident, he was invalided home to England.

Back in England, Captain A. H. C. Kenney-Herbert was appointed Deputy Assistant Quartermaster-General in March 1901 (just as Wyvern had been in 1873) on the Staff of the Northamptonshire Regiment. He was promoted to major in March 1903. Arthur seems to have found love later in life because, on 20 June 1908, at the age of forty-four, he marries Edith Harriet Evans at St Peter's Church, Eaton Square, London. Edith was one year younger than Arthur. It is highly likely that Wyvern and Agnes attended the wedding, because they were living in London at the time. In August 1915 Arthur was promoted to brevet lieutenant-colonel, although he was in the Reserve of Officers at the time (and had been since the time of his marriage), so was no longer on active service with the Northamptonshire Regiment. He never did quite equal his father's career by becoming a colonel in the British Army.

We can see from the 1939 Register – an emergency census taken on 29 September 1939 at the outbreak of the Second World War – that Arthur and Edith had retired to Royal Tunbridge Wells, Kent, and lived there at the time of the census along with one female servant. Arthur died in September 1944, aged eighty; Edith died two years before him. They did not have any children. His will was published in the local newspapers, reporting an estate valued at £9,682 (in today's money, approximately £397,000) – a reasonable amount of money for the time, but not a great fortune. His furniture and effects were sold by auction in the house that he rented in January 1945.

As we have seen in Chapter 12, Wyvern and Agnes' daughter, Enid, married Reginald Carr in August 1895. Their wedding was held in London, so Wyvern and Agnes would have been able to attend the service. After the wedding, Enid and

Reginald returned to Madras, where Reginald was employed in the Indian Civil Service. Their son, Herbert Reginald Culling, was born in Madras on 16 July 1896. They had only one child.

Herbert Carr's obituary in *The Climbers' Club Journal for 1985/86* was written by Geoff Milburn,[11] who tells us that Herbert was an adventurous boy. In 1913, aged only seventeen, he cycled on his own to the Alps, a distance of 746 miles (1200 km). Two years later he discovered the mountains of North Wales and made his first ascent. Although he had won a scholarship to Pembroke College, Oxford in 1915, he decided against taking up his place and instead joined the Royal Navy Volunteer Reserve as a second lieutenant: he was injured at Ypres, and invalided home. He eventually took up his place at Oxford after the First World War, and became a leading force behind the university's mountaineering club. He obtained an MA in Modern History, which enabled him to take up a career in teaching.

A climber by the name of Audrey Salkeld, writing Herbert Carr's obituary in the *Alpine Journal for 1987*,[12] remembers that one of the first books on climbing she had read was *The Mountains of Snowdonia*, written in 1924 by H. R. C. Carr and G. A. Lister.[13] Herbert Carr's name was well known to climbers of his era, not least because of an accident which happened in 1925 on Cwm Glas in Snowdonia. Carr's companion, Stanley Van Noorden, was killed and Carr was badly injured, but was not rescued for two days – and then only by blind chance when a shepherd happened to come across him. He never lost his passion for mountaineering and organised many alpine meetings for the Climbers' Club. He met his future wife, Evelyn Dorothy Ritchie MA, on one such trip, and they married at St Peter's Church, Berkhamsted on 28 July 1927.

Herbert Carr (better known simply by his initials H. R. C.) made a successful career in teaching and progressed in his profession to become headmaster of the prestigious Harrogate Grammar School from 1934 until he retired in 1960. H. R. C. Carr wrote an article about Wyvern, his grandfather, in *Country Life* magazine in November 1968 entitled "The Man Who Taught the Raj to Cook". He donated a photograph of Wyvern to the British Library which shows Wyvern, sometime in the last ten years of his life, still sporting his trademark bushy moustache. Carr describes him as looking just like the "quiet, courtly old gentleman as I knew him".[14] The reverse side of the photograph shows that it was taken at the studios of C. Naudin at 169 High Street, Kensington – and after reading about Wyvern's discomfort on being photographed in *Furlough Reminiscences,* I suspect he was very relieved when the posing was over. Carr also donated a copy of Wyvern's

Picnics and Suppers to the British Library. Leslie Forbes mentions it in her introduction to the Prospect Books' facsimile edition of *Culinary Jottings for Madras*, but I wanted to have a look at it myself. It was not so much the book itself I wanted to see, but more the handwritten note penned by Carr and pasted into the book. It reads:

I believe this was the last of my Grandfather's books on cookery.

His son Robert [sic], for some time an instructor at Sandhurst, lost his right arm in the Boer War. He had no issue.

His daughter, Enid, was my mother. She had only one child.

While my parents were in India I went to him for my holidays – in memory [of] a gastronomic heaven.

H. R. C. Carr, January 1978

In this short note, H. R. C. Carr gives us confirmation that he was an only child and that Wyvern's son Arthur Herbert Cleveland Kenney-Herbert (whom he confusingly calls "Robert") had no children of his own. Carr died in April 1986, shortly before his ninetieth birthday.

The conclusion has to be that no one alive today who has the surname Kenney-Herbert is a direct descendant of Wyvern's. It may be that someone alive today with the name of Kenney-Herbert is a distant relative of Wyvern's, but their relationship would be through the family line of his brother Edward.

Wyvern's headstone describes his career merely as "Late Madras Cavalry", but his life involved so much more than just his military career. His books, articles and public demonstrations made him famous in his own time. However, his cookery books are timeless. More than one hundred years after Wyvern's death, his books are still being read and his recipes are still being made. I do not think Arthur Kenney-Herbert could have hoped for a better legacy than that.

Appendix A: Recipes

Notes on Ingredients

In the following recipes, tamarind paste is sold in jars and available from good supermarkets and ethnic food stores: it has the consistency of tomato ketchup. Chilli powder is made from ground red chillies and nothing else. Creamed coconut is coconut milk reduced down into a solid block: it is best used at room temperature when it can easily be chopped into small pieces.

Wyvern's Madras Chicken Curry

Serves 2

Here is my twenty-first-century version of Wyvern's Madras Chicken Curry from 1883.

Unlike Wyvern's recipe, which uses his home-made curry powder made in bulk using 9.5 kg (21 lbs) of whole spices, my recipe uses ground spices to make enough curry powder for just one curry. I have not suggested making the curry paste which Wyvern recommends, but most of the ingredients from his paste are still included in one stage or another of the recipe.

The poppy seeds used in Wyvern's curry powder and curry paste would have been white poppy seeds. These days, white poppy seeds are not commonly sold in supermarkets and, in any case, are used primarily to thicken the curry rather than to add flavour. Therefore, I have omitted them from my recipe and added a little extra creamed coconut instead, which does an excellent job of thickening the curry and adding flavour. Wyvern adds redcurrant jelly to his curries as a "sweet-acid" agent, but the more authentic tamarind paste may be used instead.

Wyvern uses a whole chicken cut into joints with the meat still on the bone. I have used bone-in chicken thighs instead, rather than going to the bother of jointing a whole chicken. Using meat on the bone not only adds extra flavour, but also gives plenty of leeway in the cooking time because it does not overcook anywhere near as quickly as lean breast meat. You can use water instead of chicken stock if you wish, but I have kept faith with the original recipe because Wyvern considered it essential to use stock to produce "a dish of superior class".

Ingredients

For the curry powder
½ tsp ground brown (black) mustard seed
1 tsp ground cumin seed
1½ tsp ground coriander seed
1 tsp turmeric
½ tsp ground fenugreek seed
¾ tsp hot chilli powder (more if you want a hotter curry)
½ tsp dried ginger powder
¼ tsp ground black peppercorns
⅛ tsp ground cloves

For the chicken
1 tbsp vegetable oil
1 bay leaf
1 medium onion, finely chopped
2 cloves garlic, finely grated
fresh ginger, finely grated – about the same volume as garlic
1 tbsp ground almonds
1 tsp butter
6 small chicken thighs (bone-in) – about 600 g (1¼ lbs)

For the sauce
1 tbsp butter
1 medium red onion, sliced into half-rings
salt, to taste
1 tsp lime juice
1 tbsp redcurrant jelly
chicken stock (about 200 ml/7 fl oz)
2 tbsp creamed coconut, chopped into small pieces

Garnish
fresh coriander leaves (cilantro), finely chopped

Method

1. Heat a small frying pan on a medium-low heat. When the pan is hot, pour in about 1 teaspoon brown (sometimes sold as black) mustard seeds. Shake the pan from time to time and heat the seeds until they start popping. Immediately pour the seeds onto a cold plate and leave to cool. When cool, grind the mustard seeds into a fine powder with a pestle and mortar. Add ½ teaspoon to the curry powder and store the rest in a sealed plastic bag.
2. Measure out the spices for the curry powder, and mix them together in a small bowl.
3. Pull the skin off the chicken thighs with some kitchen paper. Trim the thighs of any excess fat. Set aside.
4. Heat 1 tablespoon of vegetable oil in a 20-cm (8-inch) heavy-bottomed pan on a medium heat. When the oil is hot, add the bay leaf and chopped onion to the pan and stir-fry for 5–7 minutes. The onions should not brown, so lower the heat a little if they start to fry too hard.
5. Spoon the grated garlic and ginger into the pan. Stir in well and stir-fry continuously for 2 minutes. Turn the heat down to low, and let the pan cool a little. Add the curry powder and ground almonds to the pan, and warm through the spices for about 1 minute, stirring all the time. Mix in 3 tablespoons of chicken stock to form a paste. Remove the pan from the heat.
6. In a separate, large frying pan, add 1 teaspoon butter over a medium heat. When the butter has melted, add the chicken thighs and fry, turning them over from time to time until the flesh has mostly turned white.
7. Remove the sautéed chicken thighs from the pan and place them in the onion mixture. Stir to mix, so that the chicken is coated with the spicy paste. Put a lid on the pan and set aside for about 30 minutes. (This is Wyvern's period of marination, but you can omit this stage if you wish to save time.)
8. While the chicken is marinating, trim the red onion and cut it in half down through the root end. Place the onion halves, cut-side down, and cut them into slices about 3 mm (⅛ inch) wide.

9. Reheat the pan used to cook the chicken on a medium heat. When hot, add 1 tablespoon of butter and as soon as it has melted, add the red onion slices. Stir-fry the onions for about 5 minutes until the slices are just starting to turn brown at the edges. Turn off the heat and set aside.
10. When the chicken has finished marinating in its spicy paste, return the pan to a medium heat. Add the salt, lime juice, redcurrant jelly and enough chicken stock to almost cover the chicken thighs. Stir to mix. Bring the liquid to the boil, then turn down the heat to a gentle simmer.
11. Simmer the chicken thighs in the curry sauce for about 25 minutes, turning them over from time to time. As the liquid reduces, add enough chicken stock to make sure the level of the sauce does not go below about halfway up the chicken thighs.
12. Taste the sauce and adjust the sweet/sour balance to your liking by adding some sugar or more lime juice.
13. Add the reserved onion slices and the creamed coconut to the pan, and stir to mix. Bring the sauce back to a simmer. Cook for 5 minutes, or until the chicken is thoroughly cooked. When fully cooked, the sauce should be thick but still able to be spooned. If the sauce is too runny, cook for a bit longer until the liquid has reduced (or you could add a little more creamed coconut). If the sauce is too thick, add a little more chicken stock. Bring back to a simmer.
14. Garnish with chopped coriander leaves, and serve immediately.

Ceylon Prawn Curry

Serves 2

Wyvern describes his recipe for Ceylon or Malay Curry as "delicately flavoured". He insists that cumin and coriander along with other common curry spices should be avoided, and I have followed his example. The curry is spiced with cinnamon and cloves, and the flavour is enhanced with coconut milk. Wyvern uses cucumber in his recipe, but supermarket cucumbers are far too watery for a stir-fry such as this and, in any case, are not as popular now as a cooked vegetable as they were in his day. Wyvern suggests that any member of the *Cucurbitaceae* family would be suitable for inclusion in a Ceylon curry as a substitute for cucumber, so I have chosen courgettes (zucchini) instead.

Ingredients

225g (8oz) raw peeled jumbo prawns (shrimp)
or 225g (8oz) cooked and peeled jumbo prawns (shrimp)
2 medium-sized courgettes (zucchini), washed and dried
1 medium-sized red onion
½ tsp turmeric
⅛ tsp ground cloves
3 pinches ground cinnamon
1 clove garlic, finely grated
fresh ginger, finely grated – about twice the volume of garlic
½ tsp tamarind paste
salt to taste
ghee (clarified butter) *or* vegetable oil
4 grinds black peppercorns
½ tsp sugar
½ tsp fresh lime juice
chicken stock *or* water
3 tbsp creamed coconut, chopped into small pieces
2–4 thin green chillies

Garnish
chopped coriander leaves

Method

1. Trim the onion and cut it in half down through the root end. Place the onion halves, cut-side down, onto a chopping board and cut them into slices about 3 mm (⅛ inch) wide. Then cut the slices in half to obtain short strips.
2. Top and tail the courgettes. Cut each courgette (zucchini) crossways into three pieces. Take each chunk and cut it in half down through the cut face.

You should now have 12 pieces with a semi-circular area of skin and a flat cut face. Take the pieces and cut each one into five long wedge-shaped batons, so that each strip has dark skin on the wider end and a little ribbon of seeds at the thin end. Use a sharp knife to cut out the seed area (the line where the seeds meet the flesh is clear to see). You should now have lots of little batons of seeded courgette.

3. Make sure the peeled jumbo king prawns are completely defrosted, if previously frozen. Dry the prawns thoroughly with kitchen paper. Divide the prawns into two equal batches, and set aside.
4. Chop the coriander leaves, but not too finely. Cut the stalks off the green chillies and cut them in half lengthways. Remove the seeds and the pith, and slice the chilli flesh into strips about 3 mm (⅛ inch) wide. Set aside.
5. Measure out the turmeric, ground cloves and ground cinnamon onto a plate.
6. Put half a teaspoon of ghee into a wok (or karahi if you have one) and place on a medium-high heat. When the ghee is hot, slide in the courgette batons and stir-fry for about 5 minutes, by which time the courgettes should be starting to develop small brown patches. Remove the courgette pieces from the wok and set aside.
7. Put another half teaspoon of ghee into the wok. If using raw prawns (which will be grey in colour), take the first batch and toss them into the hot wok. Stir-fry for about 1 minute, or until the prawns have turned pink on the outside and white in the middle. Remove them from the wok and set aside on a large plate.
8. Put a further half teaspoon of ghee into the wok. When the ghee is hot, stir-fry the second batch of prawns in the same way as the first. The prawns taste particularly sweet if brown patches have started to appear on the edges. When done, transfer them to the plate along with the first. Set aside.
9. Now add 1 tablespoon ghee to the wok, and lower the heat to medium. When the ghee is hot, slide in the onion strips and stir-fry for about 5 minutes – take care not to let the edges burn.
10. Turn the heat down to low, and let the wok cool down a little. Spoon the grated garlic and ginger into the wok. Stir-fry for about 2 minutes.
11. Remove the wok from the heat. Carefully tip the ground spices into the wok. Make sure the ground spices land on the onion mixture, not the sides

of the wok, or they may burn. Stir the ground spices into the onion mixture, return the wok to a low heat and warm the mixture through for about 30 seconds, stirring frequently.
12. Pour 4 tablespoons chicken stock or water into the wok along with the tamarind paste, salt, black pepper, sugar and lime juice, and stir to mix. Bring the mixture to a gentle simmer for about 10 minutes. If the sauce starts to get too thick it will burn on the bottom of the wok, so add 1 tablespoon chicken stock if needed. Repeat if necessary during the cooking, but only add 1 tablespoon stock at a time. (Be careful how much extra stock you add. Too much and the sauce will be sloppy and wet, too little and it will burn.)
13. Add the strips of chilli to the wok and simmer the sauce for a further 5 minutes.
14. Now add the creamed coconut and 3 tablespoons chicken stock to the wok. Stir to mix. Once the pieces of coconut cream have melted, simmer the sauce for a further 5 minutes, adding more stock a tablespoon at a time if the sauce gets too thick.
15. Finally, add the courgette pieces and the reserved prawns (or ready-cooked prawns if using). Return the sauce to barely a simmer, and cook for about 3 minutes or until the prawns have heated right through and the sauce is thick, but still able to be poured.
16. Garnish with chopped coriander leaves, and serve immediately.

Lamb Quoorma

Serves 2

Wyvern uses mutton in his *quoorma*, but we have the advantage of being able to use lamb which is a younger animal and its meat far more tender. Indian restaurants usually call this dish a *korma* and their modern version is often quite different from how Wyvern's recipe turns out. Nevertheless, the inclusion of almonds and cream in both styles shows that the two versions share a common root. I have followed Wyvern's instruction not to use any chillies or chilli powder in the *quoorma*. The mild heat of this curry comes from black peppercorns alone.

Ingredients

350 g (12 oz) lamb chump steaks (trimmed weight)
or the same weight of beef rump steak
ghee (clarified butter) or vegetable oil
1 large onion, finely chopped
2 tbsp ground almonds
2 cloves garlic, finely grated
fresh ginger, finely grated – about the same volume as garlic
1½ tsp ground coriander seed
½ tsp turmeric
¼ tsp ground black pepper
3 pinches ground cloves
seeds from 1 green cardamom pod, ground
water
salt, to taste
½ tsp sugar
1 tsp lime juice
3 tbsp double (heavy) cream, at room temperature

Garnish
toasted flaked (slivered) almonds

Method

1. Trim the lamb steaks to remove the fat and connective tissue. To end up with 350 g (12 oz) of lean lamb you will need to buy about 450 g (16 oz) of chump steak. If using beef rump steak, the wastage is about half as much. Cut the trimmed meat into strips about 12 mm (½ inch) across. Divide the lamb into two equal batches.
2. Heat a large, non-stick frying pan on high, add half a teaspoon of ghee and fry the first batch of lamb until the strips are brown and the edges are starting to char. Slide the pieces of lamb onto a large plate. Add another half teaspoon of ghee to the frying pan, and repeat the process with the remaining lamb. Set aside.

3. Heat 2 tbsp ghee in a 20-cm (8-inch) heavy-bottomed pan on a medium heat. When the oil is hot, add the chopped onion to the pan and stir-fry for 5–7 minutes. The onion pieces should not brown, so lower the heat a little if they start to fry too hard.
4. Add the ground almonds, grated garlic and grated ginger to the pan. Mix well and stir-fry for 2 minutes. Turn the heat to low and let the pan cool a little.
5. Add the ground coriander, turmeric, black pepper, ground cloves and ground cardamom seeds and stir to mix. Warm through the spices for about 30 seconds, stirring constantly.
6. Add 4 tablespoons water, salt, sugar and lime juice, stir to mix and simmer gently for about 15 minutes. Add more water, 1 tablespoon at a time, if the mixture gets too dry during the cooking. The sauce should be fairly dry at the point where you add the lamb, because the lamb juices will add liquid to the sauce and loosen it.
7. Slide the cooked strips of lamb (plus all the juices that have gathered on the plate) into the sauce, and bring the sauce back to a simmer. Cook the lamb for a further 8–10 minutes until tender.
8. Taste the sauce and adjust the sweet/sour balance to your liking by adding more sugar or lime juice.
9. Finally, add the double (heavy) cream, stir to mix and gently reheat the sauce. *Do not* bring the sauce to the boil, or the cream may split.
10. Garnish with toasted flaked (slivered) almonds, and serve immediately.

Plain Boiled Rice

Serves 2

I took my instruction from Wyvern many years ago in how to cook perfect boiled rice. The recipe below is from my book, *Quick Meals from The Curry House*, and I use it all the time.

Half the battle is using good-quality rice in the first place. Basmati rice has that wonderful aroma you notice in Indian restaurants, and I always use it instead of ordinary rice. But even Basmati rice comes in different qualities, so my advice is to buy the best you can afford.

Cooking boiled rice seems to be very simple, but you can easily end up with a stodgy mess if you are not careful. The key elements to success are:

- Never wash or soak the rice before you cook it.
- Use the largest pan you can find, and nearly fill it with water. It looks ridiculous cooking a small amount of dried rice in such a large pan but, believe me, it works.
- Once you have initially stirred the rice, *do not* touch it again.
- Gently simmer the water in which the rice is cooking. Do not allow the water to boil vigorously. All you want is a regular flow of little bubbles coming to the surface of the water.
- Test the rice by fishing out a few grains and biting into one. Do this at 11 and 12 minutes from when the water started to simmer.

Ingredients

125 g (4½ oz) best-quality Basmati rice
salt

Method

1. Take a large saucepan and fill it with 2 litres (3½ pints) cold water, leaving about 4 cm (1½ inches) between the the water level and the top of the pan. Do not add salt at this stage. Put a lid on the pan and bring the water to the boil.
2. Remove the lid from the pan and sprinkle the rice slowly into the boiling water. Make sure you don't dump the rice in the water in one go, or you will end up with lumps.
3. Gently stir the rice once to distribute the grains evenly over the base of the pan, and adjust the heat so that the water is *only just* simmering. *Do not* let the water boil vigorously.
4. Cook the rice for about 12 minutes. Do not stir the rice again. Add some salt to the water after about 10 minutes' cooking.
5. Test the rice regularly after about 11 minutes, and remove the pan from the heat at the point where the rice is going from a little hard to just soft in the middle.

6. Pour the rice into a sieve and drain off the water.
7. Serve the rice in a warmed serving dish.

If you want to keep the rice on hold while your curry finishes cooking, tightly cover the serving dish and place it in the oven at 150°C/300°F/Gas Mark 2 for up to 20 minutes.

Tamarind Chicken

Serves 2

This is not one of Wyvern's recipes, but it is one of my favourites from my book, *Quick Meals from The Curry House*. I thought I would include it here to give you some idea of the recipes in my book which can all be made in under one hour. Tamarind Chicken is hot, sweet and sour – the perfect combination. Because you are preparing this dish at home you can make it as hot or mild as you like. This recipe comes out medium-hot. You can also change the sweet/sour balance to your own liking by adding more tamarind paste or sugar.

Ingredients

    3 tbsp vegetable oil
    200 g (7 oz) onions, finely chopped
    2 cloves garlic, finely grated
    fresh ginger, finely grated – about the same the volume as the garlic
    water
    350 g (12 oz) chicken breast
    1 tsp ground coriander seed
    1 tsp ground cumin seed
    ½ tsp hot chilli powder
    ½ tsp turmeric
    ½ tsp paprika
    3 pinches ground cloves
    seeds of 2 green cardamom pods, ground
    2 tbsp tamarind paste

1 tbsp tomato purée (tomato paste)
¾ tsp sugar
2 grinds of black peppercorns
salt, to taste (tamarind paste contains salt, so add less than normal)
1 tbsp finely chopped coriander leaves (cilantro)

Garnish
finely chopped coriander leaves (cilantro)

Method

1. Heat 3 tablespoons of oil in a 20-cm (8-inch) heavy-bottomed pan on a medium heat. While the oil is heating up, finely chop the onion.
2. When the oil is hot, add the chopped onion to the pan and stir-fry for 5 minutes. The onion pieces should not brown, so lower the heat a little if they start to fry too hard.
3. While the onion is frying, grate the garlic and ginger onto a small plate, but remember to stir the onions occasionally to stop them from browning.
4. Spoon the grated garlic and ginger into the pan (plus any juices left on the plate). Stir in well and stir-fry continuously for 2 minutes.
5. Add 3 tablespoons water and mix thoroughly. Once the liquid starts to boil, put a lid on the pan, turn the heat down to minimum, and cook for 20 minutes. Do not remove the lid during this time.
6. While the onion mixture is cooking, skin the chicken breasts, remove any connective tissue and cut the meat into chunks about 25 mm (1 inch) across.
7. When the 20 minutes is up, take the pan off the heat and remove the lid. Now take a potato masher and thoroughly mash the onions, garlic and ginger to a fairly smooth purée.
8. Return the pan to the heat, still at its lowest setting, and add the ground coriander, ground cumin, chilli powder, turmeric, paprika, ground cloves and ground cardamom seeds. Warm through the spices for about 1 minute, stirring constantly.
9. Raise the heat to medium and add the chicken chunks. Stir round until the pieces of chicken have turned white over most of their surface. Add the tamarind paste, tomato paste, sugar, black pepper, salt and 1

tablespoon water. Stir to mix all the ingredients and bring the mixture to a simmer.
10. Simmer the chicken for 15–17 minutes. If the mixture starts to get a little dry, add just 1 tablespoon of water. Then, as the chicken is cooking, add more water if the sauce gets too dry – but only 1 tablespoon at a time.
11. Towards the end of the cooking, taste the curry and adjust the sweet/sour balance to your liking by adding a little more tamarind paste or sugar.
12. Two minutes before the chicken is ready, add 1 tablespoon finely chopped coriander leaves (cilantro) and stir. Check that the chicken is thoroughly cooked.
13. Garnish with more chopped coriander leaves (cilantro), and serve immediately.

Appendix B: Chronology

Year	Date	Event
1840	5 June	Wyvern's wife, Agnes Emily Cleveland born.
	17 August	Wyvern born.
	6 September	Wyvern baptised in St Peter's Church, Bourton-on-Dunsmore, Warwickshire. The register of baptisms is signed by his father, rector of the parish.
1841	6 June	Census: Wyvern, nine months old, is living with his father Arthur, mother Louisa, and sisters Catherine and Louisa, at Bourton Rectory.
1851	20 February	Wyvern's mother dies of typhus in Brussels.
	30 March	Census: Wyvern, aged ten, is a visitor at the house of his aunt, Mary Ann Kenney, at Binswood Terrace West, Leamington, Warwickshire.
	30 March	Census: Wyvern's father and siblings are not living at Bourton Rectory on the date of the census.
1855	8 February	Wyvern starts at Rugby School, aged fourteen.
1855–59		Wyvern is a pupil at Rugby School.
1859	Cricket season	Wyvern is Captain of the Eleven at Rugby School.
	28 May	Reverend Dr Temple, Headmaster of Rugby School, recommends Wyvern for the Madras Light Cavalry Cadetship.
	6 June	Wyvern is nominated for the Madras Light Cavalry by the Rt Hon. Lord Stanley.

	16 August	Wyvern passes examinations of the East India Military College.
	20 September	Wyvern joins the army at the rank of cornet.
	31 October	Wyvern arrives in India.
1861	7 April	Census: Wyvern's father and sisters Louisa, Harriet and Mary once again living at Bourton Rectory.
	14 March	Wyvern promoted to lieutenant.
	13 October–19 December	Wyvern on leave, medical certificate.
1862	23 April	Wyvern marries Agnes Emily Cleveland.
1863	24 September	Wyvern's son, Arthur Herbert Cleveland, born.
	3 November	Arthur Herbert Cleveland baptised at St Mark's Church, Bangalore.
	16 November–20 November	Wyvern on private affairs leave.
1864	1 September–27 December	Wyvern on a study course at Madras.
	30 November	Wyvern promoted to brevet captain.
1865	8 September	Wyvern appointed Adjutant to the Governor of Madras' Body Guard.
	24 December	Wyvern promoted to captain.
1866	19 April	Wyvern appointed Officiating Interpreter to the 16th Lancers.
	8 September	Wyvern on leave in England, medical certificate.
1868	5 June	Wyvern arrives back in India and resumes his duties with the 16th Lancers the following day.
1869	2 May	Wyvern's daughter, Enid Agnes, born.
	1 July	Enid Agnes baptised at Trinity Church,

		Bangalore.
	9 August	Wyvern appointed Officiating Quartermaster to the 16th Lancers.
	7 November	Suez Canal opens.
1871	2 April	Census: Wyvern's father still living at Bourton Rectory with Wyvern's sisters, Louisa and Mary.
	18 April	Louisa marries Reverend Humberston Skipwith.
	2 May–5 June	Wyvern on private affairs leave.
	29 May	Wyvern's daughter, Ida Louisa, born.
	7 September	Wyvern's daughter, Ida Louisa, baptised at Holy Trinity Church, Bangalore.
1872	19 January	Ida Louisa dies, aged seven months.
1873	6 April–14 June	Wyvern on private affairs leave.
	5 December	Wyvern appointed Deputy Assistant Quartermaster-General of the 1st Division Bangalore Camp.
1874	8 July–15 October	Wyvern released from duties by Colonel Bolton to attend a Garrison Course of Instruction.
	28 October	Wyvern reappointed Deputy Assistant Quartermaster-General of the Centre District.
1875	1 July	Wyvern's father, brother Edward Maxwell, and sister Mary Lucinda change their names by deed poll from Kenney to Kenney-Herbert.
	6 September	Wyvern and his wife change their names and those of their children by deed poll at Bangalore from Kenney to Kenney-Herbert.
	16 December	Horse races at Madras attended by the Prince of Wales. Wyvern's horse "Warwick"

		competes in the Sandringham Steeplechase.
1876	4 April	Wyvern appointed to the Staff of the Government of Madras as Deputy Assistant Quartermaster-General.
	1 September	Wyvern on private affairs leave to England: the subject of *Furlough Reminiscences*.
	22 December	Wyvern promoted to brevet major.
1877	17 December	Wyvern resumes duties in India.
1878	1 November (date of preface)	*Culinary Jottings for Madras* published in Madras.
1879	(title page)	Second edition of *Culinary Jottings for Madras* published.
	20 September	Wyvern promoted to major.
1880	(title page)	*Furlough Reminiscences* published in Madras.
1881	1 October (date of preface)	*Sweet Dishes* published in Madras.
	3 April	Census: Wyvern's father and sister Mary are now the only relatives living at Bourton Rectory.
	3 April	Census: Enid, Wyvern's daughter, is living at Ash Lawn, Leamington Priors with five single sisters named Crane.
	26 April	Wyvern's tour of service as Deputy Assistant Quartermaster-General expires.
	5 November	The new Governor of Madras, Mountstuart Elphinstone Grant Duff, arrives at Raichore on the Madras frontier and is met by Wyvern and others.
1883	15 February (date of preface)	Fourth edition of *Culinary Jottings for Madras* published in Madras.
	15 March	Wyvern appointed Military Secretary to Grant Duff, Governor of Madras.
	19 March	Wyvern promoted to brevet lieutenant-

CHRONOLOGY

		colonel.
	21 June	Wyvern's father dies at Bourton Rectory.
	1 November	Agnes Kenney-Herbert's father dies at Bangalore.
1884	18 January	Wyvern and Grant Duff inspect the military sanitarium at Poonamallee.
1885	16 February	Grant Duff's wife gives a "Fancy Ball" in the banqueting hall of Government House. Wyvern dresses as Clive of India.
	1 July (date of preface)	Fifth edition of *Culinary Jottings for Madras* published in Madras, retitled as *Culinary Jottings*.
	20 September	Wyvern promoted to lieutenant-colonel.
1886	8 December	Grant Duff ends his tenure as Governor of Madras.
1887	19 March	Wyvern promoted to colonel and is given the local rank of brigadier-general while employed as Secretary to the Government of Madras.
1888	8 February	Enid Kenney-Herbert attends a "Gentleman's Ball" held by the Tennis Court Club at Leamington Spa Town Hall.
1891	27 June	Wyvern takes part in amateur dramatics at Ootacamund.
	6 July	Wyvern reads the Queen's Despatch at the investiture of Major Grant VC at Ootacamund.
	November (date of preface)	Sixth edition of *Culinary Jottings* published in Madras.
	3 December	Wyvern's length of service and periods of absence from duty are calculated as at 30 November.
1892	20 April	Wyvern officially retires from the army.

	1 May (date of Wyvern's introduction)	*Moir's Preserved Food and How to Prepare It for the Table* published in London.
	August	"The Art of Dining" published in *The Nineteenth Century*.
	November	"The Art of Cooking" published in *The Nineteenth Century*.
	December	"In the Days of John Company" published in *Macmillan's Magazine*.
1893	August	"The Art of Household Management" published in *The Nineteenth Century*.
	7 December	Wyvern launches the Common-Sense Cookery Association and gives a lecture at Queen's Gate Hall, London.
1894	5 February (date of introduction)	*Fifty Breakfasts* published in London.
	4 June	Wyvern opens his cookery school in new premises at 17 Sloane Street, London.
	September	Wyvern interviewed in *The Epicure* magazine.
	October (date of preface)	*Common-Sense Cookery* published in London.
1895	January	"The Literature of Cookery" published in *The National Review*.
	1 July (date of introduction)	*Fifty Dinners* published in London.
	17 August	Wyvern's daughter, Enid, marries Reginald Childers Culling Carr at St Mary Abbotts Church, Kensington.
	31 October	Wyvern chairs The Universal Cookery and Food Association's ninth annual banquet.
1896	(title page)	*The Hare* published in London. Wyvern is a

CHRONOLOGY

		contributing author.
	9 March	Wyvern is commissioned to give instruction in cooking to the cook at the York Street Chambers and later to the cook at Chenies Street Chambers.
	27 April	Wyvern gives a lecture on "The Development of Cookery in England" at the Universal Food Cookery Exhibition, held at the Imperial Institute.
	16 July	Wyvern's grandson, Herbert Reginald Culling Carr, born in Madras.
	October (publisher's book list)	*Fifty Luncheons* published in London.
	October	"The Aesthetics of the Dining Table" published in *The National Review*.
1898	April	Wyvern is commissioned to superintend the cuisine and dining-room arrangements at Campden House Chambers.
1899		Miss Lizzie Dodwell is manageress of the Common-Sense Cookery Association at 17 Sloane Street, London according to the *Post Office London Directory* for 1899.
1900	9 January	Wyvern is commissioned to give a course of instruction to the cook at Chenies Street Chambers.
	3 November	"Journalistic Cookery" published in *The Onlooker*.
1901	(title page)	*Picnics and Suppers* published in London.
	31 March	Census: Wyvern is living at Overstrand Mansions, Prince of Wales Road, Battersea with Agnes and two female servants.
	19 June	London Distributing Kitchens Ltd incorporated.

213

	14 September	Wyvern gives a cookery demonstration at Manchester Distributive Kitchens.
1902	January	"Distributing Kitchens" published in *The National Review*.
1903	25 August (and other dates)	Series of advertisements in the *St. James' Gazette* for St James' Court for "residential flats and bachelors' suites". Those wanting full particulars are advised to contact Wyvern.
	28 October 1903 (and onwards)	Wyvern is described as "Resident Manager" in advertisements for St James' Court.
	12 December	Extraordinary General Meeting of London Distributing Kitchens Limited held and company is wound up. Official Notice signed by Wyvern in his capacity as chairman on 18 December.
1904	(title page)	*Vegetarian and Simple Diet* published in London.
	October (publisher's note)	*Wyvern's Indian Cookery Book* published in Madras and London (the retitled seventh edition of *Culinary Jottings for Madras*).
1905	June (date of preface)	Revised and expanded edition, with illustrations, of *Common-Sense Cookery* published.
1906	May	"The Teaching of Cookery" published in *The Nineteenth Century*.
	8 December	"Christmas In the Kitchen" published in *The Onlooker*.
1907	22 June	Advertisement in the *Army and Navy Gazette* outlining the prospectus for the issue of shares in the United Services Co-operative Hotel Company Limited. Wyvern is identified as a company director.

1908	20 June	Arthur Herbert Cleveland Kenney-Herbert (Wyvern's son) marries Edith Harriet Evans at St Peter's Church, Eaton Square, London.
1910	September	"The Prominence of Pastime" published in *The Nineteenth Century*.
1911	10 March	Notice in *The London Gazette* that the United Services Co-operative Hotel Company Limited has been dissolved.
	2 April	Census: Wyvern and his wife, Agnes, are living at 19a Sinclair Gardens, Ealing, London W14.
1912	24 August	Wyvern is granted the honorary rank of brigadier-general.
1916	5 March	Wyvern dies, aged 75. He is buried in Margravine (Hammersmith Old) Cemetery, London.
1920	20 January	Wyvern's wife, Agnes, dies. She is buried next to Wyvern in Margravine Cemetery, London.
1927	28 July	Herbert Reginald Culling Carr (Wyvern's grandson) marries Evelyn Dorothy Ritchie at St Peter's Church, Berkhamsted.
1944	28 August	Enid Agnes Carr (Wyvern's daughter) dies.
	23 September	Arthur Herbert Cleveland Kenney-Herbert (Wyvern's son) dies.
1986	23 April	Herbert Reginald Culling Carr dies.

Appendix C: Comparison of First and Fifth Editions of *Culinary Jottings for Madras*

First Edition – 1878	**Fifth Edition – 1885**
Introductory	Introduction
The menu	The menu
Concerning the cook and his management	The cook and his management
About certain kitchen requisites	Certain kitchen requisites
In the store-room	In the store-room
On soup-making	On stock, and clear soups
Soup-making *continued*	Thick soups and purées
Soup-making *concluded*	
Regarding our fish	Regarding our fish
Hints about entrées	Hints about entrées
Entrées *continued*	
Entrées *concluded*	Entrées *concluded*
About sauces in general	Sauces
Sauces *continued*	Sauces *continued*
Sauces *concluded*	Sauces *concluded*
Roast and boiled	Roasting and braising
Roast and boiled *continued*	Boiling and steaming
Roast and boiled *concluded*	
Our vegetables	Our vegetables
Vegetables *continued*	

Vegetables *continued*	
Vegetables *concluded*	Vegetables *concluded*
Réchauffés	Réchauffés
The savoury omelette	The savoury omelette
Our luncheons	On luncheons
Fritters	Fritters
Salads	Salads
Hors d'oeuvres	Hors d'oeuvres
	Savoury toasts
Eggs, macaroni, and cheese	Eggs, macaroni, and cheese
	Notes on the curing of meat
	Pastry-making, et cetera
	A few nice pies
	Our curries
	Curries – *continued*, and mulligatunny
Camp cookery	Camp cookery
	Addenda
	On coffee-making
To preserve meat by sulphur fumigation	To preserve meat by fumigation
	Our kitchens in India

Part II – 25 Menus	Part II – 30 Menus
6 menus – For a Party of Eight	10 menus – For a Party of Eight
1 menu – For a Dinner of Four	
	8 menus – For a Dinner of Six
4 menus – For a Party of Six	2 menus – For a Party of Six
5 menus – For a Dinner of Four Friends	
9 menus – For a Little Home Dinner	10 menus – For a Little Home Dinner

Appendix D: Ancestral relationship between Edward Kenney-Herbert and Lady Jane Hedges-White

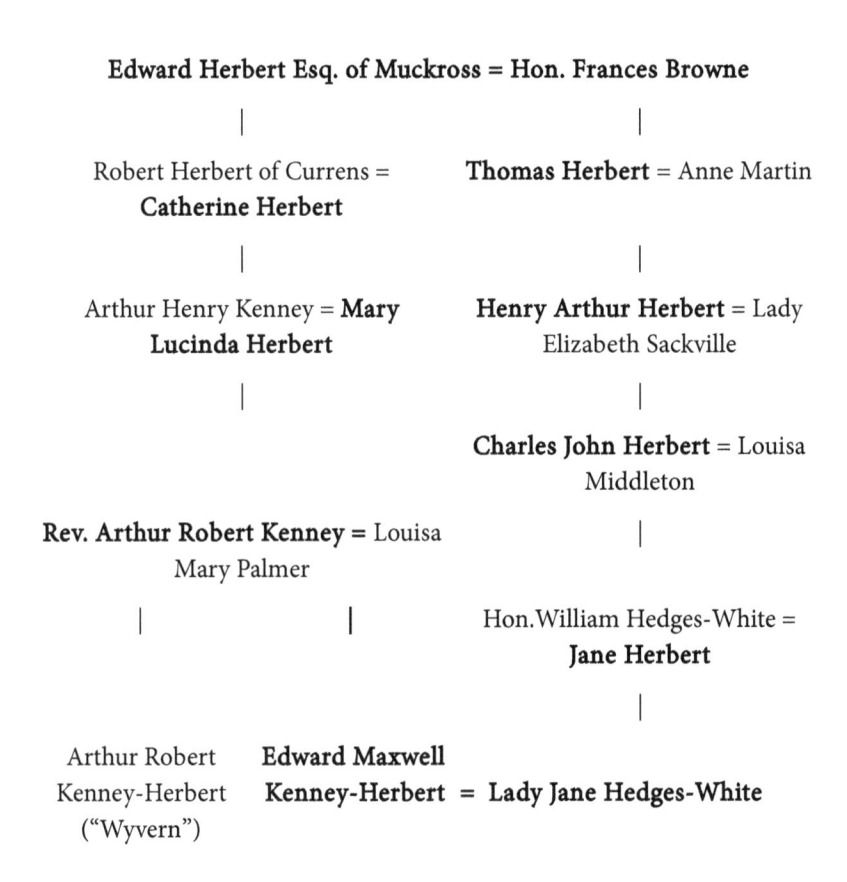

```
           Edward Herbert Esq. of Muckross = Hon. Frances Browne
                        |                              |
      Robert Herbert of Currens =        Thomas Herbert = Anne Martin
           Catherine Herbert
                        |                              |
      Arthur Henry Kenney = Mary          Henry Arthur Herbert = Lady
              Lucinda Herbert                  Elizabeth Sackville
                        |                              |
                                          Charles John Herbert = Louisa
                                                   Middleton
    Rev. Arthur Robert Kenney = Louisa                |
              Mary Palmer
                                         Hon. William Hedges-White =
                 |            |                  Jane Herbert
                                                        |
       Arthur Robert     Edward Maxwell
       Kenney-Herbert    Kenney-Herbert = Lady Jane Hedges-White
         ("Wyvern")
```

Note: **bold** lettering denotes direct line of descent.

Notes

Introduction

1. Jervoise Athelstane Baines, Census Commissioner for India, *General Report of the Census of India, 1891* (HMSO 1893), Table G, xxxix, Table C, xxii.
2. Henry Yule and A. C. Burnell, *Hobson-Jobson: The Anglo-Indian Dictionary* (John Murray 1886; Wordsworth Editions 1996), 755.
3. Mrs Murray Mitchell, *Scenes in Southern India* (American Tract Society 1885), 39.

Chapter 1: Early Years

1. Arthur Robert Kenney-Herbert ("Wyvern"), *Furlough Reminiscences* (Higginbotham & Co. 1880), 1–2.
2. *Ibid.*, 107.
3. The kind nurse was Hannah Orgill. I found this out purely by chance while wandering round the churchyard of St Peter's, where she is buried. The inscription on her headstone tells us that she was "for 32 years the dear nurse of the Rev. Arthur R. Kenney-Herbert". She died in January 1869.
4. "Wyvern", *Furlough Reminiscences*, 83–84.
5. *Ibid.*, 95.
6. *Ibid.*, 96.
7. *Ibid.*, 92.
8. Sidney H. Pardon, editor, *John Wisden's Cricketers' Almanack for 1917* (John Wisden and Co. 1917).
9. "Wyvern", *Furlough Reminiscences*, 91.
10. "Rugby", *The Northampton Mercury*, 11 June 1859.
11. The British Library, India Office Records and Private Papers, "Cadet Papers", IOR/L/MIL/9/249: 1858–1859.
12. Edward Stanley, 15th Earl of Derby, 1826–1893.

13. The British Library, India Office Records and Private Papers, "Cadet Papers".
14. *Ibid.*
15. *Ibid.*
16. Anne de Courcy, *The Fishing Fleet: Husband-Hunting in the Raj* (Phoenix 2013), 3.
17. Herbert Reginald Culling Carr, "The Man Who Taught the Raj to Cook", *Country Life*, 7 November 1968.
18. de Courcy, *The Fishing Fleet*, 62.
19. The British Library, India Office Records and Private Papers, "Roll of wives, widows and children of subscribers to Madras Military Fund", IOR/L/AG/23/10/2: 1808–c.1960.
20. The British Library, Explore Archives and Manuscripts, "Madras Military Fund", http://searcharchives.bl.uk/primo_library/libweb/action/display.do?tabs=detailsTab&ct=display&doc=IAMS037-000970859&displayMode=full&vid=IAMS_VU2 (accessed 21 April 2018).
21. The British Library, India Office Records and Private Papers, "Roll of subscribers to Madras Military Fund", IOR/L/AG/23/10/1: 1808–c.1939.
22. The British Library, India Office Records and Private Papers, "Roll of wives, widows and children of subscribers to Madras Military Fund", IOR/L/AG/23/10/2: 1808–c 1960.
23. The British Library, India Office Records and Private Papers, "Herbert, Arthur Robert Kenney–Madras Cavalry", IOR/L/MIL/11/85 f.351: 1875–1877.
24. "Bourton", *The Rugby Advertiser*, 27 October 1866.
25. Sir Mountstuart Elphinstone Grant Duff (1829–1906), Under-Secretary of State for India 1868–1874, Under-Secretary of State for the Colonies 1880–1881, and Governor of the Madras Presidency 1881–1886.
26. Sir Mountstuart Elphinstone Grant Duff, *Notes from a Diary: Kept Chiefly in Southern India 1881–1886*, Vol. 1 (John Murray 1899), 121.
27. "Change of Surname – Kenney-Herbert", *London Evening Standard*, 27 July 1875.
28. "Change of Surname – Kenney-Herbert", *London Evening Standard*, 8 December 1875.

NOTES

29. George Wheeler, *India in 1875–76: The Visit of the Prince of Wales* (Chapman and Hall 1876), 169–170.
30. "The Prince of Wales at Madras", *The Morning Post*, 10 January 1876.
31. "Wyvern", "Etcætera from Town", *The Athenaeum and Daily News*, 20 July 1877.
32. "Wyvern", "Etcætera from Town", 30 July 1877.
33. "Wyvern", "Etcætera from Town", 1 October 1877.
34. "Wyvern", "Etcætera from Town", 22 September 1877.
35. "Wyvern", "Etcætera from Town", 1 October 1877.
36. "Griffin", "Etcætera from Town", *The Athenaeum and Daily News*, 4 December 1877.
37. Cracrofts Peerage, "Pembroke, Earl of (E, 1551)", www.cracroftspeerage.co.uk/online/content/pembroke1551.htm (last updated 18 November 2012, accessed 12 April 2018).
38. Carr, "The Man Who Taught the Raj to Cook".
39. "Wyvern", "Culinary Jottings for Madras", *The Athenaeum and Daily News*, 5 January 1878.
40. "Wyvern", "Culinary Jottings for Madras", 12 January 1878.
41. "Wyvern", "Culinary Jottings for Madras", 30 September 1878.
42. Arthur Robert Kenney-Herbert ("Wyvern"), *Culinary Jottings for Madras*, first edition (Higginbotham & Co. 1878), preface.

Chapter 2: Culinary Jottings for Madras

1. "Wyvern", "Culinary Jottings for Madras", *The Athenaeum and Daily News*, 5 January 1878.
2. Arthur Robert Kenney-Herbert ("Wyvern"), *Culinary Jottings*, fifth edition (Higginbotham & Co. 1885), 1–2.
3. If you are interested in exploring Wyvern's menus and his recipes, there are a number of modern facsimile editions of *Culinary Jottings for Madras* available on the market for a reasonable price. It is not necessary to invest hundreds of pounds in a highly collectable first edition of the book. There are also a number of free digital versions available online in the public archives of libraries and universities.
4. "Wyvern", *Culinary Jottings*, 4.
5. Arthur Robert Kenney-Herbert ("Wyvern"), *Sweet Dishes*

(Higginbotham & Co. 1881), 193.
6. "Wyvern", *Culinary Jottings*, 5.
7. *Ibid.*, 5–6.
8. Jean Anthelme Brillat-Savarin (1755–1826), lawyer, politician, epicure. Author of *Physiologie du goût* (1825).
9. Brillat-Savarin, quoted in "Wyvern", *Culinary Jottings*, 6.
10. "Wyvern", *Culinary Jottings*, 12; emphasis in original.
11. *Ibid.*, 15.
12. *Ibid.*, 14.
13. *Ibid.*, 15.
14. *Ibid.*, 16.
15. Mrs Murray Mitchell, *Scenes in Southern India* (America Tract Society 1885), 53.
16. "Wyvern", *Culinary Jottings*, 17.
17. *Ibid.*, 18; emphasis in original.
18. *Ibid.*, 19.
19. *Ibid.*, 24–25.
20. *Ibid.*, 26.
21. *Ibid.*, 27.
22. *Ibid.*
23. *Ibid.*, 497–498.
24. *Ibid.*, 497.
25. *Ibid.*, 502.
26. *Ibid.*, 499.
27. *Ibid.*, 500.
28. *Ibid.*, 505.
29. *Ibid.*, 496.
30. *Ibid.*, 127.
31. *Ibid.*, 165.
32. *Ibid.*, 177–178.
33. *Ibid.*, 178.
34. *Ibid.*, 181–182.
35. *Ibid.*, 168.
36. *Ibid.*, 173.
37. *Ibid.*, 171.
38. Flora Annie Steel and Grace Gardiner, *The Complete Indian Housekeeper*

and Cook, fourth edition, edited by Ralph Crane and Anna Johnston (William Heinemann 1898; Oxford University Press 2011), 242.
39. "Wyvern", *Culinary Jottings,* 258.
40. *Ibid.,* 258.
41. *Ibid.,* 318.
42. *Ibid.,* 102; spellings in original.
43. *Ibid.*
44. *Ibid.,* 103.
45. *Ibid.,* 104.
46. *Ibid.,* 106.
47. *Ibid.,* 335.
48. *Ibid.,* 340.
49. *Ibid.,* 398.
50. *Ibid.,* 450.

Chapter 3: Furlough Reminiscences

1. Arthur Robert Kenney-Herbert ("Wyvern"), *Furlough Reminiscences* (Higginbotham & Co. 1880), preface.
2. One of the British Library's copies of *Furlough Reminiscences* (which was used for the facsimile edition) has been annotated in places by a previous, and possibly contemporary, owner and some of the notes have proved useful in determining the true identity of the people and places which appear in the book.
3. "Wyvern", *Furlough Reminiscences,* 7.
4. *Ibid.* Our guide who annotated the British Library's copy of the book has underlined part of the passage where Wyvern describes the *antipasto* as follows: "The *antipasto* is an agreeable novelty to most Englishmen" and has added a large question mark in the margin. So not all Englishmen agreed with Wyvern about the agreeability of *antipasto,* it seems!
5. *Ibid.,* 12.
6. *Ibid.,* 20.
7. *Ibid.,* 19.
8. *Ibid.*
9. *Ibid.,* 23.
10. Dane Kennedy, *The Magic Mountains: Hill Stations and the British Raj*

(University of California Press 1996), 132.
11. Wyvern", *Furlough Reminiscences*, 29.
12. Today, Blenheim Terrace is well within London, near Lord's Cricket Ground and the Abbey Road Studio, where The Beatles recorded the album of the same name some ninety years later.
13. Christian Wolmar, *The Subterranean Railway: How the London Underground Was Built & How it Changed the City Forever* (Atlantic Books 2012), 66.
14. "Wyvern", *Furlough Reminiscences*, 54.
15. *Ibid.*, 68.
16. *Ibid.*, 64.
17. *Ibid.*, 71–72; emphasis in original.
18. *Ibid.*, 75.
19. *Ibid.*, 77.
20. *Ibid.*, 67.
21. *Ibid.*, 117.
22. *Ibid.*, 216–217.
23. *Ibid.*, 80–81.
24. *Ibid.*, 21.
25. *Ibid.*, 86.
26. *Ibid.*, 94. Edward Meyrick Goulburn – "Dr G" – was headmaster of Rugby School from 1849 to 1857, and later became Dean of Norwich. In another passage, *Ibid.*, 96; Wyvern notes that he was Captain of the Eleven "under the head-mastership of my revered Dean of N-----".
27. *Ibid.*, 114.
28. *Ibid.*, 115.
29. *Ibid.*, 137.
30. *Ibid.*, 137–138.
31. *Ibid.*, 143–144.
32. *Ibid.*, 147
33. "Henry Slade", https://en.wikipedia.org/wiki/Henry_Slade (last updated 17 January 2018, accessed 9 May 2018).
34. "Wyvern", *Furlough Reminiscences*, 122.
35. "John Nevil Maskelyne", https://en.wikipedia.org/wiki/John_Nevil_Maskelyne (last updated 9 April 2018, accessed 9 May 2018).

36. "Wyvern", *Furlough Reminiscences*, 255.
37. "News of the Week", *The Spectator*, 1 April 1871.
38. Adam Bissett Thom, *The Upper Ten Thousand: An alphabetical list of all members of Noble Families, Bishops, Privy Councillors, Judges, Baronets, Members of the House of Commons, Lords-Lieutenant, Governors of Colonies, Knights and Companions of Orders, Deans and Archdeacons, and the Superior Officers of the Army and the Navy, with their official descriptions and addresses* (George Routledge & Sons 1875), title.
39. "Wyvern", *Furlough Reminiscences*, 139.
40. *Ibid.*, 132.
41. *Ibid.*, 150.
42. *Ibid.*, 150–151.
43. *Ibid.*, 151.
44. *Ibid.*, 155.
45. *Ibid.*, 174.
46. *Ibid.*, 176–177.
47. *Ibid.*, 178. See also "Christy's Minstrels", https://en.wikipedia.org/wiki/Christy%27s_Minstrels (last updated 10 April 2018, accessed 9 May 2018).
48. *Ibid.*, 169.
49. *Ibid.*, 170.
50. Advertisement, *Pall Mall Gazette*, 16 July 1894.
51. "Wyvern", *Furlough Reminiscences*, 252.
52. *Ibid.*, 2.

Chapter 4: Madras

1. S. Muthiah, *Madras Discovered* (East-West Press 1992), 237.
2. Mrs Murray Mitchell, *Scenes in Southern India* (American Tract Society 1885), 34.
3. Muthiah, *Madras Discovered*, 239.
4. *Ibid.*, 28.
5. Mitchell, *Scenes in Southern India*, 33–34.
6. "Ice for the Million", *The Athenaeum and Daily News*, 13 March 1877.
7. *The Asylum Press Almanac and Compendium of Intelligence for 1882* (Lawrence Asylum Press 1881), 740.

8. Henry Davison Love, *Short Historical Notice of the Madras Club* (Higginbotham & Co. 1902), 3.
9. *Ibid.*, 9.
10. *Ibid.*, 13.
11. *Ibid.*, 24.
12. George Wheeler, *India in 1875–76: The Visit of the Prince of Wales* (Chapman and Hall 1876), 174–175.
13. Love, *Short Historical Notice of the Madras Club*, 43.
14. "Wyvern", "Culinary Jottings for Madras", *The Athenaeum and Daily News*, 26 March 1878.
15. "Theatre Royal, Fort Saint George", *The Athenaeum and Daily News*, 28 August 1878.
16. Advertisement, *The Athenaeum and Daily News*, 2 July 1878.
17. "Wilson's Circus", *The Athenaeum and Daily News*, 12 July 1878.
18. "Wilson's Circus", *The Athenaeum and Daily News*, 29 July 1878.
19. Bradley G. Shope, *American Popular Music in Britain's Raj* (University of Rochester Press 2016), 37.
20. "Dave Carson's Performance", *The Athenaeum and Daily News*, 13 November 1876.
21. Shope, *American Popular Music in Britain's Raj*, 39.

Chapter 5: The Great Famine

1. Arthur Robert Kenney-Herbert ("Wyvern"), *Culinary Jottings*, fifth edition (Higginbotham & Co. 1885), 103.
2. "Occasional Notes", *The Athenaeum and Daily News*, 13 November 1876.
3. *Ibid.*, 30 October 1876.
4. *Ibid.*, 6 December 1876.
5. *Ibid.*, 9 January 1877.
6. Michael E. Mann, *The Hockey Stick and the Climate Wars* (Columbia University Press 2014), 28.
7. William Digby, *The Famine Campaign in Southern India 1876–1878*, Vols 1 and 2 (Longmans, Green and Co. 1878), Vol. 1, 1.
8. Mike Davis, *Late Victorian Holocausts: El Niño Famines and the Making of the Third World* (Verso 2002), Table P1, 7.
9. *Ibid.*, 26.

10. Niall Ferguson, *Empire: How Britain Made the Modern World* (Penguin Books 2004), xxii.
11. *Ibid.*, 188, footnote.
12. Simon Schama, *A History of Britain: Volume 3, The Fate of Empire, 1776–2000* (BBC Worldwide 2002), 361; emphasis in original.
13. Davis, *Late Victorian Holocausts*, 31.
14. Richard Plantagenet Campbell Temple-Nugent-Brydges-Chandos-Grenville, 3rd Duke of Buckingham and Chandos (1823–1889), Governor of the Madras Presidency 1875–1880.
15. "Wyvern", "Etcætera from Town", *The Athenaeum and Daily News*, 22 September 1877.
16. "The Famine Relief Fund", *The Athenaeum and Daily News*, 20 August 1877.
17. Sir Richard Temple (1826–1902), Famine Commissioner to the Madras Presidency, 1877.
18. "Famine and the Famine Commissioner", *The Athenaeum and Daily News*, 13 January 1877.
19. *Ibid.*
20. Davis, *Late Victorian Holocausts*, 41.
21. "Season and Prospects of the Crops", *The Athenaeum and Daily News,* 17 November 1877.

Chapter 6: Housekeeping and Life on the Move

1. Ralph Crane and Anna Johnston, editors, "Introduction", in Flora Annie Steel and Grace Gardiner, *The Complete Indian Housekeeper and Cook*, fourth edition (Oxford University Press 2011), ix.
2. Flora Annie Steel and Grace Gardiner, *The Complete Indian Housekeeper and Cook*, fourth edition, edited by Ralph Crane and Anna Johnston (William Heinemann 1898; Oxford University Press 2011), 11.
3. *Ibid.*, 11.
4. Crane and Johnston, "Introduction" in *The Complete Indian Housekeeper and Cook*, xvi.
5. Steel and Gardiner, *The Complete Indian Housekeeper and Cook*, 12.
6. *Ibid.*
7. *Ibid.*, 61.

8. *Ibid.*, 59.
9. *Ibid.*, 60.
10. *Ibid.*, 41.
11. *Ibid.*, 187.
12. *Ibid.*, 188.
13. *Ibid.*, 193.
14. *Ibid.*, 195.
15. *Ibid.*, 196.
16. *Ibid.*, 220.
17. *Ibid.*, 305.
18. *Ibid.*, 296.
19. David Burton, *The Raj at Table: A Culinary History of the British in India* (Faber & Faber 1993), 37.
20. Arthur Robert Kenney-Herbert, "In the Days of John Company", *Macmillan's Magazine*, December 1892.
21. Burton, *The Raj at Table: A Culinary History of the British in India*, 42–43.
22. Kenney-Herbert, "In the Days of John Company".
23. *Ibid.*
24. *Ibid.*
25. "Thirsty India", *The Athenaeum and Daily News*, 2 August 1878.
26. Steel and Gardiner, *The Complete Indian Housekeeper and Cook*, 156.
27. *Ibid.*, 153.
28. *Ibid.*, 155.
29. Arthur Robert Kenney-Herbert ("Wyvern"), *Culinary Jottings*, fifth edition (Higginbotham & Co. 1885), 314.
30. *Ibid.*, 316.
31. *Ibid.*, 329.

Chapter 7: On the Hills

1. Dane Kennedy, *The Magic Mountains: Hill Stations and the British Raj* (University of California Press 1996), 91.
2. Mrs Murray Mitchell, *Scenes in Southern India* (American Tract Society 1885), 341.
3. Arthur Robert Kenney-Herbert ("Wyvern"), *Culinary Jottings*, fifth

NOTES

edition (Higginbotham & Co. 1885), 259–260.
4. *Ibid.*, 284.
5. Shanta Thiagarajan, "Nilgiris sees a 20% rise in yield of hybrid vegetables", *The Times of India*, 17 February 2016, www.timesofindia.indiatimes.com/city/coimbatore/Nilgiris-sees-a-20-rise-in-yield-of-hybrid-vegetables/articleshow/51018110.cms (accessed 12 April 2018).
6. "Wyvern", *Culinary Jottings*, 149–150.
7. Mitchell, *Scenes in Southern India*, 348, 350.
8. Kennedy, *The Magic Mountains*, 47–48.
9. "Wyvern", *Culinary Jottings*, 166.
10. Kennedy, *The Magic Mountains*, 12.
11. "Ought the Madras Government Go to the Hills This Year?", *The Athenaeum and Daily News*, 1 March 1877.
12. Kenneth Ballhatchet, *Race, Sex and Class Under the Raj* (Weidenfeld and Nicolson 1980), 52.
13. *Ibid.*, drawing opposite 120.
14. "Our Hill Stations", *The Athenaeum and Daily News*, 22 June 1876.
15. Kennedy, *The Magic Mountains*, 109.
16. *Ibid.*, 132.
17. Rudyard Kipling, "Tods' Amendment" in *Plain Tales from the Hills* (Thacker Spink 1888; Penguin Books 1987), 179–184, 182.
18. Kennedy, *The Magic Mountains*, 134.
19. *Ibid.*, 141–142.
20. Rudyard Kipling, "Kidnapped", in *Plain Tales from the Hills* (Thacker Spink 1888; Penguin Books 1987), 133–137, 134; emphasis in original.
21. David Trotter, "Introduction" in Rudyard Kipling, *Plain Tales from the Hills* (Penguin Books 1987), 20; emphasis in original.

Chapter 8: Our Curries

1. Arthur Robert Kenney-Herbert ("Wyvern"), *Culinary Jottings,* fifth edition (Higginbotham & Co. 1885), 285.
2. *Ibid.*, 500.
3. John Henry Grose, *A Voyage to the East Indies,* new edition (S. Hooper 1772), 150–151.

4. *Ibid.*, 150.
5. Dr R. Riddell ("The author of *Manual of Gardening for Western India*"), *Indian Domestic Economy and Receipt Book,* fifth edition (Society for Promoting Christian Knowledge 1860), 376.
6. "Wyvern", *Culinary Jottings,* 286.
7. *Ibid.*, 287.
8. *Ibid.*, 291.
9. *Ibid.*
10. *Ibid.*, 288.
11. *Ibid.*
12. *Ibid.*, 294–295; spellings in original.
13. *Ibid.*, 295–296.
14. *Ibid.*, 298–299.
15. *Ibid.*, 299.
16. *Ibid.*, 303.
17. *Ibid.*
18. *Ibid.*, 304.
19. *Ibid.*, 305.
20. *Ibid.*, 307.
21. *Ibid.*, 308.
22. *Ibid.*, 309.
23. *Ibid.*, 244.

Chapter 9: Later Life in India

1. "Military Intelligence", *The Freeman's Journal,* 3 July 1879.
2. Arthur Robert Kenney-Herbert ("Wyvern"), *Sweet Dishes* (Higginbotham & Co. 1881), 1.
3. *Ibid.*, 4.
4. *Ibid.*
5. William Huddleston (1826–1894), acting Governor of the Madras Presidency, May–November 1881.
6. William Patrick Adam (1823–1881), Governor of the Madras Presidency, 1880–1881.
7. Sir Mountstuart Elphinstone Grant Duff, *Notes from a Diary: Kept Chiefly in Southern India 1881–1886,* Vol. 1 (John Murray 1899), 11.

NOTES

8. "Naval and Military Intelligence", *The Morning Post*, 15 March 1883.
9. Grant Duff, *Notes from a Diary*, Vol. 1, 221.
10. Wilfrid Scawen Blunt (1840–1922), poet, writer, political activist, horse breeder. Visited India 1883–1894.
11. Wilfred Scawen Blunt, *India Under Ripon: A Private Diary* (T. Fisher Unwin 1909; Elibron Classics 2005), 53.
12. Major-General Robert Clive, 1st Baron Clive (1725–1774), also known as "Clive of India". Sir Mountstuart Elphinstone Grant Duff, *Notes from a Diary: Kept Chiefly in Southern India 1881–1886*, Vol. 2 (John Murray 1899), 18.
13. *The Asylum Press Almanac and Compendium of Intelligence for 1882* (Lawrence Asylum Press 1881), 740.
14. Pusapati Ananda Gajapati Raju (1850–1897), Maharajah of the princely state of Vizianagram (now Vizianagaram), 1879–1897.
15. Robert Bourke, 1st Baron Connemara (1827–1902), Governor of the Madras Presidency, 1886–1890.
16. "Society Gossip", *York Herald*, 24 June 1891.
17. Lieutenant General Sir James Charlemagne Dormer (1834–1893).
18. "Gup", *The Homeward Mail from India, China and the East*, 15 June 1891.
19. "Charles Grant VC, 12th Regiment, Madras Infantry. Charles Grant was invested with his Victoria Cross by the Governor of Madras, Lord Wenlock, at Ootacamund on the 6 July 1891. Known as the 'hero of Thobal' for his bravery in taking and defending Thobal against a superior force." "The Grave of Colonel Charles Grant VC", www.victoriacross.org.uk/bbgrancj.htm (last updated 14 October 2014, accessed 10 May 2018).
20. The British Library, India Office Records and Private Papers, "Herbert, Arthur Robert Kenney–Madras Cavalry", IOR/L/MIL/11/92 f.57: 1891–1892.
21. "From the London Gazette of Tuesday May 24th", *London Evening Standard*, 25 May 1892.
22. "Military and Naval", *The Homeward Mail*, 21 November 1891.
23. Arthur Robert Kenney-Herbert, "In the Days of John Company", *Macmillan's Magazine*, December 1892.
24. *Ibid.*

25. *Ibid.*
26. Arthur Robert Kenney-Herbert ("Wyvern"), *Culinary Jottings*, fifth edition (Higginbotham & Co. 1885), 29; emphasis added.
27. *Ibid.*, 329.
28. "Wyvern", *Tinned Food with Advice and Recipes for Its Treatment; being John Moir and Son's (Limited) Export Catalogue – annotated by "Wyvern"* (Alf Cooke 1893), title page.
29. *Ibid.*, 3.
30. *Ibid.*, 31.
31. *Ibid.*, 13.
32. *Ibid.*, 17.

Chapter 10: Home to England

1. Arthur Robert Kenney-Herbert, "The Art of Dining", *The Nineteenth Century*, August 1892.
2. *Ibid.*
3. Marie-Antoine (Antonin) Carême (1784–1833), French chef, author of *L'Art de la cuisine Française* (1833).
4. Ian Kelly, *Cooking for Kings: The Life of Antonin Carême, the First Celebrity Chef* (Short Books 2004), 13.
5. *Ibid.*, 15.
6. Kenney-Herbert, "The Art of Dining".
7. *Ibid.*
8. "The Tatler on The Art of Dining", *The Leeds Times*, 20 August 1892.
9. *Ibid.*
10. Arthur Robert Kenney-Herbert, "The Art of Cooking", *The Nineteenth Century*, November 1892.
11. *Ibid.*
12. *Ibid.*
13. *Ibid.*; emphasis in original.
14. Arthur Robert Kenney-Herbert, "The Art of Household Management", *The Nineteenth Century*, August 1893.
15. *Ibid.*
16. *Ibid.*
17. *Ibid.*

NOTES

18. "A Man's Idea of Cookery", *The Nottingham Evening Post*, 26 August 1893.
19. "Arrangements for This Day", *The Morning Post*, 7 December 1893.
20. Arthur Robert Kenney-Herbert ("Wyvern"), *Common-Sense Cookery: For English Households, Based upon Modern English and Continental Principles, with Twenty Menus for Little Dinners Worked Out in Detail* (Edward Arnold 1894), title page.
21. *Ibid.*, 1.
22. *Ibid.*, 369.
23. Isabella Beeton, *Mrs Beeton's Book of Household Management* (S. O. Beeton 1861).
24. "Wyvern", *Common-Sense Cookery*, 409–410.
25. *Ibid.*, 417.
26. Elizabeth David, *Spices, Salt and Aromatics in the English Kitchen* (Penguin Books 1970; Grub Street 2000), 159.
27. Sir Henry Thompson FRCS (1820–1904), surgeon, author.
28. Sir Henry Thompson, *Food and Feeding*, eleventh edition (Frederick Warne 1901), 168 (footnote).
29. Arthur Robert Kenney-Herbert ("Wyvern"), *Common-Sense Cookery*, second edition (Edward Arnold, undated, c. 1898), advertisements following index.
30. *Ibid.*
31. *Ibid.*
32. "The Wares of Autolycus – Fifty Breakfasts", *Pall Mall Gazette*, 24 March 1894.
33. Kenney-Herbert, *Common-Sense Cookery*, second edition, advertisements following index.
34. "A Woman's Chit-Chat", *The Cheltenham Looker-On*, 28 April 1894.
35. Kenney-Herbert, *Common-Sense Cookery*, second edition, advertisements following index.
36. Arthur Robert Kenney-Herbert ("Wyvern"), *Fifty Breakfasts*, second edition (Edward Arnold, undated, c. 1895), advertisements following index.
37. *Ibid.*
38. "Notes from Cookery Schools", *The Epicure*, February 1894.
39. In more recent times, the building originally known as Queen's Gate

Hall housed The Harrington, a club founded by rock guitarist and Rolling Stone, Ronnie Wood.
40. "A Woman's Chit-Chat", *The Cheltenham Looker-On*, 14 April 1894.
41. "Our London Correspondent", *The Glasgow Herald*, 27 June 1894.
42. "Notes from Cookery Schools", *The Epicure*, July 1894.
43. "Pall Mall Gazette Office", *Pall Mall Gazette*, 4 June 1894.
44. Millennium Hotel London Knightsbridge, "About the Hotel", www.millenniumhotels.com/en/london/millennium-hotel-london-knightsbridge, (accessed 24 April 2018).
45. Advertisement, *Pall Mall Gazette*, 16 July 1894.
46. Advertisement, *The Morning Post*, 25 August 1894.
47. Advertisement, *The Morning Post*, 27 October 1894.

Chapter 11: The Servant Problem

1. "Amara Veritas", *The Servant Problem: An Attempt at Its Solution by an Experienced Mistress* (Simpkin, Marshall, Hamilton, Kent & Co. 1899), 6–7.
2. *Ibid.*, 7.
3. *Ibid.*, 6.
4. *Ibid.*, 5.
5. "Wyvern", "Etcætera from Town", *The Athenaeum and Daily News*, 1 October 1877.
6. *Ibid.*
7. "Amara Veritas", *The Servant Problem*, 121.
8. *Ibid.*, 22.
9. *Ibid.*, 34.
10. "Wyvern", "Etcætera from Town", 1 October 1877.
11. "Amara Veritas", *The Servant Problem*, 35.
12. Arthur Robert Kenney-Herbert, "The Teaching of Cookery", *The Nineteenth Century*, May 1906.
13. Sir Henry Cole (1808–1882), Commissioner, Royal Commission for the Exhibition of 1851 ("The Great Exhibition").
14. John Charles Buckmaster (1820–unknown), author of *Buckmaster's Cookery: Being an abridgement of some of the lectures delivered at the International Exhibition for 1873 and 1874* (George Routledge and Sons

1874).
15. Dorothy Stone, *The National: The Story of a Pioneer College* (Robert Hale & Company 1976), 8.
16. Mrs Charles Clarke, née Edith Nicolls (1844–1926), Principal of the National Training School for Cookery 1875–1919.
17. Eliza Youmans, quoted in Stone, *The National*, 26.
18. Charles Herman Senn MBE (1862–1934), Founder and Honorary Secretary of the Universal Cookery and Food Association.
19. Georges Auguste Escoffier (1846–1935), head chef at the Savoy Hotel, London, author of *Le Guide Culinaire* (1903).
20. Advertisement, *The Epicure*, December 1894.
21. Advertisement, *The Morning Post*, 27 October 1894.
22. Advertisement, *The Morning Post*, 27 June 1894.
23. Agnes B. Marshall, *Mrs. A. B. Marshall's Cookery Book*, fifty-fifth thousand (Simpkin, Marshall, Hamilton, Kent & Co., undated, c.1894), Advertisements, 24.
24. "The Colonel and his Cookery School", *The Epicure*, September 1894.
25. Elizabeth Alicia M. Lewis, "A Reformation of Domestic Service", *The Nineteenth Century*, January 1893.
26. Arthur Robert Kenney-Herbert, "Distributing Kitchens", *The National Review*, January 1902.

Chapter 12: Victorian Celebrity Chef

1. "The Colonel and his Cookery School", *The Epicure*, September 1894.
2. *Ibid.*
3. *Ibid.*
4. *Ibid.*
5. Arthur Robert Kenney-Herbert ("Wyvern"), *Fifty Breakfasts*, second edition (Edward Arnold, undated, c. 1895), advertisements following index.
6. Advertisement, *The Morning Post*, 3 May 1895.
7. Arthur Robert Kenney-Herbert, "The Literature of Cookery", *The National Review*, January 1895.
8. "Universal Cookery and Food Association", *The Morning Post*, 1 November 1895.

9. "The Wares of Autolycus – Fifty Dinners", *Pall Mall Gazette*, 16 November 1895.
10. "New Books and New Editions", *Leeds Mercury*, 29 January 1896.
11. Arthur Robert Kenney-Herbert, "Cookery of the Hare", in *The Hare* (Fur and Feather Series), edited by Alfred E. T. Watson (Longmans Green 1896), 229–263.
12. Advertisement, *The Morning Post*, 14 March 1896.
13. Advertisement, *The Morning Post*, 11 April 1896.
14. Advertisement, *The Morning Post*, 2 May 1896.
15. Arthur Robert Kenney-Herbert, "The Business of Pleasure – Cookery", *The Onlooker*, 3 November 1900.
16. Advertisement, *London Evening Standard*, 19 May 1896.
17. Advertisements, *The Morning Post*, 8 September 1896.
18. Arthur Robert Kenney-Herbert, "The Aesthetics of the Dining Table", *The National Review*, October 1896.
19. Agnes Garrett (1845–1935), interior designer and founder of Ladies' Residential Chambers Ltd. Co-author (with Rhoda Garrett) of *Suggestions for House Decoration in Painting, Woodwork, and Furniture* (Macmillan and Co. 1876).
20. Rhoda Garrett (1841–1882), interior designer and co-author (with Agnes Garrett) of *Suggestions for House Decoration in Painting, Woodwork, and Furniture* (Macmillan and Co. 1876).
21. Millicent Fawcett (1847–1929), suffragist, President of the National Union of Women's Suffrage Societies, and co-founder of Newnham College, Cambridge.
22. Elizabeth Garrett Anderson (1836–1917), physician and co-founder of the London School of Medicine for Women.
23. Elizabeth Crawford, "Spirited Women of Gower Street: The Garretts and their Circle", UCL Bloomsbury Project conference papers, 15 April 2011, www.ucl.ac.uk/bloomsbury-project/articles/events/conference2011/crawford.pdf (accessed 24 April 2018).
24. City of Westminster Archives Centre, "Ladies Residential Chambers Ltd. – Minute Books of the Management Committee 1895–1911", system ID 0975.
25. *Ibid.*

NOTES

26. *Ibid.*
27. *Ibid.*
28. "Campden House Chambers", *The Morning Post*, 4 April 1898.
29. Advertisement, *The Morning Post*, 22 September 1898.
30. "Penelope", "Letter to the Ladies", *Dundee Evening Telegraph,* 23 April 1898.
31. Advertisement, *The Morning Post*, 28 September 1899.
32. Advertisement, *The Morning Post*, 27 July 1898.
33. Arthur Robert Kenney-Herbert, "The Business of Pleasure – Cookery", *The Onlooker*, 3 November 1900.
34. *Ibid.*
35. Agnes B. Marshall, *Mrs. A. B. Marshall's Cookery Book,* fifty-fifth thousand (Simpkin, Marshall, Hamilton, Kent & Co., undated, c. 1894), title page.
36. Arthur Robert Kenney-Herbert, "The Business of Pleasure – Plain Cooking", *The Onlooker*, 24 November 1900.
37. Arthur Robert Kenney-Herbert, "Christmas in the Kitchen", *The Onlooker*, 29 December 1900.
38. The British Library, India Office Records and Private Papers, "Roll of wives, widows and children of subscribers to Madras Military Fund", IOR/L/AG/23/10/2: 1808–c.1960.
39. The National Archives, BT 31 – Board of Trade: Companies Registration Office: Files of Dissolved Companies, "Distributing Kitchens Ltd. Incorporated in 1900", BT 31/8856/65115.
40. "Prospectus – The Reformed Food (Vegetarian) Company Limited", *Northern Daily Telegraph*, 1 August 1900.
41. The National Archives, BT 31/8856/65115.
42. *Ibid.*
43. "Manchester Distributive Kitchens", *Manchester Courier and Lancashire General Advertiser*, 14 September 1901.
44. The National Archives, BT 31 – Board of Trade: Companies Registration Office: Files of Dissolved Companies, "London Distributing Kitchens Ltd. Incorporated in 1901", BT 31/9499/70577.
45. Elizabeth Alicia M. Lewis, "A Reformation of Domestic Service", *The Nineteenth Century*, January 1893.
46. Arthur Robert Kenney-Herbert, "Distributing Kitchens", *The National*

Review, January 1902.
47. *Ibid.*
48. "Dinner Ordered from the Wrong Colonel", *Yorkshire Evening Post*, 7 April 1903.
49. Advertisement, *St. James' Gazette*, 25 August 1903.
50. The National Archives, BT 31/9499/70577.
51. The National Archives, BT 31/8856/65115.
52. "Minor Books", *The Scotsman*, 27 October 1904.
53. Arthur Robert Kenney-Herbert ("Wyvern"), *Common-Sense Cookery*, revised and enlarged edition with illustrations (Edward Arnold 1905), v.
54. Arthur Robert Kenney-Herbert, "Christmas in the Kitchen", *The Onlooker*, 8 December 1906.
55. *Ibid.*
56. The National Archives, BT 31 – Board of Trade: Companies Registration Office: Files of Dissolved Companies, "United Services Co-operative Hotel Company Ltd. Incorporated in 1907", BT 31/11966/93329.
57. "From the The Naval and Military Record of Nov. 18", *Homeward Mail from India, China and the East*, 20 November 1909.
58. The National Archives, BT 31/11966/93329.
59. "Joint Stock Companies", *The London Gazette*, 10 March 1911.
60. Arthur Robert Kenney-Herbert, "The Prominence of Pastime", *The Nineteenth Century*, September 1910.
61. *Ibid.*
62. *Ibid.*
63. "Has Our King Blundered?", *Athletic News*, 5 September 1910.
64. *Ibid.*
65. Kenney-Herbert, "The Prominence of Pastime".
66. "Memoranda", *The London Gazette*, 23 August 1912.
67. "General Kenney-Herbert", *Coventry Standard*, 24 March 1916.
68. Herbert Reginald Culling Carr, "The Man Who Taught the Raj to Cook", *Country Life*, 7 November 1968.

Chapter 13: Wyvern's Legacy

1. "Military and Naval", *The Homeward Mail*, 21 November 1891.
2. *Ibid.*

NOTES

3. Leslie Forbes, *Culinary Jottings for Madras* (Prospect Books 2007), xxii.
4. Florence White, *Good Things in England* (Jonathan Cape 1932; seventh impression 1951), 178.
5. Elizabeth David, *A Book of Mediterranean Food* (John Lehmann 1950); *French Country Cooking* (John Lehmann 1951).
6. Elizabeth David, *Spices, Salt and Aromatics in the English Kitchen* (Penguin Books 1970; Grub Street 2000), 20.
7. *Ibid.*, 158.
8. *Ibid.*, 158–159.
9. Caroline Conran, Terence Conran and Simon Hopkinson, *The Conran Cookbook* (Conran Octopus 2002), 308.
10. "Accident to Captain Kenney Herbert", *Leamington Spa Courier*, 21 April 1900.
11. Geoff Milburn, "Herbert Reginald Culling Carr", *The Climbers' Club Journal for 1985/86* (The Climbers' Club 1986), 189–195.
12. Audrey Salkeld, "Herbert Reginald Culling Carr 1896–1986", *Alpine Journal for 1987* (The Alpine Club 1987), 297–298.
13. Herbert Reginald Culling Carr and George. A. Lister, *The Mountains of Snowdonia in History, the Sciences, Literature and Sport* (John Lane 1924).
14. Herbert Reginald Culling Carr, "The Man Who Taught the Raj to Cook", *Country Life*, 7 November 1968.

Glossary

Names and duties of Indian servants

ayah	lady's maid, a nursemaid
box-wallah	travelling salesman
butler	head servant of the household
consama/consumah	house-steward, chef
cook	widely used English name (see also "Ramasamy")
dhoby	laundry servant, washerman/washerwoman
khitmutgâr/matey	serves meals and waits at table
munshi	secretary
"Ramasamy"	generic name used by the British for a male from southern India (Wyvern uses it referring to his cook – see Introduction)
sweeper	cleaner, servant who empties the latrines
tunny ketch/tunnycutch	cook's help (female)

Indian terms used by the British

bazaar	market, street of shops
bungalow	single-storey house used widely by the British in India, particularly in military cantonments
burra khana	big dinner, feast
chatty	earthenware pot
dak bungalow	guest house for travellers, often established by the government
degchee	type of cooking pan, saucepan
godown	warehouse or storage building

gup	gossip
memsahib	married British lady, equivalent to *ma'am*
mofussil	country stations and districts, remote areas
pugri	kind of turban
pyjamas	loose-fitting traditional Indian trousers, with a drawstring waist
ryot	peasant farmer
sahib	British gentleman; equivalent to *sir*
tiffin	lunch
verandah	covered platform surrounding a bungalow

Place names: colonial–modern

Bangalore	Bengaluru
Bombay	Mumbai
Calcutta	Kolkata
Ceylon	Sri Lanka
India	India, Pakistan and Bangladesh
Madras	Chennai
Neilgherries/The Hills	Nilgiri Hills
Ootacamund/Ooty	Udhagamandalam (but still commonly called Ooty)
Raichore	Raichur
Simla	Shimla

Social definitions

Anglo-Indian (colonial)	British citizens living in India
Anglo-Indian (modern)	Indian citizens with mixed British and Indian ancestry
châtelaine	mistress of an important house
Eurasian	British colonial term for modern-day Anglo-Indian
gentleman	upper-class male, man of superior social

GLOSSARY

	position
lady	upper-class female, woman of superior social position
Upper Ten Thousand	the upper classes, the Establishment

Food: Wyvern's local terms–English

bandecai	okra (ladies' fingers)
brinjal	aubergine (eggplant)
chapatti	unleavened flatbread
dâl/dhal	pulses – lentils, peas, beans, etc.
dhunnia	coriander seed
huldi	turmeric
jeera	cumin seed
kala mirrch	black peppercorns
karay-pauk	curry leaves
kasoundé	Mango pickle
khush-khush	poppy seed
maythi	fenugreek seed
maythi bajee	fenugreek leaves
moringa pods	drumsticks
mucka cholum	maize
pomfret	a type of fish
rai	mustard seed
seer	a type of fish
sooka mirrch	chilli powder
sont	ginger

Online Pictures

There is a special area on The Curry House website for owners of *The Cooking Colonel of Madras*. The bonus material includes photographs of Wyvern, drawings from 19th century illustrated magazines, and pictures of material used in David Smith's research for this book. Please visit:

www.curryhouse.co.uk/wyvern

Selected Bibliography

Kenney-Herbert, Colonel Arthur Robert, "Wyvern"

Common-Sense Cookery: For English Households, Based upon Modern English and Continental Principles, with Twenty Menus for Little Dinners Worked Out in Detail (Edward Arnold 1894).
Common-Sense Cookery, revised and enlarged edition with illustrations (Edward Arnold 1905).
"Cookery of the Hare", in *The Hare* (Fur and Feather Series), edited by Alfred E. T. Watson (Longmans Green 1896).
Culinary Jottings for Madras: A Treatise in Thirty Chapters on Reformed Cookery for Anglo-Indian Exiles, Based Upon Modern English, & Continental Principles, with Twenty-Five Menus for Little Dinners Worked Out in Detail, first edition (Higginbotham & Co. 1878).
Culinary Jottings for Madras, second edition (Higginbotham & Co. 1879).
Culinary Jottings for Madras, fourth edition (Higginbotham & Co. 1883).
Culinary Jottings, fifth edition (Higginbotham & Co. 1885).
Culinary Jottings, sixth edition (Higginbotham & Co. 1891).
Fifty Breakfasts (Edward Arnold 1894).
Fifty Dinners (Edward Arnold 1895).
Fifty Luncheons (Edward Arnold 1896).
Furlough Reminiscences (Higginbotham & Co. 1880).
Picnics and Suppers (Swan Sonnenschein 1901).
Sweet Dishes (Higginbotham & Co. 1881).
Tinned Food with Advice and Recipes for Its Treatment; being John Moir and Son's (Limited) Export Catalogue – annotated by "Wyvern" (Alf Cooke 1893).
Vegetarian and Simple Diet (Swan Sonnenschein 1904).
Wyvern's Indian Cookery Book, seventh edition (Higginbotham & Co., Madras; Simpkin Marshall & Co., London; 1904).

Primary Sources

Asylum Press Almanac and Compendium of Intelligence for 1882 (Lawrence Asylum Press 1881).
Beeton, Isabella, *Mrs Beeton's Book of Household Management* (S. O. Beeton 1861).
Bissett Thom, Adam, *The Upper Ten Thousand: An alphabetical list of all members of Noble Families, Bishops, Privy Councillors, Judges, Baronets, Members of the House of Commons, Lords-Lieutenant, Governors of Colonies, Knights and Companions of Orders, Deans and Archdeacons, and the Superior Officers of the Army and the Navy, with their official descriptions and addresses* (George Routledge and Sons 1875).
Blunt, Wilfred Scawen, *India Under Ripon: A Private Diary* (T. Fisher Unwin 1909; Elibron Classics 2005).
Clarke, Mrs Charles, *High-Class Cookery Recipes* (William Clowes 1909).
Cole, Rose Owen, *The Official Handbook for the National Training School for Cookery*, twenty-six thousand (Chapman & Hall, undated, c.1896).
Digby, William, *The Famine Campaign in Southern India 1876–1878*, Vols 1 and 2 (Longmans, Green and Co. 1878).
Eagan, J. S. C., *The Nilgiri Guide and Directory* (SPCK Press 1916).
Grant Duff, Sir Mountstuart Elphinstone, *Notes from a Diary: Kept Chiefly in Southern India 1881–1886*, vols 1 and 2 (John Murray 1899).
Grigg, H. B., *A Manual of the Nilagiri District in the Madras Presidency* (E. Keys 1880).
Grose, John Henry, *A Voyage to the East Indies*, new edition (S. Hooper 1772).
Kipling, Rudyard, *Plain Tales from the Hills*, introduction by David Trotter (Thacker Spink 1888; Penguin Books 1987).
Love, Henry Davison, *Short Historical Notice of the Madras Club* (Higginbotham & Co. 1902).
Marshall, Agnes B., *Mrs. A. B. Marshall's Cookery Book,* fifty-fifth thousand (Simpkin, Marshall, Hamilton, Kent & Co., undated, c.1894).
Mitchell, Mrs Murray, *Scenes in Southern India* (American Tract Society 1885).
Pardon, Sidney H., editor, *John Wisden's Cricketers' Almanack for 1917* (John Wisden and Co. 1917).
Riddell, Dr R. ("The author of *Manual of Gardening for Western India*"), *Indian Domestic Economy and Receipt Book,* fifth edition (Society for Promoting

Christian Knowledge 1860).

Steel, Flora Annie and Grace Gardiner, *The Complete Indian Housekeeper and Cook*, fourth edition, edited by Ralph Crane and Anna Johnston (William Heinemann 1898; Oxford University Press 2011).

Thompson, Sir Henry, *Food and Feeding,* eleventh edition (Frederick Warne 1901).

Thurston, Edgar, *The Madras Presidency: with Mysore, Coorg and the Associated States* (Cambridge University Press 1914).

Veritas, Amara, *The Servant Problem: An Attempt at its Solution by an Experienced Mistress* (Simpkin, Marshall, Hamilton, Kent & Co. 1899).

Wheeler, George, *India in 1875–76: The Visit of the Prince of Wales* (Chapman and Hall 1876).

Yule, Henry and A. C. Burnell, *Hobson-Jobson: The Anglo-Indian Dictionary* (John Murray 1886; Wordsworth Editions 1996).

Secondary Sources

Achaya, K. T., *A Historical Dictionary of Indian Food* (Oxford University Press 2002).

Ballhatchet, Kenneth, *Race, Sex and Class Under the Raj* (Weidenfeld and Nicolson 1980).

Burton, David, *The Raj at Table: A Culinary History of the British in India* (Faber & Faber 1993).

Carr, Herbert Reginald Culling and George. A. Lister, *The Mountains of Snowdonia in History, the Sciences, Literature and Sport* (John Lane 1924).

Conran, Caroline, Terence Conran and Simon Hopkinson, *The Conran Cookbook* (Conran Octopus 2002).

David, Elizabeth, *A Book of Mediterranean Food* (John Lehmann 1950).

David, Elizabeth, *French Country Cooking* (John Lehmann 1951).

David, Elizabeth, *Spices, Salt and Aromatics in the English Kitchen* (Penguin Books 1970; Grub Street 2000).

Davis, Mike, *Late Victorian Holocausts: El Niño Famines and the Making of the Third World* (Verso 2002).

de Courcy, Anne, *The Fishing Fleet: Husband-Hunting in the Raj* (Phoenix 2013).

Ferguson, Niall, *Empire: How Britain Made the Modern World* (Penguin Books

2004).

Forbes, Leslie, *Culinary Jottings for Madras* (Prospect Books 2007).

James, Lawrence, *Raj: The Making of British India* (Abacus 1998).

Kelly, Ian, *Cooking for Kings: The Life of Antonin Carême, the First Celebrity Chef* (Short Books 2004).

Kennedy, Dane, *The Magic Mountains: Hill Stations and the British Raj* (University of California Press 1996).

Mann, Michael E., *The Hockey Stick and the Climate Wars* (Columbia University Press 2014).

Muthiah, S., *Madras Discovered* (East-West Press 1992).

Narasiah, K. R. A., *Madras: Tracing the Growth of the City Since 1639* (Oxygen Books 2008).

Schama, Simon, *A History of Britain: Volume 3, The Fate of Empire, 1776–2000* (BBC Worldwide 2002).

Shope, Bradley G., *American Popular Music in Britain's Raj* (University of Rochester Press 2016).

Stone, Dorothy, *The National: The Story of a Pioneer College* (Robert Hale & Company 1976).

White, Florence, *Good Things in England* (Jonathan Cape 1932; seventh impression 1951).

Wolmar, Christian, *The Subterranean Railway: How the London Underground Was Built & How it Changed the City Forever* (Atlantic Books 2012).

Index

A

Ablett, John, 172, 177
Anglo-French school of cookery, 137
Anglo-Indian, 5, 6, 19, 23, 27, 28, 36, 37, 44, 77, 83, 90, 105, 106, 109, 110, 111, 120, 121, 124, 145, 186, 187, 246
Ascot, 19, 20, 60
Athenaeum and Daily News, 15, 19, 22, 24, 28, 65, 72, 74, 75, 76, 78, 79, 80, 82, 101, 103, 152
Athletic News, 182
Avonby, 9, 59
ayah, 57, 105, 125, 152, 245

B

Bangalore, 12, 14, 15, 16, 17, 35, 40, 43, 60, 75, 98, 107, 125, 189, 246
Barings bank, 82
Barnes, 61
Barrie's curry powder, 113, 114, 121
beef, 20, 36, 43, 45, 46, 47, 48, 116, 129, 130, 132, 140, 166, 200
beer, 9, 13, 52, 92, 93
   Bass, 64
   India Pale Ale (IPA), 93
   porter, 65
Beeton, Isabella – Mrs Beeton, 143
Bengalee Babu, 76
Birdingbury, 9, 14, 22
Blunt, Wilfrid Scawen, 126
Bombay, 12, 33, 52, 53, 73, 81, 96, 108, 125, 246
Bombay ducks, 129
botanical garden, 99, 100, 104
Bourton rectory, 7, 8, 14, 16, 21, 59, 125
Bourton-on-Dunsmore, 7, 14, 21, 58
bread making, 45, 94, 95
Brillat-Savarin, Jean Anthelme, 31, 135, 146, 167, 185
Brompton Oratory, 180
Buckmaster, John Charles, 156
bullock cart, 89, 92, 129
burra khana, 129, 245
butler, 32, 34, 88, 92, 124, 125, 245

C

Calcutta, 22, 33, 69, 73, 246
Campden House Chambers, 168, 169, 175
Carême, Antonin, 134, 167

Carr, Herbert Reginald Culling (H.R.C.), 164, 183, 191, 192
Carr, Reginald Childers Culling, 164, 190
Carson, Dave, 75, 76, 77
census
  1851, 8
  1871, 55
  1881, 21, 55, 59, 108
  1891, 4
  1901, 88, 170, 171, 172, 183
  1911, 182
  1939 Register, 190
Ceylon, 12, 18, 117, 118, 180, 185, 196, 246
Ceylon curry, 118, 187, 197
champagne, 60, 61, 64, 65, 130
charcoal, 35, 47, 124, 137
Chenies Street Chambers, 167, 168, 175
chicken, 37, 48, 49, 87, 94, 95, 116, 117, 118, 120, 129, 130, 137, 144, 166, 193, 203
children - sent back to school in Britain, 4, 12, 54, 104–5, 189
chutneys, 73, 74, 91, 111, 114, 116, 119, 120, 121, 129, 148
Clarke, Mrs Charles, 156, 157, 158
Cleveland, Agnes, 12
  born, 13
  marries Wyvern, 11

Cleveland, Lieutenant-General John Wheeler, 12, 14, 125, 189
Cleveland, Louisa Elizabeth, 14
Clive, Robert - Clive of India, 126
coconut milk, 114, 116, 117, 118, 193
Cole, Sir Henry, 155, 156
College Hall, Madras, 75, 77
Common-Sense Cookery, 5, 109, 139, 140, 141, 142, 143, 144, 145, 146, 162, 164, 177, 178, 183, 186, 187
Common-Sense Cookery Association, 6, 67, 139, 140, 147, 148, 155, 158, 159, 161, 162, 163, 165, 169, 186
Complete Indian Housekeeper and Cook, 83, 84, 85, 87, 88, 90, 91, 94, 185
cookery schools, 138, 147, 148, 149, 150, 155, 157, 158, 159, 165, 169, 172
cookery teaching, 155, 156, 157
Coonoor, 80, 97, 98, 103
country vegetables, 40, 41, 94
Culinary Jottings for Madras, 3, 4, 5, 6, 23, 24, 25, 26, 27, 28, 29, 30, 36, 41, 46, 48, 51, 71, 74, 78, 84, 87, 90, 91, 96, 98, 99, 106, 109, 123, 124, 129, 132, 141, 142, 143, 162, 167, 183, 185, 186, 192
curry, 1, 27, 28, 29, 32, 36, 38, 73, 74, 90, 91, 108, 109, 110, 111, 112, 113, 114, 115, 116, 117, 118, 119, 120,

121, 122, 129, 130, 132, 142, 143, 145, 148, 150, 163, 165, 166, 186, 187, 188, 194, 196, 199, 203, 205, 247
curry powder, 44, 112, 113, 114, 115, 117, 132, 142, 159, 193, 194, 195

D

dak bungalows, 91, 92, 93
David, Elizabeth, 1, 144, 161, 187, 188
Delhi, 36, 188
dessert, 21, 29, 30, 31, 49, 50, 53, 88, 130, 134, 144, 148, 171
Digby, William, 80, 81
distributing kitchen, 174, 175, 176
Distributing Kitchens Ltd, 172, 173, 177, 186
Dodwell, Dorothy, 170
Dodwell, Lizzie, 169, 170
doepeaza, 111
drunken cooks, 152, 153
Duke of Buckingham, Governor of Madras, 82

E

Earl of Pembroke, 23
East India Company, 4, 5, 69, 100, 101, 110, 128
East India Military College, 11, 14
Edward Arnold, 140, 162, 178
El Niño, 79
English vegetables, 40, 41, 94, 99

entrée, 21, 29, 31, 53, 87, 123, 134, 135, 143, 144, 148, 150
entremet, 29, 30, 31, 123, 124, 134, 135, 144
Epicure, The, 147, 149, 158, 159, 161, 165
Epsom Derby, 18, 19, 20, 60, 64
Escoffier, Auguste, 158
Etcætera from Town, 19, 20, 22, 23, 65
Eurasian, 6, 106, 246
Evans, Reverend Charles, 11

F

famine, 46, 78, 79, 80, 81, 82, 83, 101
Fawcett, Millicent, 3, 167
Feltham. A F, 158
Fifty Breakfasts, 140, 145, 146, 147, 164
Fifty Dinners, 145, 146, 164
Fifty Luncheons, 146, 166
First War of Independence. See Indian uprising of 1857
fish, 21, 29, 31, 35, 43, 44, 49, 95, 118, 134, 135, 137, 139, 144, 148, 166, 175
fishing fleet, 12, 13, 83
Forbes, Leslie, 186, 192
Fort St George, 71, 74, 75
Fulham, 65, 67

Furlough Reminiscences, 5, 7, 8, 9, 15, 19, 20, 21, 50, 51, 52, 54, 64, 71, 106, 128, 150, 152, 178, 191

G

game, 7, 21, 22, 29, 30, 31, 35, 36, 92, 93, 121, 137, 150, 166
Gandhi, Mahatma, 3, 70, 83
Gardiner, Grace. See Steel, Flora Annie
Garrett Anderson, Elizabeth, 167
Garrett, Agnes, 3, 167, 168
Garrett, Rhoda, 167
godowns, 36, 37, 38, 39, 130, 245
Gospel Purity Association, 102
Government House, 126
Grant Duff, Sir Mountstuart Elphinstone, 15, 70, 125, 126, 127
Great Exhibition, 155
Grose, John Henry, 110

H

Hammersmith Old Cemetery. See Margravine Cemetery
Hare, The - Fur and Feather Series, 164
Harrogate Grammar School, 191
Hedges-White, Lady Jane, 17
Higginbotham and Co, 26, 51, 71, 132, 145
hill stations, 4, 15, 45, 88, 89, 96, 98, 99, 100, 101, 102, 103, 104, 106

Hindustani, 11, 14, 33, 86
Hopkinson, Simon, 188
hors d'oeuvres, 24, 29, 30, 48, 49, 50, 87, 144
Hurlingham, 19, 65

I

ice, 30, 71, 72, 73, 98, 130
Ice House - Madras, 71
Indian Civil Service, 13, 85, 164, 191
Indian Domestic Economy and Receipt Book, 27, 111, 119
Indian Mutiny. See Indian uprising of 1857
Indian servants
　adults treated as children by the British, 32, 86
　perceived as dishonest by the British, 32, 35, 47, 113, 124, 125
Indian uprising of 1857, 4, 107, 128
insulated containers, 160, 172, 173
　thermaphor, 173, 175

J

John Bull, 46
John Company, 91, 128, 129, 133, 181

K

kedgeree, 44
Kenney, Louisa, 8
Kenney, Reverend Arthur Robert, 8
Kenney-Herbert

change of surname from Kenney, 8, 16–17
Kenney-Herbert, Agnes
  birth of daughter, 15
  birth of son, 13
  burial, 189
  headstone, 189
  marries Wyvern, 11
Kenney-Herbert, Arthur Herbert Cleveland
  baptised, 14
  born, 13, 189
  dies, 190
  marries, 190
  military career, 189, 190
  school in England, 55, 107
Kenney-Herbert, Colonel Arthur Robert. See Wyvern
Kenney-Herbert, Edward, 58, 192
  born, 8
  career, 16, 172
  marries, 17
Kenney-Herbert, Enid
  baptised, 15
  born, 15
  gives birth to son, 191
  marries, 164, 190
  school in England, 54, 107
Kenney-Herbert, Reverend A R, 8, 16, 21, 59, 125, 183
Kensington, 55, 63, 67, 140, 147, 155, 156, 164, 168, 179, 182, 191

khitmutgâr, 85, 127, 245
King George V, 182
Kipling, Rudyard, 4, 5, 102, 105, 106, 107, 108
kitchens in India, 27, 36, 39, 85, 86, 110, 124, 188
korma. See quoorma

L

Ladies' Residential Chambers, 167, 168
lamb, 20, 95, 166, 199
Lewis, Elizabeth, 159, 160, 174
lock hospitals, 102
London Distributing Kitchens Ltd, 173, 176
London Distributing Kitchens Lts, 177
London Gazette, 181
Lord Mayor of London, 82
Lord's Cricket Ground, 10, 19, 21, 55, 63
Lytton, Lord - Viceroy, 81, 82

M

Macmillan's Magazine. See periodicals
Madras Club, 39, 72, 73, 74, 119, 126, 181
Madras curry. See Wyvern's Madras Chicken Curry
Madras harbour, 69, 70

Madras houses, 71
Madras Light Cavalry, 10, 13, 14
Madras Mail, 20, 36, 51
Madras Military Fund, 13
Madras Presidency, 5, 12, 15, 36, 47,
    67, 69, 77, 78, 81, 83, 88, 91, 92, 93,
    96, 125, 127
Madras Times, 123
Malay curry, 118
Manchester Distributive Kitchens,
    173, 175
Margravine Cemetery, 188
Marina, The, 70, 71
Marshall, Agnes, 158, 159, 170
Marshall's School of Cookery, 150,
    158, 159
Mary-Jane, 4, 31, 86, 121, 122, 136,
    137, 138, 142
Maskelyne and Cooke, 63
masula boat, 69, 70
memsahibs, 84, 85, 187, 246
men and women - proportions in
    British society, 12, 102
Metropolitan Railway, 55
Mettupalayam, 97, 103
missionaries, 5, 69, 81, 91, 94, 95, 102
Mitchell, Mrs Murray, 5, 33, 69, 71,
    97, 99, 103
mofussil, 68, 92, 93, 246
Moir, John & Son, 96, 130, 131, 132
Mount Road, Madras, 71, 72

Mrs A. B. Marshall's Cookery Book,
    158, 171
mulligatawny, 27, 28, 90, 110, 117,
    119, 120, 121, 132, 142, 150
mulligatunny. See mulligatawny
Museum Theatre, Madras, 74
mutton, 32, 43, 46, 47, 48, 49, 74, 87,
    117, 119, 120, 129, 166, 171, 199
Mysore, 79, 95

N

National Review. See periodicals
National Training School for
    Cookery, 150, 155, 156, 157, 158
Naudin, C - photographer, 67, 191
Naval and Military Record, 180
Neilgherries. See Nilgiri Hills
Nilgiri Hills, 1, 15, 33, 40, 97, 98, 100,
    101, 108, 123, 246
Nilgiri Mountain Railway, 1, 97
Nineteenth Century. See periodicals

O

omelette, 41, 42, 43, 44, 92, 171, 175
Onlooker. See periodicals
Ootacamund. See Ooty
Ooty, 1, 4, 15, 22, 40, 78, 80, 97, 98,
    99, 100, 101, 102, 103, 104, 106,
    108, 127, 128, 246
oriental cookery, 28, 111, 119, 148,
    163, 180
Oriental Depot, Leicester Square, 114

Orleans, 19, 20, 65
Oxford and Cambridge boat race, 15, 60, 64

P

papad or poppadum, 129
partridge, 30, 92
passive resistance, 83
Pennaconda, 42, 43
periodicals publishing articles by Wyvern
    Macmillan's Magazine, 91, 128, 133
    National Review, 160, 163, 167, 174
    The Nineteenth Century, 133, 138, 141, 155, 159, 161, 162, 174, 179, 181, 186
    The Onlooker, 170, 171, 178, 179
Picnics and Suppers, 146, 171, 192
pilau, 119, 148, 150
Pioneer, The, 27, 109
Poonamallee, 126
Post Office London Directory, 163, 169
Prince of Wales (Edward VII), 18, 73
Princess Louise, 166
prostitution, 102

Q

Queen of Ices, 158
Queen Victoria, 3, 156, 158, 166
Queen's Gate Hall, 147, 148, 149
quoorma, 111, 119, 199

R

racism, 4, 57, 59, 66, 72, 105, 106, 107
Raichore, 125
Ramasamy, 4, 31, 32, 33, 35, 39, 41, 45, 121, 122, 142, 245
redcurrant jelly, 114, 121, 142, 194
Reformed Food (Vegetarian) Company, 172
Regimental Theatre Company, 74, 76
relevé, 29, 31, 87, 134, 135, 144
relief strikes, 83
rice - boiled, 117, 121, 187, 201
Riddell, Dr R, 27, 111, 119
Ripon, Lord, 126
Ritchie, Evelyn Dorothy, 191
rôt, 30, 31, 49, 135, 136, 144
Rothschild
    bank, 82
    Baron de, 134, 167
Rubattino Line, 52
Rugby School, 9, 10, 11, 59, 181

S

Saint Lèger, G M de, 174
sanitaria, 100, 101, 102, 103, 126
Secunderabad, 40, 43
Senn, Charles Herman, 157, 158, 163, 166

servant problem, 150, 151, 152, 153, 155, 159, 174
servants registry, 56, 58, 147, 148, 149, 153, 154, 155, 163, 165, 169
service à la Française, 30, 66, 134, 135
service à la Russe, 66, 134, 135
sexually-transmitted infections, 102
Shakespeare, William, 23
sherry, 92, 93
Simla, 36, 97, 100, 102, 105, 106, 246
Simpkin Marshall, 26
Slade, Henry, 62
Sloane Street, 147, 148, 149, 150, 161, 163, 165, 166, 169, 170
snipe, 22, 49, 92
St James' Court, 174, 176, 177, 180, 181
St Mary's Church, Madras, 71
St Peter's Church, Bourton-on-Dunsmore, 7
Stanley, Rt Hon. Lord, 10
Steel, Flora Annie and Gardiner, Grace, 44, 84, 85, 86, 87, 88, 89, 90, 91, 93, 94, 95, 185
Suez Canal, 12, 52, 53
Swan Sonnenschein, 171, 177
Sweet Dishes, 30, 48, 50, 71, 123, 124, 162

T

tamarind, 91, 114, 120, 143, 193, 197, 203

tamarind chicken, 203
Tamil, 33, 118, 120
Tamil Nadu, 1, 69
Temple, Reverend Dr Frederick, 11
Temple, Sir Richard, 82, 83
Theatre Royal, Madras, 74
Thompson, Sir Henry, 144, 145, 146
tinned food, 34, 35, 36, 46, 92, 93, 94, 95, 116, 129, 130, 131, 132
Toda, 1, 100
Tommy Atkins, 5
tricycle cart, 160, 173, 175, 176
Tudor, Frederic - the Ice King, 71, 72, 73
Twickenham, 19, 65

U

United Services Co-operative Hotel Company, 179, 181, 186
Universal Cookery and Food Association, 157, 158, 163
Universal Cookery and Food Exhibition, 166
upper ten, 63, 64, 151, 247

V

Vegetarian and Simple Diet, 177
vegetarian dishes, 27, 166, 173, 177
Vegetarian, The, 172, 177
Vivekanandar Illam, 71

W

Warburton, Kate, 172, 175
Wellington, 103
White, Florence, 187
Wilkinson, Fanny, 167
Wilson's Circus, 75
wine, 20, 28, 44, 52, 66, 92, 93, 96, 116, 124, 130
Wisden's Cricketers' Almanack, 10
Wyvern
   baptised, 7
   birth of daughter, 15
   birth of son, 13
   born, 7
   burial, 188
   dies, 183
   first use of pseudonym, 8, 19
   granted honorary rank of brigadier-general, 183
   headstone, 188, 192
   interviewed in The Epicure, 161, 162, 163
   joins army, 11
   marries Agnes Cleveland, 11
   meaning of pseudonym, 23
   promoted to captain, 14
   promoted to colonel, 127
   promoted to lieutenant, 11
   promoted to lieutenant-colonel, 127
   promoted to major, 123
   retires from army, 128, 133
   Rugby school, 9, 10, 59, 183
Wyvern as Deputy Assistant Quartermaster-General, 15, 16, 17, 23, 123, 125, 190
Wyvern as Military Secretary to the Governor of Madras, 15, 64, 125, 127, 179
Wyvern's Indian Cookery Book, 26, 109
Wyvern's Madras Chicken Curry, 115, 117, 187, 193

Y

York Street Chambers, 167, 168
Youmans, Eliza, 157

Lightning Source UK Ltd.
Milton Keynes UK
UKHW021524140420
361682UK00016B/4358